JOURNAL FOR THE STUDY OF THE NEW TESTAMENT
SUPPLEMENT SERIES
149

Executive Editor
Stanley E. Porter

Sheffield Academic Press

Sister or Wife?

1 Corinthians 7 and Cultural Anthropology

J. Dorcas Gordon

Journal for the Study of the New Testament
Supplement Series 149

Copyright © 1997 Sheffield Academic Press

Published by Sheffield Academic Press Ltd
Mansion House
19 Kingfield Road
Sheffield S11 9AS
England

Printed on acid-free paper in Great Britain
by Bookcraft Ltd
Midsomer Norton, Bath

British Library Cataloguing in Publication Data

A catalogue record for this book is available
from the British Library

ISBN 1-85075-685-6

CONTENTS

ACKNOWLEDGMENTS

This work, which began as my doctoral thesis, has been long in the process, and there are many people who have contributed to its successful completion. To them I give my thanks: to Schuyler Brown for accepting the risk of acting as my Director in a field of study that was new at the Toronto School of Theology; to Raymond Humphries for his support and Irish humour throughout; to Joan Watson for her friendship and willingness to guide me through the computer 'jungle'; to Ron Williams and Chris Love for taking on the arduous role of proofreaders; to Kathleen Gibson, not just for her promptness in obtaining library materials, but for her listening ear. Especially do I acknowledge my great debt to my husband, Noel, and to my children, Mark, Sarah, Tim and Aaron. Words cannot express my thanks to them for their support and encouragement not only at the thesis stage, but as this work moves on to publication.

AJT	*American Journal of Theology*
ANRW	*Aufstieg und Niedergang der römischen Welt*
ATR	*Anglican Theological Review*
BA	*Biblical Archaeologist*
BAGD	W. Bauer, W.F. Arndt, F.W. Gingrich and F.W. Danker, *Greek–English Lexicon of the New Testament*
Bib	*Biblica*
BJRL	*Bulletin of the John Rylands University Library of Manchester*
BR	*Biblical Research*
BT	*The Bible Translator*
BTB	*Biblical Theology Bulletin*
BZNW	Beihefte zur *ZNW*
CBQ	*Catholic Biblical Quarterly*
CH	*Church History*
CTM	*Concordia Theological Monthly*
HeyJ	*Heythrop Journal*
HR	*History of Religions*
HTR	*Harvard Theological Review*
Int	*Interpretation*
JAAR	*Journal of the American Academy of Religion*
JAC	Jahrbuch für Antike und Christentum
JBL	*Journal of Biblical Literature*
JETS	*Journal of the Evangelical Theological Society*
JFSR	*Journal of Feminist Studies in Religion*
JJS	*Journal of Jewish Studies*
JR	*Journal of Religion*
JRE	*Journal of Religious Ethics*
JRH	*Journal of Religious History*
JRS	*Journal of Roman Studies*
JSNT	*Journal for the Study of the New Testament*
JSOT	*Journal for the Study of the Old Testament*
NICNT	New International Commentary on the New Testament
NovT	*Novum Testamentum*
NovTSup	*Novum Testamentum* Supplements
NTS	*New Testament Studies*
RelSRev	*Religious Studies Review*
ResQ	*Restoration Quarterly*
RevExp	*Review and Expositor*
RTR	*Reformed Theological Review*

SBLDS	SBL Dissertation Series
SBLSP	SBL Seminar Papers
SJT	*Scottish Journal of Theology*
SNTSMS	Society for New Testament Studies Monograph Series
TBT	*The Bible Today*
TDNT	G. Kittel and G. Friedrich (eds.), *Theological Dictionary of the New Testament*
TS	*Theological Studies*
TynBul	*Tyndale Bulletin*
UBSGNT	United Bible Societies' *Greek New Testament*
VC	*Vigiliae christianae*
ZNW	*Zeitschrift für die neutestamentliche Wissenschaft*

INTRODUCTION

1 Corinthians 7 has caused numerous difficulties for traditional exegesis.[1] A lack of clarity exists as to how Paul's words on marriage and celibacy are to be understood. Although many biblical scholars would agree that Paul is responding to a question or questions asked by the Corinthians, differences of opinion remain over the specific focus of the Corinthian enquiry.[2]

One group understands the basic question to be, 'Is marriage

1. See John C. Hurd, *The Origin of 1 Corinthians* (Macon, GA: Mercer University Press, 2nd edn, 1983), pp. 43-71 for a history of interpretation concerning the integrity of 1 Cor. It is the working hypothesis of this thesis that 1 Cor. is a single letter.

2. Hurd, *Origin*, p. 68 provides a chart which lists fourteen scholars out of twenty-four who regard verse 1b as Pauline. Hans Conzelmann, *1 Corinthians: A Commentary on the First Epistle to the Corinthians* (Philadelphia: Fortress Press, 1975), pp. 114-16; Elisabeth Schüssler Fiorenza (*In Memory of Her: A Feminist Theological Reconstruction of Christian Origins* [New York: Crossroads, 1983], p. 223) should be added to the list of those who view this verse as Pauline. The interpretation that understands this verse to be a quote from the Corinthian letter to Paul began with Origen in the third century, and is finding increasing support. To those listed by Hurd should be added: Hurd, *Origin*, p. 163; W. Meeks, *The First Urban Christians: The Social World of the Apostle Paul* (New Haven: Yale University Press, 1983), p. 102; C.K. Barrett, *Commentary on the First Epistle to the Corinthians* (BNTC; London: A. & C. Black, 1968), p. 267; F.F. Bruce, *Paul, Apostle of the Heart Set Free* (Grand Rapids: Eerdmans, 1977), p. 267; J. Murphy-O'Connor, 'The Divorced Woman in 1 Cor. 7.10-11', *JBL* 100 (1981), pp. 601-606 (603). Most who accept this position understand Paul to be citing the Corinthians' words in order to qualify them. A variation holds that Paul cites the Corinthian letter in order to set himself against their opinion. See David Smith, *The Life and Letters of St Paul* (New York: Harper & Row, 1920), p. 262; also Charles Giblin, '1 Corinthians 7: A Negative Theology of Marriage and Celibacy?' *TBT* 41 (1969), pp. 2839-55 (2842); William Orr and James Walther, *1 Corinthians: A New Translation* (AB; Garden City, NY: Doubleday, 1976), p. 205. See William E. Phipps, 'Is Paul's Attitude toward Sexual Relations Contained in 1 Cor. 7.1?', *NTS* 28 (1982), pp. 125-31 for further discussion of these three opinions.

desirable?',[3] while other exegetes focus on the question, 'Is sexual intercourse between married persons allowed?'[4] These reconstructions depend upon the varied interpretations given to v. 1b, καλὸν ἀνθρώπῳ γυναικὸς μὴ ἅπτεσθαι, and more specifically the meaning of ἅπτεσθαι[5] and the implications of καλόν.[6] This verse provides a good example of the exegetical problems that arise within 1 Corinthians 7.

Since vv. 8-16 are an abrupt transition from v. 7, some exegetes reconstruct four further questions addressed to Paul by the Corinthians.[7] They also agree that there was an ascetic group in Corinth that

3. A. Robertson and A. Plummer, *A Critical and Exegetical Commentary on the First Epistle of St Paul to the Corinthians* (ICC; Edinburgh: T. & T. Clark, 2nd edn, 1914 [1911]), p. 132; Leon Morris, *The First Epistle of Paul to the Corinthians: An Introduction and Commentary* (The Tyndale New Testament Commentaries; London: Tyndale Press, 1958), p. 105; James Moffatt, *The First Epistle of Paul to the Corinthians* (London: Hodder & Stoughton, 2nd edn, 1959), p. 73.

4. J. Héring, *The First Epistle of Saint Paul to the Corinthians* (trans. A.W. Heathcote and P.J. Allcock; London: Epworth Press, 1962), p. 48; J. Murphy-O'Connor, *1 Corinthians* (New Testament Message; Wilmington: Michael Glazier, 1979), p. 59; Kirsopp Lake, *The Earlier Epistles of St Paul: Their Motive and Origin* (London: Rivingtons, 1914), p. 180; Conzelmann, *1 Corinthians*, p. 114; Charles Talbert, *Reading Corinthians: A Literary and Theological Commentary on 1 and 2 Corinthians* (New York: Crossroads, 1987), pp. 37-38.

5. Scholars divide into two groups over what is intended by this verb meaning 'to touch'. Most state that it is a euphemism for sexual relations. Some maintain it refers to sexual intercourse, and more specifically sexual intercourse between married persons. Others understand Paul to be referring to the relationship based upon sexual intercourse, that is marriage. F.W. Grosheide (*Commentary on the First Epistle to the Corinthians* [NICNT; Grand Rapids, MI: Eerdmans 1953], p. 155) is representative of this last opinion: 'The general nature of this expression shows that Paul does not speak about what should happen in marriage but about the question whether or not one should marry. Nor does he say: no woman, or: his wife, but: a woman.'

6. Some scholars give καλόν a purely utilitarian and pragmatic meaning, while others interpret this word to refer to moral 'good' as one 'good' among several 'goods'. For others it was the goal of morality, the highest member of a series of lesser 'goods'. A few of the Fathers understood it to mean the absolute of ethical conduct. See Hurd, *Origin*, pp. 158-61 for a complete discussion of this word.

7. E. Evans, *The Epistles of Paul the Apostle to the Corinthians in the Revised Version* (The Clarendon Bible; Oxford: Clarendon Press, 1930), p. 90; W.G.H. Simon, (*The First Epistle to the Corinthians: Introduction and Commentary* [Torch Bible Commentaries; London: SCM Press, 1959], pp. 88-90), expresses these questions as follows: '1-9. Here there are two problems on which the apostle has been consulted; in the case of married people ought sexual relations to be abandoned, and

was suspicious of all sexual relations. Differences in emphasis occur, however, depending on how the individual exegete views the strength and the extent of the ascetic tendency.[8]

Exegetical Problems in 1 Corinthians 7

Each section in ch. 7 has a number of specific exegetical questions. The problems attached to v. 1 have been presented. Other questions in this section (vv. 1-7) include Paul's monotonous balancing of statements in vv. 2-4[9] and the relationship of vv. 6-7 to vv. 1-5.[10]

Verses 8-9

In vv. 8-9 differences of opinion are found among scholars as to who is addressed in this section: whether unmarried men and widows or widowers and widows.[11] As well, the word πυροῦσθαι suggests that

in the case of those who are not married, ought they to aim at the celibate life, and not marry at all?. . . 10-11. The third Corinthian question concerned the possibility of divorce. . . 12-16. The fourth question follows: what about a marriage in which one partner is converted to Christianity while the other remains heathen?' Scholars who explain vv. 1-16 as the result of four distinct questions fall into two groups: those who, like Simon, believe Paul answered the first two questions simultaneously in vv. 1-9; those who consider vv. 1-7 as directed solely to the first question, the answer to the second comprising vv. 8-9. See Hurd, *Origin*, pp. 157-58 for further details.

8. W.M. Ramsay ('Historical Commentary on the Epistle to the Corinthians', *The Expositor*, Series 6.1 [1900], p. 381) provides an example. He suggests that the Corinthians were demanding that Paul support them in their belief that marriage should be the *rule* for all Christians.

9. Wayne Meeks, 'The Image of the Androgyne: Some Uses of a Symbol in Earliest Christianity, *HR* 13 (1974), pp. 165-208 (199-200); Robin Scroggs, 'Paul and the Eschatological Woman', *JAAR* 40 (1972), pp. 283-303 (294-95). Qualifications are made to Scroggs's interpretation by Elaine Pagels, 'Paul and Women: A Response to Recent Discussion', *JAAR* 42 (1974), pp. 538-49.

10. The words συγγνώμην and ἐπιταγήν in v. 6 are at the heart of the debate as is the use of the adversative particle in v. 7.

11. Orr and Walther (*1 Corinthians*, p. 210) view it as addressed to widowers and widows. Barrett (*First Epistle*, p. 77) renders it 'those who are at present unmarried', that is, as divorced, separated or widowers. He then proceeds to account for the naming of widows as a special class. Scroggs ('Eschatological', p. 295) translates it 'unmarried and widows' and sees this as one point at which the parallelism between men and women in ch. 7 is broken.

Paul places a low value on marriage.[12]

Verses 10-11

In vv. 10-11 the first question concerns Paul's introduction of a dominical logion, especially when it contradicts his response here which
allows divorce as well as the permission to divorce in v. 15. The way
in which he presents the logion in his argument adds to this difficulty.
Instead of, τοῖς δὲ γεγαμηκόσιν ὁ κύριος παραγγέλλει, he writes
τοῖς δὲ γεγαμηκόσιν παραγγέλλω and then is forced to qualify his
statement with the words, οὐκ ἐγὼ ἀλλὰ ὁ κύριος. Further, the fact
that he specifically relates the parenthetical clause (v. 11) to the woman
and not to the man as in the synoptic form, and his reversal of the
order husband/wife as in vv. 2-8, 12-13 to wife/husband, raises questions about the involvement of wives in this conflict about marriage
and sexual intercourse, singleness and celibacy.[13]

The word χωρισθῆναι (vv. 10, 11, 15) has been variously translated. While the RSV rendering, 'the wife should not separate from
her husband', reflects the consensus of modern commentators,[14] others,
because of the aorist passive form, insist that it should be translated,
'the wife should not be separated from her husband'.[15]

As a result of these exegetical questions in vv. 10-11, two reconstructions of the historical situation reflected in the text have been
suggested. One group of exegetes concludes that the husband belonged
to an ascetic group and was denying the wife her conjugal rights.
Since the marriage was no longer a marriage, the wife desired to be

---

12. M.L. Barre ('To Marry or to Burn: πυροῦσθαι in 1 Cor. 7.9', *CBQ* 36
[1974], pp. 193-202 [193]). recognizes that, although this can be offset to a certain
extent by the significantly strong eschatological tone in vv. 29-31, the fact remains
that Paul has a 'rather unwholesome attitude towards marriage and the place of sex in
Christian life'.

13. As early as 1936, James Moffatt (*First Epistle*, p. 78) advocated a feminist
party in the local church which claimed freedom to desert or divorce a husband.

14. For example, William Baird, *1 Corinthians, 2 Corinthians* (Atlanta: John
Knox, 1980), p. 30; J. Ruef, *Paul's First Letter to Corinth* (Harmondsworth: Pen-
guin, 1971), p. 55; Robertson and Plummer, *First Epistle*, p. 140; Barrett, *First
Epistle*, p. 162; Conzelmann, *1 Corinthians*, p. 119.

15. For example, Orr and Walther, *1 Corinthians*, p. 211; Murphy-O'Connor,
'Divorced Woman', p. 601. The fact of the passive leads Murphy-O'Connor to argue
for a Jewish milieu in v. 10b.

free from him and possibly wished to marry another.[16] The second possibility affirms that the wife belonged to the ascetic group and has abstained from sexual intercourse with her husband. To make the abstinence permanent, she wished to be divorced from her husband.[17]

Verses 12-16
Commentators agree on the general context in vv. 12-16: Paul is addressing himself to Christians married to unbelievers. However, differences of opinion about the relationship of v. 16 to the previous verses leave it uncertain as to whether Paul is encouraging divorce or maintenance of the marriage.[18]

The question of the emphasis in vv. 12-16 is an important one. A number of scholars view Paul as extending the dominical saying in v. 10 as far as is possible in his advice in vv. 12-16.[19] The emphasis, then, is on Christians not dissolving their marriage with unbelievers. This interpretation, however, neglects the unifying aspect of these verses: Paul leaves it to the unbeliever to decide whether or not the marriage continues.

16. Murphy-O'Connor, *1 Corinthians*, pp. 63-64; Murphy-O'Connor, 'Divorced Woman', p. 604.

17. Robertson and Plummer, *First Epistle*, p. 140; Moffatt, *First Epistle*, p. 78. Conzelmann, *1 Corinthians*, p. 120, and Dungan, *The Sayings of Jesus in the Churches of Paul* (Philadelphia: Fortress Press, 1971), pp. 91-92, contend that 7.11a refers to a wife who has already divorced her husband while Murphy-O'Connor ('Divorced Woman', p. 603) emphasizes the possible future reference in ἵνα with the subjunctive. Robertson and Plummer (*1 Corinthians*, p. 140) states that both are possible: either she had divorced her husband or was mentioned in the Corinthians' letter as likely to divorce her husband.

18. If v. 16 refers back to vv. 12-14 then it functions as another reason for the Christian spouse to remain married to the non-Christian. For example, J. Jeremias, 'Die missionarische Aufgabe in der Mischehe (1 Kor. 7, 16)', in W. Eltester (ed.), *Neutestamentliche Studien für Rudolf Bultmann zu seinem 70 Geburtstag am August 1954* (BZNW, 21; Berlin: Töpelmann, 2nd rev. edn, 1957), pp. 255-60. Barrett (*1 Corinthians*, p. 167) offers the paraphrase, 'wife/husband, it may be that you will save your husband/wife'. On the other hand, if the questions in v. 16 are taken as a continuation of Paul's argument in v. 15, then they function as a reason to permit divorce. See S. Kubo, '1 Corinthians 7.16: Optimistic or Pessimistic?', *NTS* 24 (1978), p. 544; Robertson and Plummer, *First Epistle*, p. 143.

19. Robertson and Plummer, *First Epistle*, p. 141.

Verses 17-24

The history of interpretation of vv. 17-24, especially as it relates to v. 21, is extensive, and disagreements continue over whether Paul's response is that of a social conservative who is determined to hold the *status quo* concerning slavery or a social realist who would have wanted slaves to accept freedom if it were offered to them.[20] A further question asks whether vv. 21-23 reflect a real situation in the Corinthian church involving slave and free or whether Paul's argument is merely illustrative.[21]

This pericope appears out of place in the middle of Paul's lengthy discussion of marriage and sexual intercourse, singleness and celibacy. While some scholars view it as an interpolation or, at least, an excursus, others conclude that it relates closely to the argument in the rest of ch. 7.[22] For some, these verses link ch. 7 to the baptismal formula in Gal. 3.26-28.[23]

Verses 25-40

In 7.25 the περὶ δὲ signals that Paul is once again responding directly to a question from the Corinthians' letter.[24] While this section contains a number of exegetical problems, such as the relationship of vv. 25-35 to vv. 36-38,[25] the meaning of παρθένων,[26] and the relationship of

20. See S. Scott Bartchy, μαλλον χρεσαι: *First Century Slavery and 1 Corinthians 7.21* (SBLDS; Missoula, MT: Society of Biblical Literature, 1973), pp. 1-27, for a history of interpretation of v. 21.

21. Murphy-O'Connor (*1 Corinthians*, p. 69) and Bartchy (*Slavery*, pp. 129-31) argue that it is illustrative contra Orr and Walther (*1 Corinthians*, pp. 216-17).

22. Robertson and Plummer (*First Epistle*, p. 144) refer to those who view it as an interpolation; Orr and Walther (*1 Corinthians*, p. 216) call it a 'digression' and suggest that these verses might be a commentary on peace. Those who view these verses as related specifically to the argument in the rest of ch. 7 include: Hurd, *Origin*, pp. 89, 178; Bartchy, *Slavery*, pp. 161-62. N.W. Lund (*Chiasmus in the New Testament: A Study in Formgeschichte* [Chapel Hill: University of North Carolina, 1942], pp. 151-61), sets out these verses as 'b' in an a-b-a pattern.

23. For example, Bartchy, *Slavery*, pp. 131, 163-65; Scroggs, 'Eschatological', p. 293; Fiorenza, *Memory*, pp. 220-21. Scholars who do not make this connection include David Cartlidge, 'Competing Theologies of Asceticism in the Church' (PhD dissertation; Cambridge, MA: Harvard University, 1969). On p. 57 n.1, he links the formula to other parts of 1 Cor. but not specifically to ch. 7.

24. Barrett, *First Epistle*, p. 173; Conzelmann, *1 Corinthians*, p. 137

25. See Hurd, *Origin*, pp. 177-78.

26. Does παρθένων refer to 'young women'? So Robertson and Plummer, *First*

vv. 39-40 to the rest of the chapter,[27] one question in particular has fostered a lengthy discussion. This concerns the reconstruction of the specific context of vv. 36-38.

The explanation of these verses (in which there are no textual uncertainties) divides scholars into three groups. Does the concern over 'the virgins' reflect a situation in which fathers are anxious to know what to do with unmarried daughters,[28] or a set of circumstances in which a number of engaged couples[29] or couples bound in a spiritual marriage are asking for advice?[30] This lack of agreement arises out of the various meanings that can be given to certain words in vv. 36-38.[31]

Epistle, p. 151; Moffatt, *First Epistle*, p. 91; or does the double form of the address in v. 28 mean Paul is answering a question about both men and women who have never married? See Barrett, *First Corinthians*, p. 173; Orr and Walther, *1 Corinthians*, p. 220; Conzelmann, *1 Corinthians*, p. 131 n. 7.

27. While the majority of commentators relate vv. 39-40 back to vv. 8-9 where Paul has previously addressed the question of widows, it is recognized that they do not neatly fit there or at the end of the chapter. According to Barrett *(First Epistle*, p. 186), their formal attachment to the rest of the chapter is loose; they seem to be an afterthought.

28. Supporters of this theory include Robertson and Plummer, *First Epistle*, p. 158; Henry L. Goudge, *The First Epistle to the Corinthians* (Westminster Commentaries; London: Methuen, 3rd edn, 1911), p. 60; Morris, *First Epistle of Paul to the Corinthians*, p. 105; E.B. Allo, *Saint Paul: Première épître aux corinthiens* (Paris: Gabalda, 1935), p. 177; W.F. Orr, 'Paul's Treatment of Marriage in 1 Corinthians 7', *Pittsburg Perspective* 8 (1967), pp. 5-22 (21-22); Grosheide, *Commentary*, pp. 182-84.

29. Supporters of this theory include: J.K. Elliott, 'Paul's Teaching on Marriage in I Corinthians: Some Problems Considered', *NTS* 19 (1973), p. 220; S. Belkin, 'The Problem of Paul's Background. III. Marrying One's Virgin', *JBL* 54 (1935), pp. 49-52; H. Chadwick, 'All Things to All Men', *NTS* 1 (1954–1955), pp. 261-75; Barrett, *First Epistle*, pp. 184-85; Conzelmann, *1 Corinthians*, p. 136; Talbert, *Reading Corinthians*, p. 49.

30. Supporters of this theory include: Murphy-O'Connor, *1 Corinthians*, p. 75; J. Ruef, *Paul's First Letter*, p. 68; T.W. Manson, 'The Corinthian Correspondence 1', in *Studies in the Gospels and Epistles* (Manchester: Manchester University Press, 1962), pp. 190-209; Moffatt, *First Epistle*, pp. 98-100; with caution, Hurd, *Origin*, pp. 169-81.

31. The first set of questions surrounds the rare word ὑπέρακμος. While some translators take it to mean 'past the bloom of youth' (of the women), others translate it 'with strong passions' (of the man). Both Max Zerwick and Mary Grosvenor (*A Grammatical Analysis of the Greek New Testament* [Rome: Biblical Institute Press, 1981], p. 512) and *BAGD*, p. 839, give an either/or translation for this word. A

Style and Content of Paul's Argument

As well as the specific exegetical questions, a general sense of unease exists about the style and content of Paul's arguments. This chapter contains: (1) a high percentage of verbs of persuasion and appeal, and (2) many concessions. In his arguments Paul uses a number of hortatory verbs and verbs in the first person. The latter are, however, verbs that are weak and lacking in authority. Paul thinks or believes (δοκέω), he supposes or expresses an opinion (νομίζω), he wishes (θέλω). Nowhere in 1 Corinthians 7 does Paul specifically claim apostolic status; rather,

> the only authority Paul claims for himself is the moral authority of one who is more experienced and mature. . . There is nothing in principle to exclude other mature Christians from the role Paul assumes here in chapter 7: although it is an apostle who speaks, there is no appeal to status.[32]

Even when he uses himself as an example of preferred behaviour, it is not as a command to all (v. 7). A weakened use of personal authority within this chapter presents difficulty for the exegete.

second word, ἀσχημονεῖν, can be used intransitively with the meaning of 'to be ashamed' or transitively with the meaning 'to do base or not fitting things'. Paul uses it in Rom. 1.27 with reference to homosexual acts and the adjective τὰ ἀσχήμονα (1 Cor. 12.23) as a euphemism for genitalia. Such usage would support either the spiritual marriage or engaged couples theory. Chadwick suggests that the word ὀφείλει has a more natural ring if the pressure is external and is being imposed from the usages of society rather than merely a reference to inward ἀνάγκη (Chadwick, 'All Things', p. 67). Hurd *(Origin*, p. 173) and J.J. O'Rourke ('Hypotheses Regarding I Corinthians 7, 36-38', *CBQ* 20 [1958], p. 293) disagree with Chadwick's conclusion. The principal philological difficulty for the 'fathers and daughters' theory is found in the plural γαμείτωσαν, in that the most natural explanation of the plural, occurring after a series of singular nouns and verbs, is that the understood subjects are the persons previously mentioned. In another form, γαμίζω, now yielding a causative translation, provides the strongest argument for the validity of this theory. Other items of vocabulary which inform this debate include: (a) τὴν παρθένον αὐτοῦ (v. 36) or τὴν ἑαυτοῦ παρθένον (vv. 37-38), both of which are understood to mean variously 'virgin daughter', 'spiritual bride' or 'betrothed girl'; (b) θελήμα-τος (v. 37) can mean both 'purpose' and 'desire'.

32. Paul Gooch, 'Ethical Authorities: 1 Corinthians 7', in *idem, Partial Knowledge: Philosophical Studies in Paul* (Notre Dame: University of Notre Dame Press, 1987), p. 94.

The first of many concessions occurs in vv. 1-5. Paul takes the statement in v. 1, καλὸν ἀνθρώπῳ... ἅπτεσθαι and qualifies it in v. 2. This qualification is elaborated in vv. 3-4 in which male and female marital responsibilities are expressed in identical language. The prohibition, μὴ ἀποστερεῖτε, completes this argument. Paul then proceeds to qualify the qualification, and in this same argument, which emphasizes maintaining a sexual relationship within marriage, he makes an exception, thus undermining the force of the prohibition.

Verses 10-11 provide a second example. Paul quotes a dominical saying, which in itself is unusual, and orders obedience to it. Yet in the next statement he allows the exact opposite.[33] Another use of concessions appears in Paul's good/better arguments found in vv. 8-9. Here he makes a statement affirming the value of singleness/celibacy, makes an exception to it, and then gives a reason justifying the exception. A variation on this good/better argument is also found in vv. 36-38 and 39-40. These concessions occur in the context of imperatives that are more frequent here than in Paul's ethical teaching in the surrounding chapters.[34]

The ambiguity caused by these concessions has raised questions for theologians and moralists as well as for biblical scholars. There is a sense of embarrassment that Paul betrays little enthusiasm for the married state. The result is that his words on marriage/sexual intercourse and singleness/celibacy are often interpreted in light of Ephesians 5, or explained as being necessary because of Corinthian immorality.[35]

---

33. Paul does this in only one other place, 1 Cor. 9.14.

34. This chapter contains almost two dozen imperatives. In ch. 8 there is only one. In other letters where imperatives are extensively used (Gal. 6 and Rom. 12), there is not the same heightened use of the first person or the explicit distinction between Paul's own opinion and the Lord's. See Gooch, 'Ethical Authorities', p. 92.

35. P. Benoit ('Christian Marriage according to Saint Paul', *Clergy Review* 65 [1980], pp. 309-21) gives an example of this: 'This is not an easy chapter to read. Paul's thought moves back and forth. It is not a complete and systematic account of Christian marriage. It is not a theological treatise, and we will not find in it a teaching on the nature and ends of marriage that is as profound as that of the letter to the Ephesians.' He continues, 'As prisoners of their environment and of their old personal habits, they wondered especially how to lead their sexual lives' (p. 311). Other examples include: J.A. Fischer, 'Paul on Virginity', *TBT* 72 (1974), pp. 1633-38 and H. Ridderbos, *Paul: An Outline of his Theology* (Grand Rapids: Eerdmans, 1975), pp. 306-14. Ridderbos, in his section on marriage in Paul, interprets ch. 7 in

In later centuries, his ambiguous statements in ch. 7 have provided justifications for the proponents of both marriage and celibacy.[36]

The question of Pauline inconsistency and ambiguity in ch. 7 is a serious one. One scholar describes Paul's arguments as 'awkward', and accounts for this by speaking of a delicate and novel situation prompting the questions on marriage and celibacy.[37] Because of the oscillation between statements which surrender virtually everything to the ascetics and qualifications which tell for the opposite viewpoint, H. Chadwick views this chapter as apostolic opportunism.[38] Peter Richardson and Paul Gooch, in their study on Pauline accommodation, address the question of charges of inconsistency to Paul, and suggest that while his accommodating manner exposes him to these charges, 'Paul deliberately acted in ways that were accommodating for a specific goal.'[39]

Social Dynamics

The goal that Paul hoped to achieve by the ambiguity created in ch. 7 can be made clear only when the social dynamics of the conflict reflected in this chapter are understood. To uncover these dynamics involves asking a series of questions not only about what is being argued but also how it is being argued and who is involved in the conflict: Is it an outside influence? Is it the whole community that stands over against Paul? Are there distinct groups within the community who oppose each other?

light of Eph. 5.22-23. Of ch. 7 he states, 'Even in 1 Corinthians 7, the chapter to which appeal is made for an opposite opinion [that Paul does not value marriage], in our view no ascetic-dualistic motives are to be discovered with reference to marriage' (p. 312).

36. Elaine Pagels ('Adam and Eve, Christ and the Church: A Survey of Second Century Controversies Concerning Marriage', in A.H.B. Logan and A.J.M. Wedderburn [eds.], *The New Testament and Gnosis: Essays in Honor of Robert McL. Wilson* [Edinburgh: T. & T. Clark, 1983], pp. 146-75) traces how Paul's statements in 1 Cor. were used during the second century by pro-singleness/celibacy and pro-marriage/sexual intercourse forces.

37. Vincent L. Wimbush, *Paul, the Worldly Ascetic: Response to the World and Self-Understanding according to 1 Corinthians 7* (Macon: Mercer University Press, 1987), p. 13.

38. Chadwick, 'All Things', pp. 264-65.

39. Peter Richardson and Paul Gooch, 'Accommodation Ethics', *TynBul* 29 (1978), pp. 89-142 (100).

Until recently, attention has focused on the competing theological ideas lying behind the discord in 1 Corinthians, and on opponents. Traditional exegesis, therefore, has frequently concentrated on delineating the theology of these opponents. The results have been widely divergent.[40] Paul's opponents and their theology have been categorized as Judaizers, Gnostics (either Hellenistic or Jewish) who laid claim to special revelation, or Jewish Christians who espoused an Alexandrian wisdom Christology.[41] The conflicts regarding the issues raised in the Corinthians' letter to Paul are then explained in terms of the competing theologies of Paul and his opponents.

An understanding of the dissension in 1 Corinthians begins with 1.12 and Paul's delineation of four names: Paul, Apollos, Cephas, and Christ. Yet it is difficult to find specific information about these four parties anywhere else in 1 Corinthians. Johannes Weiss, who tries hard to differentiate these groups, in the end concludes as follows:

> The difficulty of forming a judgment about the Cephas party is. . . due to the fact that they do not stand out in clear distinction from the Apollos party. After Paul has spoken about the leaders in 3.5-9 and 3.10-17, he includes both together under one verdict, and this continues up to 4.13. It is as though in this section both parties combined in his mind into one perverse, insubordinate, arrogant and hostile group.[42]

An important essay by Ferdinand Baur (1831) argued that in spite of four slogans reported in 1.12, there were only two parties involved in the strife at Corinth. Against the adherents of Paul and Apollos stood those of Peter who claimed to be the ones who belonged to Christ.[43]

---

40. N. Dahl states in 'Paul and the Church at Corinth according to 1 Corinthians 1.10–4.21', in *Studies in Paul* (Minneapolis: Augsburg Press, 1977), p. 421, that there is 'no consensus with regard to the background and nature of the controversies (reflected in 1.12)'.

41. John J. Gunther, *St Paul's Opponents and their Background: A Study of Apocalyptic and Sectarian Teachings* (NovTSup, 35; Leiden: Brill, 1973), has isolated thirteen different hypotheses.

42. Johannes Weiss, *The History of Primitive Christianity* (trans. and ed. Frederick Grant, A.H. Forster, P.S. Kramer and S.E. Johnson; New York: Wilson Erickson, 1936), p. 336.

43. Although by no means the first to write along these lines, Baur's influence was felt greatly. See E.E. Ellis, 'Paul and his Opponents: Trends in Research', in Jacob Neusner (ed.), *Christianity, Judaism and Other Greco-Roman Cults: Studies for Morton Smith at Sixty*. I. *The New Testament* (Leiden: Brill, 1975), pp. 226-27.

Most scholars begin by reconstructing a single point of view which was opposed to Paul and then seek to identify it with one of the parties mentioned in 1.12. At one time or another each of the three parties, Apollos, Cephas and Christ, has been viewed as representing Paul's chief opposition.[44] Although he does not speak of parties, Johannes Munck's conclusion is similar, in that he sees the Corinthians as a whole, owing to their Greek background, misunderstanding Christianity as wisdom.[45] Like Munck, John Hurd rejects any outside influence upon the congregation as the cause of the controversies. Instead he relates them to Paul's own change of mind in the time between his Corinthian ministry and the Previous Letter mentioned in 1 Cor. 5.9-11.[46]

In a recent article, Peter Richardson, noting the absence of anti-Judaism in 1 Corinthians, draws a connection between it and Paul's accommodating and deliberately conciliatory manner of argumentation. Based specifically on his analysis of the food issues in chs. 8–11, he concludes that within the community Paul is faced with two viewpoints, those of Apollos and Cephas, who lie to either side of him. Paul's goal is to effect compromise in the interests of the continued health of the congregation.[47]

Gerd Theissen has studied the conflict at Corinth in order to determine what these conflicts say about the social make-up and organization of the early Christian communities. Using a number of factors, he shows that the Corinthian community was comprised of groups with widely divergent social backgrounds. He then uses a range of sociological theories of conflict management and status determination to delineate the controversies in 8.1–11.1 and 11.17-32. His conclusion: the conflicts at Corinth are not so much the results of differing theologies as they are the results of differing social expectations.[48]

44. See history of interpretation in Hurd, *Origin*, pp. 97-107.

45. Johannes Munck, 'The Church without Factions: Studies in 1 Corinthians 1–4', in *Paul and the Salvation of Mankind* (London: SCM Press, 1959), pp. 135-67.

46. Hurd, *Origin*, esp. pp. 240-70.

47. Peter Richardson, 'On the Absence of Anti-Judaism in 1 Corinthians', in Peter Richardson and David Granskou (eds.), *Anti-Judaism in Early Christianity*. I. *Paul and the Gospels* (Waterloo: Wilfrid Laurier Press, 1986), pp. 59-74.

48. Gerd Theissen, *The Social Setting of Pauline Christianity: Essays on Corinth* (trans. and ed. John H. Schütz; Philadelphia: Fortress Press, 1982). See especially the chapters: 'Social Stratification within the Corinthian Community: A Contribution to the Sociology of Early Hellenistic Christianity', pp. 69-120; 'The Strong and the

Larry Yarborough, in an unpublished paper presented at the SBL Annual Meeting in 1987, relates Theissen's conclusions to ch. 7. He draws on the contrast between the 'weak and strong' in 8.1–11.1 and the 'rich and poor' in 11.17-32, and applies these categories to marriage and celibacy.[49] As a result of his study, he determines that the conflict in ch. 7 involved a few wealthy and influential celibates who sought to impose their values on the rest of the church. This emphasis in Richardson, Theissen and Yarborough on the relationship between conflict and Paul's manner of argumentation and on the rhetoric of the conflicting groups within the community provides a starting point for this study.

Position of this Study

Richardson and Theissen argue that the conflicts in 1 Corinthians are the result of two distinct groups operating within that community, even though they disagree over the composition of these groups.[50] Within ch. 7, although some scholars point out the existence of two viewpoints,[51] little has been done to develop this conclusion by means of a detailed analysis of the text. For example, in his understanding of the problem in vv. 25-40 as spiritual marriages, Murphy-O'Connor concludes,

> It would be unrealistic to imagine that all members of the Corinthian community thought alike on all issues. Hence, it is not at all impossible that the question that Paul here tries to resolve came from a group opposed to

Weak in Corinth: A Sociological Analysis of a Theological Quarrel', pp. 121-44; 'Social Integration and Sacramental Activity: An Analysis of 1 Cor. 11.17-34', pp. 145-74.

49. Larry Yarborough, 'Elitist Sexual Ethics in Corinth', unpublished paper presented at SBL Bible and Ethics Consultation, Boston, MA, 6 December 1987.

50. In his analysis of the food controversies in 1 Cor., Richardson ('Absence', p. 72) delineates the protagonists ethnically. Over against a conservative, Cephas-led group which was primarily, if not exclusively, Jewish, stands a more liberal, non-Jewish group under Apollos. Paul stands in the middle as he seeks to appeal to both Jews and Greeks. Theissen (*Social Setting*, pp. 123-24) describes these same divisions as being the result of wealth and social status, and concludes that membership in the factions is not to be situated ethnically or socioculturally. He concludes that Greeks, Jews and Romans belonged to both groups in the conflict.

51. For example, S. Kubo, '1 Corinthians VII.16: Optimistic or Pessimistic?', *NTS* 24 (1978), pp. 539-44 (543).

those who wrote 7.1. In fact we do more justice to the complexity of
Paul's answer if we assume this to be the case. Our hypothesis, therefore,
is that some members of the community at Corinth informed Paul of their
opposition to spiritual marriages, and may have gone on to substantiate
their point by presenting the difficulties of a particular case.[52]

He does not, however, attempt to analyze the position of the two
groups, but concentrates instead on Paul's response to the celibates.
Similarly, although Yarborough recognizes that not all within the
community were in agreement with the ascetic group, his exegesis is
primarily in terms of Paul's response to the celibates as if the arguments of those opposing them were not represented in ch. 7.[53] In
addition, his explanation of the conflict in socio-economic terms, the
wealthy celibates against the poor who argued for marriage, runs into
difficulty in light of specific evidence from the first century which
shows that celibacy was not just an option for the rich but cut across
socio-economic lines.[54]

This investigation begins with the fact that ch. 7 is written to address a substantial difference of opinion within the community about
marriage/sexual intercourse and singleness/celibacy. In an attempt to
uncover the dynamics of the conflict, the analysis will concentrate on
the breaks in pattern and the concessions in Paul's argument. The
understanding is that they provide vital clues that will facilitate a
historical reconstruction of the situation reflected in ch. 7. As well,
this kind of investigation will lead to an increased understanding of
the issues in the text.

52. Murphy-O'Connor, *1 Corinthians*, p. 72.

53. In a response to Yarborough's argument, Margaret Mitchell ('Response to
O. Larry Yarborough, "Elitist Sexual Ethics in Corinth"', unpublished paper presented at SBL Bible and Ethics Consultation, Boston, MA, 6 December 1987), after
acknowledging his insight in viewing marriage issues as an expression and cause of
the factionalism within the community, states that in the end he proceeds to analyze
Paul's response and to reconstruct the Corinthians' position as a single, unified
position.

54. The evidence that celibacy did cut across socio-economic lines was presented
in Margaret Mitchell's 'Response', pp. 6-11.

Structure of Breaks in Pattern and Concessions

Breaks in Pattern in vv. 29b-31 and vv. 32-34:

ὁ καιρὸς συνεσταλμένος ἐστίν τὸ λοιπόν ἵνα
    καὶ οἱ ἔχοντες γυναῖκας ὡς μὴ ἔχοντες ὦσιν,
    καὶ οἱ κλαίοντες ὡς μὴ κλαίοντες,
    καὶ οἱ χαίροντες ὡς μὴ χαίροντες,
    καὶ οἱ ἀγοράζοντες ὡς μὴ <u>κατέχοντες</u>
    καὶ οἱ χρώμενοι τὸν κόσμον ὡς μὴ <u>καταχρώμενοι</u>
παράγει γὰρ τὸ σχῆμα τοῦ κόσμου τούτου.

θέλω δὲ ὑμᾶς ἀμερίμνους εἶναι.
    ὁ ἄγαμος μεριμνᾷ τὰ τοῦ κυρίου πῶς ἀρέσῃ τῷ κυρίῳ
    ὁ δὲ γαμήσας μεριμνᾷ τὰ τοῦ κόσμου, πῶς ἀρέσῃ τῇ γυναικί
        <u>καὶ μεμέρισται.</u>
    καὶ ἡ γυνὴ ἡ ἄγαμος <u>καὶ ἡ παρθένος</u> μεριμνᾷ τὰ τοῦ κυρίου,
        <u>ἵνα ᾖ ἁγία καὶ τῷ σώματι καὶ τῷ πνεύματι</u>
    ἡ δὲ γαμήσασα μεριμνᾷ τὰ τοῦ κόσμου, πῶς ἀρέσῃ τῷ ἀνδρί.

Concessions in ch. 7 include the following:

	General Principle	*Concession*	*Rationale*
vv. 1-7 v. 1	καλὸν ἀνθρώπῳ γυναικὸς μὴ ἅπτεσθαι		
v. 2		ἕκαστος τὴν ἑαυτοῦ γυναῖκα ἐχέτω, καὶ ἑκάστη τὸν ἴδιον ἄνδρα ἐχέτω.	διὰ δὲ τὰς πορνείας
vv. 3-4		τῇ γυναικὶ ὁ ἀνὴρ τὴν ὀφειλὴν ἀποδιδότω, ὁμοίως δὲ καὶ ἡ γυνὴ τῷ ἀνδρί	ἡ γυνὴ τοῦ ἰδίου σώματος οὐκ ἐξουσιάζει ἀλλὰ ὁ ἀνήρ ὁμοίως δὲ καὶ ὁ ἀνὴρ τοῦ ἰδίου σώματος οὐκ ἐξουσιάζει ἀλλὰ ἡ γυνή

Sister or Wife?

	General Principle	*Concession*	*Rationale*
v. 5	μὴ ἀποστερεῖτε ἀλλήλους,	εἰ μήτι ἂν ἐκ συμφώνου πρὸς καιρὸν	ἵνα σχολάσητε τῇ προσευχῇ
		καὶ πάλιν ἐπὶ τὸ αὐτὸ ἦτε	ἵνα μὴ πειράζῃ. . . διὰ τὴν ἀκρασίαν ὑμῶν
v. 6	(τοῦτο δὲ λέγω κατὰ συγγνώμην, οὐ κατ᾿ ἐπιταγήν)		
v. 7	θέλω δὲ πάντας ἀνθώπους εἶναι ὡς καὶ ἐμαυτόν	ἀλλὰ	ἕκαστος ἴδιον ἔχει χάρισμα ἐκ θεοῦ. . .
vv. 8-9	(λέγω δὲ τοῖς ἀγάμοις καὶ ταῖς χήραις)		
	καλὸν αὐτοῖς ἐὰν μείνωσιν ὡς κἀγώ	εἰ δὲ οὐκ ἐγκρατεύονται γαμησάτωσαν,	κρεῖττον γάρ ἐστιν γαμῆσαι ἢ πυροῦσθαι,
vv. 10-11	(τοῖς δὲ γεγαμηκόσιν παραγγέλλω, οὐκ ἐγὼ ἀλλὰ ὁ κύριος)		
	γυναῖκα ἀπὸ ἀνδρὸς μὴ χωρισθῆναι—	ἐὰν δὲ καὶ χωρισθῇ, μενέτω ἄγαμος ἢ τῷ ἀνδρὶ καταλλαγήτω—	
	καὶ ἄνδρα γυναῖκα μὴ ἀφιέναι.		
vv. 12-16	(τοῖς δὲ λοιποῖς λέγω ἐγώ, οὐχ ὁ κύριος)		
vv. 12-14		εἴ τις ἀδελφὸς γυναῖκα ἔχει ἄπιστον, καὶ αὕτη συνευδοκεῖ οἰκεῖν μετ᾿ αὐτοῦ, μὴ ἀφιέτω αὐτήν	ἡγίασται γὰρ ὁ ἀνὴρ ὁ ἄπιστος ἐν τῇ γυναικὶ, καὶ ἡγίασται ἡ γυνὴ ἡ ἄπιστος ἐν τῷ ἀδελφῷ.
		καὶ γυνὴ εἴ τις ἔχει ἄνδρα ἄπιστον, καὶ οὗτος συνευδοκεῖ οἰκεῖν μετ᾿ αὐτῆς, μὴ ἀφιέτω τὸν ἄνδρα.	ἐπεὶ ἄρα τὰ τέκνα ὑμῶν ἀκάθαρτά ἐστιν, νῦν δὲ ἅγιά ἐστιν.

	General Principle	Concession	Rationale
vv. 15-16		εἰ δὲ ὁ ἄπιστος χωρίζεται, χωριζέσθω	οὐ δεδούλωται ὁ ἀδελφὸς ἢ ἡ ἀδελφὴ ἐν τοῖς τοιούτοις; ἐν δὲ εἰρήνῃ κέκληκεν ὑμᾶς ὁ θεός.
vv. 20-22 v. 20	ἕκαστος ἐν τῇ κλήσει ᾗ ἐκλήθη ἐν ταύτῃ μενέτω.		τί γὰρ οἶδας, γύναι, εἰ τὸν ἄνδρα σώσεις; ἢ τί οἶδας, ἄνερ, εἰ τὴν γυναῖκα σώσεις;
vv. 21-22	δοῦλος ἐκλήθης; μή σοι μελέτω	ἀλλ᾿ εἰ καὶ δύνασαι ἐλεύθερος γενέσθαι, μᾶλλον χρῆσαι	ὁ γὰρ ἐν κυρίῳ κληθεὶς δοῦλος ἀπελεύθερος κυρίου ἐστίν ὁμοίως ὁ ἐλεύθερος κληθεὶς δοῦλός ἐστιν χριστοῦ (rationale relates to general principle, v. 20)
vv. 26-28 v. 26	(νομίζω οὖν. . .) καλὸν ἀνθρώπῳ τὸ οὕτως εἶναι.		
vv. 27-28	δέδεσαι γυναικί; μὴ ζήτει λύσιν λέλυσαι ἀπὸ γυναικός; μὴ ζήτει γυναῖκα.	ἐὰν δὲ καὶ γαμήσῃς, οὐχ ἥμαρτες καὶ ἐὰν γήμῃ ἡ παρθένος, οὐχ ἥμαρτεν.	θλῖψιν δὲ τῇ σαρκὶ ἕξουσιν οἱ τοιοῦτοι, ἐγὼ δὲ ὑμῶν φείδομαι. (rationale relates to general principle, v. 26)
vv. 36-38	(Reversal of general principle/concession)		
v. 37	ὃς δὲ ἕστηκεν ἐν τῇ καρδίᾳ αὐτοῦ ἑδραῖος, μὴ ἔχων	v. 36 εἰ δέ τις ἀσχημονεῖν ἐπὶ τὴν	

	General Principle	*Concession*	*Rationale*
	ἀνάγκην, ἐξουσίαν δὲ ἔχει περὶ τοῦ ἰδίου θελήματος, καὶ τοῦτο κέκρικεν ἐν τῇ ἰδίᾳ καρδίᾳ τηρεῖν τὴν ἑαυτοῦ παρθένον, καλῶς ποιήσει	παρθένον αὐτοῦ νομίζει ἐὰν ᾖ ὑπέρακμος, καὶ οὕτως ὀφείλει γίνεσθαι, ὃ θέλει ποιείτω οὐχ ἁμαρτάνει γαμείτωσαν.	
	(v. 38: evaluation of the two situations set out in vv. 36-37)		
vv. 39-40	γυνὴ δέδεται ἐφ' ὅσον χρόνον ζῇ ὁ ἀνὴρ αὐτῆς	ἐὰν δὲ κοιμηθῇ ὁ ἀνὴρ ἐλευθέρα ἐστὶν ᾧ θέλει γαμηθῆναι, μόνον ἐν κυρίῳ.	
	(v. 40 is similar to vv. 25-26)		

Summary Analysis of the Concessions and Breaks in Pattern

This method of analyzing ch. 7 reveals a pattern of concessions and exceptions throughout Paul's argument. A visual presentation of the argument seeks to identify recurring patterns indicated under the headings of general principle, concession and rationale. Only those parts of ch. 7 that relate directly to these patterns have been set out.

Patterns within this chapter have also been delineated by scholars such as Nils Lund, Robin Scroggs and Scott Bartchy. Lund's concern is to uncover chiastic structures, and in his delineation of the text he is primarily interested in the similarities and the continuity between various sections of the text rather than in breaks in pattern and discontinuity.[55] Scroggs has emphasized Paul's consistency throughout the chapter in addressing his remarks to both males and females, while Bartchy's interest in structure arises out of an analysis that concentrates on showing that vv. 17-24 belong to the structure of the argument in ch. 7.[56] One of Bartchy's important contributions is his arguments relating this chapter to Gal. 3.26-28. However, because he defines the conflict exclusively in terms of Paul's struggle with the πνευματικοι, he fails to see other breaks in pattern that are important

55. Lund, *Chiasmus*, pp. 151-63.
56. Scroggs, 'Eschatological', pp. 294-97; Bartchy, *Slavery*, pp. 167-71.

to an understanding of the social dynamics in this chapter.

In 7.2 an exception is introduced to the statement about absolute celibacy in v. lb. Paul elaborates on this exception in vv. 3-4, and then, after a strong statement in v. 5 in which he denounces any move on the Corinthians' part to deprive one another of marital rights, he presents a qualification that lessens the absoluteness of this stance on sexual intercourse in marriage. The original principle affirming sexual intercourse is restated in v. 5c; however, in v. 6, its authoritative nature is undermined.

In vv. 8-9 and 10-11 general statements which affirm, in turn, the value of singleness/celibacy and the stability of marriage are followed by concessions. In vv. 8-9 a reason is given as to why the concession is necessary, whereas in vv. 10-11 no reason is given as to why an exception is being made to a dominical saying. In addition, not only does the form of Paul's opening remarks in vv. 10-11 (τοῖς δὲ γεγαμηκό-σιν παραγγέλλω, οὐκ ἐγὼ ἀλλὰ ὁ κύριος) differ from vv. 8-9 (λέγω δὲ τοῖς ἀγάμοις καὶ ταῖς χήραις), but the concession, in the way it separates the two halves of the general statement, is awkward.[57]

Verses 26-28 follow a pattern similar to vv. 8-9 and 10-11, in that they too contain a general principle and a concession. The general statement in v. 26 in which people are urged to remain as they are, is defined in v. 27 in terms of those who are bound and those who are free from marriage. A concession follows in v. 28a which allows a man and a virgin to marry. Verse 28b, like v. 9, presents the rationale. However, this rationale, instead of presenting a reason for the concession, speaks of the distress that accompanies the married state.

Verses 39-40 follow the pattern of general statement and concession. However, the concluding remarks in v. 40 closely resemble the introductory remarks in v. 25 and the general principle in v. 26. The words in v. 40 (μακαριωτέρα δέ ἐστιν ἐὰν οὕτως μείνῃ) compare closely with those found in v. 26 (καλὸν ἀνθρώπῳ τὸ οὕτως εἶναι).

Verses 12-16 begin in the same manner as vv. 8-9 and 10-11 with a verb of saying and those addressed in the dative plural. At this point the structure changes. The next element in the sentence contains what has, in other sections, formed the concession (εἴ). An imperative follows, as do the reasons why this condition should apply. The pattern occurs not only in vv. 12-14, but again in vv. 15-16 drawing attention

---

57. In the *UBSGNT*, the concession is preceded and followed by a dash indicating that it marks a break in the normal flow of the sentence.

to the fact that these verses address two opposite situations: those who
have unbelieving spouses who consent to live with them and those
whose unbelieving spouses do not. In effect there is no general principle in this section. Rather, the recommended course of action arises
out of the specific situation in which the believer finds (him)herself. In
addition, the lack of consistency in the vocabulary used to address the
Christian partner affected by this advice (as underlined in the text) is
integral to an understanding of the text.

Verses 36-38 are similar to vv. 12-16 in that they also seem to be
addressing two distinct situations. Verse 36, like v. 12, begins with εἴ
τις; however, unlike vv. 12-16, the second statement, v. 37, is introduced by ὃς δὲ. In effect, Paul reverses the pattern of vv. 8-9, 10-11
and 26-28. The concession comes first (v. 36) and is followed by the
general principle (v. 37). These verses are then completed by a comparison and evaluation of the two situations (v. 38).

The general statement in v. 20, which speaks of remaining as one is
when called, is followed in v. 21 by an example of someone called as a
slave (δοῦλος ἐκλήθης; μή σοι μελέτω). This is accompanied, in turn,
by an exception (v. 21b) and a reason for the exception (v. 22). The
latter, which speaks of the situation of both slave and free, relates
more specifically to the general statement in v. 20.

Two sections in which there are no concession forms, vv. 29-31 and
vv. 32-34, exhibit breaks in pattern which assist in an understanding
of Paul's argument. In vv. 29-31, in the first, second and third examples, the predicate is the same as the subject, although without the
article and modified by μή. In the fourth and fifth statements the predicate changes. Two breaks in the structure of vv. 32-34 call for particular attention: the ἵνα clause which modifies the reference to the
unmarried woman and the virgin in v. 34a, and the absence of the καὶ
μεμέρισται in v. 34b.

It is the intention of this work to analyze closely the concessions and
breaks in pattern in ch. 7 in an attempt to uncover the dynamics of the
social context. Once these dynamics have been investigated, the
analysis will focus on the function of Paul's argumentation in light of
the social situation that has been uncovered. What is needed is a
methodology that specializes in analyzing conflict situations reflected
in a text.

Methodological Framework

The renewed interest in cross-disciplinary analysis has given rise to a series of analytical presentations using the methods and models of the social sciences. The observations and research made available by psychology, sociology and anthropology are viewed as a means of complementing, controlling and correcting exegetical and historical analysis and conclusions.[58] While this has not been viewed by all with unrestrained enthusiasm,[59] there are notable achievements in studies using this approach.[60] Since new answers arise not so much from new data as new questions, 1 Corinthians 7 with its many difficulties can benefit from questions asked from the perspective of another discipline.[61] This work will use the insights of anthropological theory in two ways to assist in its investigation of the conflict in ch. 7.

First, anthropologists place marriage and sexual intercourse, singleness and celibacy, under the heading of kinship, which is defined as a system linking people together in an orderly social life.[62] It is

58. Victor Turner, 'Process, System and Symbol: A New Anthropological Synthesis', in *idem*, *On the Edge of the Bush: Anthropology as Experience* (Tucson: University of Arizona Press, 1985), p. 152, states, generally, of such interaction, 'The validly new never negates the seriously researched immediate past in any science; it incorporates it in a "wider orbit of recovered law".'

59. C.S. Rodd states bluntly that historical sociology is impossible. See 'On Applying a Sociological Theory to Biblical Studies', *JSOT* 19 (1981), pp. 95-106. See also O.C. Edwards, Jr, 'Sociology as a Tool for Interpreting the New Testament', *ATR* 65 (1985), pp. 431-48; Thomas Best, 'The Sociological Study of the New Testament: Promise and Peril of a Discipline', *SJT* 36 (1983), pp. 184-94. In *Social Aspects of Early Christianity* (Philadelphia: Fortress Press, 2nd edn, 1983), p. 11, Malherbe calls his approach sociological yet warns against using methods and models drawn from the social sciences. He is concerned about 'excessive enthusiasm' for social interpretations.

60. One early survey of research involving a social-scientific approach to the New Testament is found in Daniel Harrington, 'Second Testament Exegesis and the Social Sciences: A Bibliography', *BTB* 18 (1988), pp. 77-85.

61. Michelle Rosaldo speaking within her own discipline, anthropology, states, 'New questions demand new kinds of answers. The development of science depends in discovering in facts previously taken for granted, a field for serious investigation and research.' See Michelle Rosaldo and Louise Lamphere (eds.), *Women, Culture and Society* (Stanford: Stanford University Press, 1976), p. 21.

62. A kinship system is a group of relationships which result from family and marriage. The concept of the family produces three special kinds of social

understood that in any given society a certain number of relationships are recognized, for social purposes, in that they have attached to them certain rights and duties or distinctive modes of behaviour.[63]

A society's kinship system presents a complex set of norms, usages and patterns of behaviour which are instrumental in determining succession to property, office, social position or rank. Deviations from the norm are important in providing a measure of the relative condition of equilibrium or disequilibrium in the system. Since marriage/ sexual intercourse represents a fundamental expression of social structure, its opposite, singleness/celibacy, presents a different model of social organization.[64] Therefore, the use of the anthropological category of kinship as a framework by which to describe Corinth's system of marriage provides a different lens by which to view the problems in 1 Corinthians 7.

relationships: parent/child, sibling, husband/wife. All other social relationships arising as a result of this unit include the connection of two elementary families through a common member. Kinship links people together in a convergence of interest and sentiment, and controls and limits those conflicts which occur because of a divergence of such sentiment or interest. To persist, kinship has to provide an orderly workable system of social relations defined by social usage. See Robin Fox, *Kinship and Marriage: An Anthropological Perspective* (Harmondsworth: Penguin Books, 1967), pp. 13-26; Rodney Needham (ed.), *Rethinking Kinship and Marriage* (London: Tavistock Publications, 1971).

63. According to W.H.R. Rivers, *Kinship and Social Organization* (London School of Economic Monographs on Social Anthropology, 334; London: Athlone Press, 1968), p. 75, 'marriage is only one of the social institutions which have molded the terminology of relationship. It is, however, so fundamental a social institution that it is difficult to get far away from it in any argument which deals with social organization.'

64. Another way to understand this is to speak of descent. Descent has biological meaning, but also jural meaning when it refers to a method of determining succession to property, social position or rank. It can be traced in a number of ways: unilineal, which is descent through relatives of the same sex, father/son/grandson, mother/ daughter/granddaughter; cognatic, of which there are two types, kindred and nonunilineal. This type of descent is defined laterally. See Burton Pasternak, *Introduction to Kinship and Social Organization* (Englewood Cliffs: Prentice–Hall, 1976) pp. 101-104. The conflict between these two types of social organization is presented in Roger M. Keesing and Felix M. Keesing's view of society as containing a set of battle-lines that are always being fought or negotiated (*New Perspectives in Cultural Anthropology* [New York: Holt, Rinehart and Winston, 1971], pp. 181-82). One of these battle-lines involves the relative importance of the tie between husband and wife (marriage) and that between brother and sister (non marriage/non sexual).

In ch. 7 there is a conflict about whether the Christian calling demands singleness and celibacy or allows marriage and sexual activity. Victor Turner's model of social drama provides a way of uncovering the social dynamics of this quarrel. In his analysis of social process, tensions in a conflict represent different expressions of a root metaphor.[65] He labels these opposing elements structure and anti-structure,[66] and describes the course of their contestation as a social drama. He states,

> Through the social drama one can sometimes look beneath the surface of social regularities into the hidden contradictions and conflicts in the social system. The kinds of redressive mechanism deployed to handle conflict, the pattern of factional struggle, and the sources of initiative to end crisis, which are all clearly manifest in the social drama, provide valuable clues to the character of the social system.[67]

A social drama[68] takes place in an observable sequence: breach, crisis, redressive action and reintegration. Each of these categories is a distinct stage in the social process and has its own qualities and

65. Turner labels the foundational principle grounding a culture's world view a root metaphor. He refers to Stephen Pepper's 'root metaphor' (*World Hypotheses* [Berkeley: University of California Press, 1942], pp. 38-39) and to Max Black's 'conceptual archetype' (*Models and Metaphors: Studies in Language and Philosophy* [Ithaca, NY: Cornell University Press, 1962], p. 241). For Pepper a 'root metaphor' is the product arising from attempts to understand the world in terms of an analogy with some common-sense fact. A 'conceptual archetype' is defined as a 'systematic repertoire of ideas by means of which a given thinker describes, by *analogical extension*, some domain to which those ideas do not immediately and literally apply'.

66. In *Dramas, Fields and Metaphors: Symbolic Action in Human Society* (Ithaca, NY: Cornell University Press, 1974), p. 44, Turner defines structure and anti-structure in terms of a mathematical equation needing its minus signs as well as its pluses, negatives as well as positives, zeros as well as numbers. In its essence anti-structure is not negative.

67. Victor Turner, *Schism and Continuity in an African Society* (Manchester: Manchester University Press, 1957), p. xvii.

68. The term 'social drama' arises out of an explicit comparison of the temporal structure of certain types of social processes with that of dramas on the stage. As the latter has actors and actresses, scenes, acts and climax, so too does the 'social' drama. It is a conflict situation in which 'fundamental aspects of society, normally overlaid by the customs and habits of daily intercourse [are brought] into frightening prominence. People have to take sides in terms of deeply entrenched moral imperatives and constraints often against their own personal preferences.' See Turner, *Dramas*, p. 35.

identifiable structure. The order and characteristics of these sequences will delimit how ch. 7 is to be analyzed.

The model of social drama will be augmented by the work of Mary Douglas on grid and group.[69] According to her theory, 'grid' measures individual ties; that is, connections between particular individuals that do not carry with them group-centred consequences. 'Group' measures group loyalties which includes any form of structuring that is dependent upon group organization. A use of her model enables the exegete to situate conflicting groups on a social map according to two variables: their group loyalties and those that are concerned with individual networks. The latter category, for example, includes a person's sex or age or kinship ties. Douglas's model also defines the kinds of arguments and justifications that are needed to move a particular group on this social map to a particular action. She states that given certain social circumstances, people can be expected to hold such-and-such views. More particularly, different social biases will find different beliefs plausible. When this tool is used to analyze Paul's arguments in ch. 7, what he expects of the factions becomes clearer as does the reason for the type of justification that he offers.

The final phase of Turner's social drama, a reintegration of the opposing expressions of the root metaphor or a social recognition and legitimation of an irreparable schism between the contesting parties,[70] is not observable in 1 Corinthians. It can be examined from later information about that community which is found in 2 Corinthians and 1 Clement. Other communities that operated within Paul's symbolic universe also give insight into the resolution of the tensions in 1 Corinthians 7.

Before the data on Corinth's kinship system is presented or the social drama analyzed, it is necessary to examine previous attempts to apply sociological categories to the New Testament and more particularly the cross-cultural perspective provided by modern anthropological theory.

---

69. Mary Douglas, *Purity and Danger: An Analysis of Concepts of Pollution and Taboo* (London: Routledge & Kegan Paul, 1966); Mary Douglas (ed.), *Essays on the Sociology of Perception* (London: Routledge & Kegan Paul, 1982); Mary Douglas, *Natural Symbols: Explorations in Cosmology* (London: The Cressit Press, 1970); Mary Douglas, *Cultural Bias* (Occasional Paper, 34, Royal Anthropological Institute of Great Britain and Ireland; London: Bakers Trade Finishers, 1978).

70. Turner, *Dramas*, pp. 40-41.

Chapter 1

SOCIAL SCIENCE METHODOLOGY AND THE NEW TESTAMENT

> The validly new never negates the seriously researched immediate past in
> any science, it incorporates it in a wider orbit of recovered law.[1]

In Biblical Studies, the interest in Christianity as a social phenomenon
is not new. Adolf Deissmann investigated the papyri discoveries made
at the turn of the century to help to clarify two difficult problems: the
first concerned the nature of the Greek language that is used in the
New Testament and the second the social class of the earliest Christians. Although Deissmann's *Light From the Ancient East* (1908) does
not identify any formal commitment to social theory or ideology, it is
full of asides in which he reacts against the assumption that theological
discourse was the central concern of biblical writers.

Earlier Uses of the Social Sciences

Deissmann's discontent with the over-emphasis on a theological
interpretation of biblical texts was presented more formally in two
approaches that used social categories. The work of Shirley Jackson
Case, centred at the University of Chicago, focused on early Christianity as a social reality and Jesus as a social reformer. Case argued
for what is called a socio-historical method in biblical studies.[2] In his
final work, *The Christian Philosophy of History* (1943), he protests
that the history of Christianity has been conceived too narrowly as literary history and not broadly enough to include social process, and

---

1. Victor Turner, 'Process, System and Symbol', p. 152.
2. Two names are prominent in the Chicago School: Shirley Jackson Case and
Shailer Mathews. Case's work provides an analysis of the socio-historical method as
it pertains to biblical studies. Mathews was interested in the way the social mind
affected theology. Because he worked primarily in the area of the history of Christian
thought, his work is suggestive for the sociology of knowledge.

that the life situations behind the documents need to be recovered:

> Religion could no longer be studied without reference to the social envi-
> ronment of its adherents living at a specific time and place in history.
> Account had to be taken of the local circumstances that motivated conduct
> and shaped opinion. The historian of Christian theology, when sensitive
> to this new demand, could not content himself with the mere assembling
> of texts from ancient documents, he must discover not only what beliefs
> had been current but why they had been devised and promulgated.[3]

To grasp this social reality, historians need aid from the social sciences—from sociologists, psychologists, and anthropologists.[4]

Today Case's program is critiqued in terms of the difference between its intentions and its accomplishments. He did not analyze sociologically the groups and communities which composed early Christianity, but, instead, generalized on the basic ideas and social aspects
of the Graeco-Roman world. With valid reason, critics accused him of
being reductionist, and of using socio-economic factors in a simplistic
way.[5] His social-historical method lost out to neo-orthodoxy with its
emphasis on theology and the word,[6] and by the late 1940s the Chicago

---

3.   Shirley J. Case, 'Whither Historicism in Theology?', in M.H. Krumbine
(ed.), *The Process of Religion: Essays in Honor of Dean Shailer Mathews* (New
York: The Macmillan Company, 1933), p. 61. On p. 64 he continues: 'No study is
capable of revealing the true history of the Christian movement which does not
exhibit its past in the full light of the conditions and processes of the actual life of real
people, as individuals and groups within a concrete social nexus during all the years
and in every land when and where the Christian religion is a-making'.

4.   The historian needs the sociologist to provide information on characteristic
human motivations and activities, the psychologist to know how mental interests may
determine behaviour, and the anthropologist to clear up the contrast 'between the
presuppositions of a primitive age and those postulates by which. . . a man of the
twentieth century is accustomed to regulate his conduct and thinking'. See William J.
Hynes, *Shirley Jackson Case and the Chicago School* (Chico, CA: Scholars Press,
1981), p. 127.

5.   See L.E. Keck, 'On the Ethos of Early Christians', *JAAR* 42 (1974),
pp. 435-51 (438); Paul Schubert, 'Shirley Jackson Case, Historian of Early Christianity: An Appraisal', *JR* 29 (1949), pp. 30-47; C.C. McCown, 'Shirley Jackson
Case's Contribution to the Theory of Sociohistorical Interpretation', *JR* 29 (1949),
pp. 15-29; Robert W. Funk, 'The Watershed of the American Biblical Tradition: The
Chicago School, First Phase, 1892-1920', *JBL* 95 (1976), pp. 4-22 (15-17).

6.   In 'Sociology and the New Testament', *Listening* 21 (1986), pp. 138-47
(139), Robin Scroggs says that even today he considers the controversy surrounding
this method to be theological. He states: 'At the extreme, the disagreement is about

School was no longer a part of American theological discussion.[7] However, his basic insight, that Christianity does not exist apart from particular persons or communities, has been appropriated in modern discussions of the social world of the early Christian communities.[8]

Form criticism, which was contemporary with the Chicago School, also asked questions about Christianity as a social phenomenon, and scholars like Oscar Cullmann recognized the importance of form criticism's sociological orientation. He called for the development of a kind of sociology capable of studying the norms governing the growth of popular tradition.[9] This never materialized, and so form criticism failed to fulfil its own promise. The popularity of the dialectical theology of Barth led to theological interests forming the questions to which biblical scholarship responded, and Bultmann's insistence that kerygma was a theological category minimized the importance of rigorous historical questions in tracing the earliest traditions.[10] A

the status of theological affirmations in Scripture. Is revelation linguistic in character? Should one begin with an austere theology of the *Word*, such that the *words* are divinely ordered?'

7. Frederick Grant's monograph, *The Economic Background of the Gospels* (London: Oxford University Press, 1926) was the only major work on the economics of first-century Palestine. The book was republished in unaltered form in 1973 because nothing comparable had appeared in the intervening years. The importance of the Chicago School to the Canadian academic scene is seen in Marlene Gay Shore, *The Science of Social Redemption: McGill, the Chicago School and the Origins of Social Research in Canada* (Toronto: University of Toronto Press, 1987).

8. Case's functional approach to interpreting social history parallels the use of a similar method within anthropology. Hynes *(Case and the Chicago School*, p. 139) states that 'a number of potentially positive correlations between the socio-historical method of Shirley Jackson Case and contemporary methodological developments within functional and cultural anthropology suggest themselves to the interested and inquisitive student for the future'.

9. He stated: 'There needs to be a special branch of sociology, devoted to the laws which govern the growth of popular traditions. Form criticism will only be able to function profitably if conclusive results can be established in this area. In fact, the most serious defect in [form critical] studies which has appeared thus far is the absence of any sociological basis.' See Oscar Cullmann, 'Les recéntes études sur la formation de la tradition evangelique', *RHPhR* 5.573 (Strasbourg: 1925) as translated and quoted by John G. Gager, 'Shall we Marry our Enemies? Sociology and the New Testament', *Int* 37 (1983), pp. 256-65 (260).

10. Theissen, *Social Setting*, p. 8. Edwin Judge agrees: 'The reason for the delay was, of course, the existential hermeneutic of Bultmann, and the interest of Barth in the Word of God which prevented the conclusions of form criticism being applied

third reason for form criticism's failure is summed up by Leander
Keck, who describes how far its present meaning is removed from
what was originally intended by Hermann Gunkel:

> For him [Gunkel], it was a sociological category pointing to the direct
> relation between the forms of oral tradition and their uses in culture. But
> today the term has been so deformed that it means little more than the
> context. . . Ascertaining the full Sitz im Leben requires us to do what
> Case envisioned: to 'exhibit its [Christianity's] past in the full light of the
> conditions and processes of the actual life of real people, as individuals
> and groups, within a concrete social nexus. . .'[11]

The fact that social scientific approaches to the study of early Christianity have had to compete particularly with the interpretative interests of theology, has resulted in a devaluation of their potential within
biblical scholarship.

Renewed Interest in the Social Sciences

In the early 1970s a renewed interest in the social sciences occurred
because of a crisis of confidence in the historical-critical method.
William Herzog points out that scientists have come to question many
of the assumptions underlying the enlightenment paradigm for investigating the world, especially the notion of 'objectivity'. Within science,
reality is no longer seen as an objective and static world operating by
immutable laws and awaiting discovery. On the contrary, it is ever-
evolving and dynamically changing. Objectivity in pure form is not
attainable. What the researcher conceives as possible or impossible, as
serious or superfluous, will influence how one works and what one
finds.[12] Herzog declares,

> It [historical critical method] pretends to suspend evaluations which is
> simply impossible, since research proceeds on the basis of questions
> asked and a ranked priority in their asking. But such judgments presup-

sociologically for fifty years.' This statement appears in a transcript of a colloquium
published in Bruce Malina, *The Gospel of John in Sociolinguistic Perspective*
(Berkeley: Centre for Hermeneutical Studies, 1984), p. 49.

    11. Keck, 'On the Ethos', p. 446.

    12. William Herzog, 'Interpretation as Discovery and Creation: Sociological
Dimensions of Biblical Hermeneutics', *American Baptist Quarterly* 2 (1983), pp.
105-18 (109).

>3

pose a system of values and an ontology of meaning which not only give weight to the questions asked but make it possible to ask them at all.[13]

In other words, the biblical scholar's relation to the subject matter prompts the questions (s)he brings to the text and elicits the answers obtained from the text. Since the texts do not speak until scholars speak to them, and since they always answer in the scholar's own language, no interpreter is neutral, and no text a simple object that yields a single meaning.[14]

A renewed interest in the social sciences and their potential in the interpretation of biblical texts has also been furthered by what John Stanley calls 'a blurring of paradigms'.[15] In the early 1970s James Robinson declared that scholarship had entered a period of crisis with regard to the basic categories by which it assembled its data. He spoke of the need to dismantle and reassemble the basic categories of the scholarly discipline in order to determine direction for the future.[16] Ten years later, O.C. Edwards points to 'historical-critical method's failure of nerve',[17] while D. Harrington notes the lack of any movement in the field of biblical study during the previous decade. Although Harrington recognizes that there have been good presentations of the topics that constitute the agenda of this approach, he sees a need to infuse new life into the student of the church by moving beyond methods and positions that were in fashion in the 1960s.[18]

13. Herzog, 'Interpretation', p. 109, quoting Walter Wink, *The Bible in Human Transformation* (Philadelphia: Fortress Press, 1973), p. 7.

14. Herzog, 'Interpretation', p. 111.

15. He defines a paradigm as a shared example of how to do things. John Stanley, 'The Sociology of Knowledge and New Testament Interpretation', in Barbara Hargrove (ed.), *Religion and the Sociology of Knowledge: Modernization and Pluralism in Christian Thought and Structure* (Lewiston: Edward Mellen Press, 1984), p. 123.

16. James Robinson, 'Introduction: The Dismantling and Reassembling of the Categories of New Testament Scholarship', in James Robinson and Helmut Koester, *Trajectories through Early Christianity* (Philadelphia: Fortress Press, 1971), pp. 1-19.

17. O.C. Edwards, Jr, 'Historical-Critical Method's Failure of Nerve and a Prescription for a Tonic: A Review of Some Recent Literature', *ATR* 59 (1977), pp. 115-34.

18. Daniel Harrington, 'Sociological Concepts and the Early Church: A Decade of Research', *TS* 41 (1980), pp. 181-90 (181).

Such statements affirm the inadequacies, sensed by many exegetes, of historical critical inquiry alone.

In science, when a paradigm shift occurs the previous methodology is discarded. Stanley suggests that in biblical studies the blurring of paradigms will, instead, allow exegetes to travel diverse routes toward the meaning of the text and to celebrate methodological diversity.[19] David Bartlett reports on five different models for biblical studies, one of which draws upon sociology and anthropology to understand the world which produced the biblical texts. His conclusions are similar to those of Stanley:

> The very variety of approaches to the task of biblical scholarship may imply that no single scholarly paradigm can be adequate to the varieties of biblical literature... I doubt very much that one ruling paradigm of biblical studies will emerge in this century, and I suspect that the diversity of approaches will help us to appreciate the diversity of the texts and enrich our understanding of Scripture itself.[20]

Social Sciences and Biblical Exegesis

Biblical scholars have begun to ask new questions and to formulate new hypotheses by linking the historical critical method with the social sciences. While previous accomplishments in philology, literary analysis, history of traditions and theological insight are honoured, these scholars combine the social sciences with the historical-critical method to counteract the abstractions of the history of ideas:[21]

John Gager's *Kingdom and Community: The Social World of Early Christianity*[22] is one of the first works to be published in North America which has used the social sciences as tools for investigating the life of the church in its first two centuries. Suffering from many of the difficulties which one might expect in any emerging branch of

19. Stanley, 'Sociology of Knowledge', p. 130.

20. David L. Bartlett, 'Biblical Scholarship Today: A Diversity of New Approaches', *The Christian Century* 98 (1981), pp. 1090-94 (1094).

21. Robin Scroggs has charged biblical studies with 'methodological docetism' because it emphasizes ideas almost exclusively. He identifies this as the most appropriate description of the impasse which exists within biblical scholarship ('The Sociological Interpretation of the New Testament: The Present State of Research', *NTS* 26 [1980], pp. 164-79 [165-66]).

22. John Gager, *Kingdom and Community: The Social World of Early Christianity* (Englewood Cliffs, NJ: Prentice–Hall, 1975).

research, especially one aimed at aligning previously isolated academic disciplines, his work has raised a number of questions which have helped to clarify procedures in subsequent research.

What Gager hopes to accomplish is uncertain. The subtitle speaks of 'the social world of early Christianity', and in the opening pages he clarifies this with the statement: 'I do not intend to produce social history. This is not primarily a study of social teachings, social impact, social surroundings or social institutions'.[23] He will explore early Christian 'processes of world construction and world maintenance'. A paragraph which follows outlines what he means by this:

> All new religions, then, are directed toward the creation of new worlds: old symbols are given new meaning and new symbols come to life; new communities define themselves in opposition to previous traditions; a new order of the sacred is brought into being and perceived by the community as the source of all power and meaning; new rituals emerge to remind the community of this sacred order by creating it anew in the act of ritual celebration; mechanisms are established for preserving this new world and for adapting it to changing circumstances; and eventually an integrated world view may emerge. . . whose task is to give meaning not just to the community itself but to all other worlds as well.[24]

Only the second point, a new group defining itself in opposition to previous traditions, is treated at any length.[25]

Gager states his 'basic conviction that the process of generating a sacred cosmos or a symbolic universe is always rooted in concrete communities of believers'.[26] Yet he fails to locate or describe these communities.[27] The resultant homogenization of early Christianity does a disservice to its diversity. To apply Burridge's understanding of millenarian morality to a first century generation of Christianity through applying it to Paul totally neglects other strains such as the Jerusalem church, to which it would not apply.[28]

23. Gager, *Kingdom*, pp. 10-11.
24. Gager, *Kingdom*, p. 11.
25. Jonathan Z. Smith, 'Too Much Kingdom, Too Little Community', *Zygon* 13 (1978), pp. 123-30 (125).
26. Gager, *Kingdom*, p. 10.
27. Smith ('Too Much Kingdom', p. 125) states: 'There are no realia, no dates, no places, no names, no anything except vague generalizations and ideas attributed to any of the communities Gager describes. Indeed, he calmly declares "whatever its date and location" (p. 50) of the only text which he analyzes in detail.'
28. David L. Bartlett, 'John G. Gager's "Kingdom and Community": A Summary

Gager's use of models to provide new data draws on Melanesian cargo cults to explain one aspect of Christianity, while, at the same time, using a group of people who expected the end of the world to explain another. This apocalyptic model runs into two difficulties. Not only are there theoretical differences among the scholars cited to explain this model, but the traits which Gager applies to Christianity are traits originally derived from Palestinian Jewish eschatology and from Christianity.[29] In addition, cognitive dissonance and Coser's theory of the functions of social conflict, the models which Gager uses, have been challenged as heuristic models by sociologists.[30]

This early work defined the issues that needed clarification so that the methods and models of the social sciences could be used in biblical studies in a way that maintained the integrity of each discipline. Biblical studies require that the diversity within early Christianity be respected, and that any analysis be limited to a reasonably coherent and identifiable segment of it. The biblical text must be primary. The social sciences require that the models be valid within their own disciplines.[31] A discussion of the writings of Wayne Meeks, Gerd Theissen, John Elliott, Bruce Malina and Norman Petersen demon-

and Response', *Zygon* 13 (1978), pp. 109-22 (119).

29. Smith, 'Too Much Kingdom', p. 127.

30. On cognitive dissonance: Aronson Elliot, 'The Theory of Cognitive Dissonance in Current Perspective', in Leonard Berkowitz (ed.), *Cognitive Theory in Social Psychology* (New York: Academic Press, 1978), pp. 181-220; on Coser's functions of social conflict: John Rex, *Key Problems of Sociological Theory* (London: Routledge & Kegan Paul, 1961), pp. 115-20 and Michael Phillipson, 'Theory, Methodology and Conceptualization', in Paul Filmer, Michael Phillipson, David Silverman and David Walsh, *New Directions in Sociological Theory* (London: Macmillan, 1972). For a general discussion of models and biblical interpretation see Bruce Malina, 'Why Interpret the Bible with the Social Sciences?', *American Baptist Quarterly* 2 (1983), pp. 119-33 (131); Cyril S. Rodd, 'On Applying a Sociological Theory to Biblical Studies', *JSOT* 19 (1981), pp. 95-106; Bruce J. Malina, 'Normative Dissonance and Christian Origins', *Semeia* 35 (1986), pp. 35-58 (35).

31. Gager's failure to reflect carefully on the models used can perhaps be explained by his disclaimer: 'In the long run I am less committed to particular models. . . than I am to the more general program of rapprochement between historians of religion and theorists in other fields' (Gager, *Kingdom*, pp. xii-xiii). It is the need to investigate social science models more fully which has challenged biblical scholars since Gager's book. See John Elliott, 'Social Scientific Criticism of the New Testament: More on Methods and Models', *Semeia* 35 (1986), pp. 1-33.

strates the increasing sophistication and precision in the application of the social sciences to biblical interpretation.

In his major work, *The First Urban Christians*,[32] Wayne Meeks avoids the generalizations of Gager by recognizing the diversity within early Christianity and choosing the extended missionary activity of Paul as a coherent and identifiable unit for description. The scope of his inquiry is the social world of the Apostle Paul, and the use and exegesis of particular texts are vital to that task. Although his goal is social history, he does acknowledge the need for the social sciences in the interpretation of Paul's social world, and his use of anthropological and sociological research suggests that he shares the aims of the social-scientific study of the Bible and the biblical world. However, he uses words such as 'suggestive rather than generative', and 'eclectic', 'piecemeal',[33] to describe his approach to social-scientific theory, and this results in a cautious and rather apologetic analysis at the level of explanation.[34] John Elliott states,

> Meeks, it would appear, would like to have it both ways—the safety of theory free social description and the occasional dalliance with sociological research. But can a historian implanted with the seed of the social sciences plausibly claim to be 'only a little bit pregnant'? Meeks' entire enterprise would have gained considerably in methodological clarity and perhaps also cogency if he had identified his theories and their sources, explicated his conceptual models, and clarified his sociological as well as historical and theological premises and thus provided a more precise basis for the verification and critique of conclusions reached. What is gained by such methodological obfuscation other than the possible appeasement of those naive about their own social premises and unwilling to acknowledge the role theory plays in any authentic scientific undertaking?[35]

32. Wayne Meeks, *The First Urban Christians: The Social World of the Apostle Paul* (New Haven: Yale University Press, 1983).

33. Meeks, *First Urban*, p. 5.

34. His concern is to appease the skepticism concerning the social sciences which he perceives within theologians and historians of Christianity. See Meeks, *First Urban*, pp. 2-4. On p. 5 he states: 'As Peter Brown said in one of his elegant essays, the historian's attitude toward the social sciences is like that of the African tribal chief who described the neighbouring tribe for the enquiring ethnographer: "they are our enemies, we marry them"'.

35. John Elliott, 'A Review of *The First Urban Christians: The Social World of the Apostle Paul* by Wayne A. Marshall', *RelSRev*, 11 (1985), pp. 329-34 (332).

In spite of this criticism, it is recognized that the sifting through, arranging and appropriating of the social data is, itself, a subtle and sometimes tricky activity since it involves moving from what is generally true of the larger culture to what may specifically be applicable with regard to the New Testament texts. Meeks's ability to infer the social context from what is primarily a discussion of theological or ethical matters is masterful.[36]

Gerd Theissen provides another example of this ability to infer social context from theological and ethical discussions. His writings are concerned with the integrity of biblical exegesis. Each concentrates on one distinct group within early Christianity, the Corinthian community or Palestinian Christianity,[37] and his conclusions are grounded in a wealth of detailed exegesis.

In his studies on Corinth, Theissen chooses functional analysis to explain how the earliest movement which arose in Palestine could function in different surroundings. Functionalism takes seriously the intentionality of religious phenomena, but interprets them in terms of their contribution to the solution of basic social problems.[38] Theissen articulates the sociological theory that he appropriates without apology, yet he remains more properly a social historian.[39]

36. Robin Scroggs, 'Sociology', p. 141.

37. Theissen, *Social Setting*; Gerd Theissen, *The First Followers of Jesus: A Sociological Analysis of the Earliest Christianity* (trans. J. Bowden; London: SCM Press, 1978). Another work, *Psychological Aspects of Pauline Theology* (trans. J.P. Galvin; Philadelphia: Fortress Press, 1987) presents a psychological exegesis of significant theological subjects and key Pauline texts. He states that the goal of psychological exegesis is to describe and explain behaviour and experience in ancient Christianity, and Theissen is aware of the controversial nature of this pioneering enterprise. It is described by reviewers as an exciting and insightful work. See Merlin H. Hoops, 'Review of Gerd Theissen, *Psychological Aspects of Pauline Theology*', *Int* 42 (1988), p. 318.

38. Functionalism is defined against phenomenological analysis and the causal-genetic approach. The former concludes that, at its core, religion is inaccessible to sociological analysis. The latter denies the distinctive intentionality of religious phenomena and traces them back to non-religious factors. See John Schütz in Theissen, *Social Setting*, p. 16.

39. Theissen, *Social Setting*, pp. 17, 20. In his review of Theissen's *The First Followers of Jesus*, Elliott ('Social Scientific', pp. 10-25) points out that he offers no cross-cultural models to generate heuristic explanations of the factors he describes. Both Malina (Review of Gerd Theissen *Sociology of Early Palestinian Christianity*, *CBQ* 41 [1979], p. 178) and Elliott are critical of the psychological paradigm which

In *A Home for the Homeless: A Sociological Exegesis of 1 Peter, its Situation and Strategy*,[40] John Elliott has attempted to recover the political situation of the addressees of 1 Peter. Investigating two terms used in the letter which have traditionally been given metaphorical, religious significance ('aliens and exiles' 1 Pet. 2.11), he argues that these should be given their literal meanings to denote the political and legal deprivations of the members of the communities in Asia Minor.

In his introductory chapter he is explicit about his sociological perspective. The task he sets is a sociological exegesis that he describes as 'the analytic and synthetic interpretation of a text through the combined exercise of the exegetical and sociological disciplines, their principles, theories and techniques'.[41] Elliott's method involves the employment of the perspectives, presuppositions, modes of analysis, comparative models, theories and research of the discipline of sociology, yet it focuses upon a biblical document, and through the employment of all the sub-disciplines of exegesis attempts to determine the meaning and impact of the text within its various contexts.

He states,

> The literary text serves as the primary focus, starting point, and empirical control of sociological analysis. Its primary goal is the interpretation of the text as it has been designed to serve as a vehicle of socioreligious interaction. Sociological exegesis asks not only what a text said 'then and there' but also how and why that text was designed to function and what its impact upon the life and activity of its formulators was intended to be.[42]

Antoinette Wire astutely observes that Elliott's sympathies are towards the author of 1 Peter, and notes his difficulty in taking a critical stance against the writer. This raises questions about the comprehensiveness of the model he uses,[43] and Elliott admits in a later article that more

he uses. Malina states (p. 178): 'The "sociology" is rather social description and/or social history in which the implicit sociological models are never clearly articulated'.

40. John Elliott, *A Home for the Homeless: A Sociological Exegesis of 1 Peter, its Situation and Strategy* (Philadelphia: Fortress Press, 1981).

41. Elliott, *Home for the Homeless*, pp. 7-8.

42. Elliott, *Home for the Homeless*, p. 8.

43. Antoinette Wire, A Review of John H. Elliott, *A Home for the Homeless: A Sociological Exegesis of 1 Peter, its Situation and Strategy* and David Balch, *Let Wives Be Submissive: The Domestic Code in 1 Peter*, *RelSRev* 10 (1984), pp. 209-16 (214).

work needs to be done both in defining what a sociological 'model' is, and in determining how models are best used.[44] In this criticism he includes the studies of Meeks, Theissen and his own.[45]

In spite of certain weaknesses in the final product,[46] the approach of Elliott is sound and one that needs to be acknowledged in any attempt at an interdisciplinary analysis. His method takes seriously the need to make an exhaustive exegetical study as well as an unapologetic use of the social sciences. In spite of the fact that he, too, fails sufficiently 'to explicate, clarify and justify the sociological perspectives adopted and the methods employed',[47] his insistence on an equal emphasis on exegesis and the methods of the social sciences is basic to a proper interdisciplinary study.

The strength of Bruce Malina's work, *Christian Origins and Cultural Anthropology*[48] lies in his analysis of social science models within cultural anthropology. This represents a move away from using the social sciences in general to a specific use of anthropology and an exploration of the possibilities of the theory of Mary Douglas on 'grid and group' for biblical interpretation.

Fasting is used as a test for models drawn from anthropology, and, although the New Testament passages are laid out in the text, there is little exegesis.[49] Malina asks only about the social meaning of fasting, and while one recognizes that his primary consideration is to make Mary Douglas's theory understandable to biblical scholars, its full

44. Elliott, 'Social Scientific', pp. 1-26.

45. Elliott, 'Social Scientific', p. 26 n. 29.

46. Elliott has been reproached for his lack of reflection on the text which he is analyzing. See *New Testament Abstracts* 29 (1985), p. 163.

47. Elliott, 'Social Scientific', p. 24 n. 29 critiques his own work in these words.

48. Bruce Malina, *Christian Origins and Cultural Anthropology: Practical Models for Biblical Interpretation* (Atlanta: John Knox, 1986).

49. In A Review of Bruce J. Malina's *New Testament World: Insights from Cultural Anthropology*, *CBQ* 45 (1983), p. 498, Pheme Perkins recognizes this lack of concreteness in his *New Testament World*, and has commented that Malina's purpose would be better served had he made a more detailed analysis of one or two New Testament examples and then commented on the differences this perspective from anthropology makes. Adrian Edwards (A Review of Bruce Malina *The New Testament World*, *New Blackfriars* 65 [1984], pp. 42-44 [43]) is critical of Malina's failure to give an account of the social worlds of Jesus and Paul. Commenting on the chapter on 'Clean and Unclean' which relies on the theory of Mary Douglas, he states, 'this approach is not significantly related to the political and social realities of first century Palestine'.

potential is realized only when exegesis is complete.

Norman Peterson (*Rediscovering Paul: Philemon and the Sociology of Paul's Narrative World*),[50] situates his analysis of Philemon within an anthropological framework. He explains his preference for anthropology by juxtaposing two statements which differentiate the goals of sociology and anthropology. One is from the work of Gerd Theissen and the other from that of T.O. Beidelman, an anthropologist with strong interests in the study of religion. The quotation from Theissen contains a definition of what a sociological statement is:

> A sociological question is less concerned with what is individual than with what is typical, recurrent, general. Second, it is less concerned with the singular conditions of a specific situation than with structural relationships which apply to several situations. Therefore a sociology of primitive Christianity has the task of describing and analyzing the interpersonal behaviour of members of primitive Christian groups.[51]

Now Beidelman:

> We cannot get far in understanding a society before decoding the ways its members communicate their wants and needs to one another, and in order to do that, we must first understand the ways in which these persons see and define themselves and the world in which they live. . . the sum total of ways in which the members of a society symbolize or categorize their experience so that they may give it order and form and thereby manipulate it and also deal with their fellows who share this experience with them. Language not only includes words but gestures, facial expressions, clothing and even household furnishings—in short total symbolic behaviour. Those with a common language share common values and perceptions and thus form a moral group, a kind of church.[52]

What Petersen finds valuable in Beidelman's approach is anthropology's emphasis on decoding the ways in which members of a society see and define themselves and the world in which they live. An understanding of this system of meanings allows the modern interpreter to comprehend that society's 'social systems or institutions, the social arrangements pertinent to its social life, such as the family, kinship

---

50. Norman Petersen, *Rediscovering Paul: Philemon and the Sociology of Paul's Narrative World* (Philadelphia: Fortress Press, 1985).

51. Petersen, *Narrative*, p. 18, citing Theissen, *Social Setting*, pp. 176-77 and Schütz's introduction to this volume.

52. Petersen, *Narrative*, pp. 18-19 citing T.O. Beidelman, *The Kaguru: A Matrilineal People of East Africa* (New York: Holt, Rinehart & Winston, 1971), p. 30.

systems, political organizations, legal procedures, religious cults, and the like'.[53] Although Petersen's work is complicated, it is evaluated by reviewers as an ambitious and innovative attempt to advance and consolidate some of the fresh hermeneutical developments in Pauline studies.[54]

Towards a Viable Social Scientific Methodology

In spite of the growing methodological precision of sociological inquiry, questions still arise as to the validity and usefulness of such a study. Traditionally, a wariness has informed the relationship between biblical studies and the social sciences, and has resulted in an anti-sociological stance within biblical scholarship.[55] Some scholars have feared that sociological interpretations would deny religious phenomena any distinctive character by treating them as effects of non-religious causes, and that the questions the social scientist addressed to religious texts would extract from them something contrary to, or at least different from, their manifest content or intention.[56]

Early sociologists, such as Emile Durkheim, believed that social factors could fully explain religion; however, a number of more recent theories view religion in a more positive way.[57] Even so, the

53. Petersen, *Narrative*, pp. 19-20.

54. Robert Tannehill, 'Exploring Paul in New Ways', *Int* 44 (1987), pp. 76-78; John A. Darr and Vincent L. Wimbush, 'A Review, *Rediscovering Paul: Philemon and the Sociology of Paul's Narrative World* by Norman R. Petersen', *RelSRev* 14 (1988), p. 118-24 (118).

55. Gager, 'Enemies', p. 257. Scroggs, 'Sociology', pp. 138-39.

56. See Meeks, *First Urban*, pp. 2-3. Carolyn Osiek (*What are they saying about the Social Setting of the New Testament?* [Ramsey, NJ: Paulist Press, 1984], pp. 5-6), states of these difficulties: 'There is the danger that social and sociological study of early Christianity can take the reductionist approach of limiting religious experience to patterns of group behaviour where it can be observed and categorized, rather than recognizing it as the bridge between everyday existence and the Transcendent'. Contrast Scroggs's statement ('Sociology', p. 140): '*No* "scientific" approach needs to be reductionist. Every "scientific" approach—including the historical *can* be reductionistic. That is, reductionism does not lie in the methodology itself, but in the theological presuppositions which one brings to sociological or any other methodology.'

57. In 'The Application of Symbolic Anthropology to Religions of the Greco-Roman World', *RelSRev* 10 (1984), pp. 216-23 (216-18), Robert A. Segal discusses the difference between the social sciences now and their predecessors. The true difference, he states, 'is over the *distinctiveness* of the *intellectual* function

suspicion still lingers in some circles that a social scientific analysis of the New Testament poses a threat to the authority of scripture and to faith itself.[58]

As this approach struggles to develop a controlling orthodoxy of method and intent, questions persist as to what constitutes a proper social science methodology. The fluidity of the situation can be seen in the results expected: social description or an unfolding of a sociology of early Christianity.[59] This has caused a lack of agreement about basic procedures. Some scholars utilize the theoretical views of sociology and the interpretative models from across the range of the social sciences, while others vary little from traditional historians.

Two levels of application of social categories need to be distinguished: description and explanation. In reaction to earlier theological approaches, description emphasizes the importance of historical, social and economic factors in the understanding of the early church. The findings of archaeology, history and literature contemporary to the texts, are used to gather data and form concepts concerning social life and organization, political life, institutions and social dynamics. This data is then arranged and the social context extrapolated from the theological and ethical discussion.[60]

The second level, explanation, uses the tools and techniques of

religion serves. However important and beneficial religion was to them, classical social scientists invariably assumed its function to be either nonintellectual altogether or, if intellectual, better served by modern science. . . Whether or not for them [contemporary social scientists], religion best, let alone exclusively serves its intellectual function, that function is not pre-scientific and so is not merely primitive. Religion runs askew to modern science and so is not closed to moderns.' (p. 217)

58. Gager, 'Enemies', p. 257; Best ('Sociological Study', p. 192) warns the 'New Testament sociologist' to insist upon the importance of the faith-dimension in the texts.

59. This confusion surrounding the question of using the words 'social' or 'sociological' can be clearly seen in Malherbe's work. See Malherbe, *Social Aspects*. On p. 20 he uses 'sociological description' to define both social history and the use of social science theory. He states that 'the sociological description of early Christianity can concentrate either on social facts or sociological theory as a means of describing the "sacred cosmos" or "symbolic universe" of early Christian communities'. His interest is in social description, and he warns against 'excessive enthusiasm' for social interpretations.

60. While older handbooks and commentaries have drawn parallel religious and theological material from the ancient world, they do not demonstrate similar knowledge of the social reality that influenced peoples' lives.

modern social-scientific study, not merely to describe but also to probe the inner dynamics of the early Christian movement, regarded not as a unique event but as an example of patterns of behaviour which may be widely observed and objectively studied.[61] In any study both are needed if the social sciences are to be used with integrity.[62] Theoretical explanations without descriptions are incomplete, while meaningful descriptions contain within them assumptions that verge on being theories in disguise. By definition, however, a sociological study is one that openly uses models from the social sciences.

Other critics suggest that this methodology creates a set of problems which will outweigh its usefulness. E.A. Judge, in a critique of Holmberg's *Paul and Power*, states,

> His methodological stance does not bestride ideas and facts in an equally secure manner. In particular he does not have his foot on firm ground on the factual side. The extensive reading list conceals a dangerous gap. It couples with New Testament studies a strong admixture of modern sociology, as though social theories can be safely transposed across centuries without verification. The basic question remains unasked: What are the social facts of life characteristic of the world to which the New Testament belongs? Until the painstaking field work is better done, the importation of social models that have been defined in other cultures is methodologically no improvement on the 'idealistic fallacy'. We may fairly call this the sociological fallacy.[63]

Philip Esler names three assumptions in this objection: (1) that socio-logical models must be historically tested or 'verified' before they can be applied; (2) that sociological models are defined with respect to particular cultures and, therefore, cannot be applied to first century

---

61. Best, 'Sociological Study', p. 185.

62. Norman Petersen is criticized for not describing the system of slavery as it existed in the first century. See Tannehill, 'Exploring Paul in New Ways', p. 77.

63. E.A. Judge, 'The Social Identity of the First Christians: A Question of Method in Religious History', *JRH* 11 (1980), pp. 201-17 (210) as quoted in Philip Esler, *Community and Gospel in Luke–Acts* (Cambridge: Cambridge University Press, 1987), p. 13. The work of Judge, the classical historian, on the social identity of the early Christians is seminal, and has resulted in a growing consensus which affirms the diversity of status within the early Christian communities. While he does not use social scientific models in his analysis, his warning of the need for adequate description in any sociological study must be heeded. See Judge, 'Social Identity', pp. 211-12.

society; (3) that historical field work is a totally 'objective' enterprise.[64]

The third assumption provides an example of the need for models to identify the whole range of theoretical presuppositions that a researcher has already subscribed to in defining a field of inquiry. By not consciously and deliberately acknowledging and reflecting upon such preconceptions, any researcher runs the risk of imposing modern notions of categorization and significance upon data from a period where they might be quite inappropriate.[65]

The first two assumptions point out the need to define the term 'model'. In the social sciences models are mental constructs, research tools, not social laws, and sociologists and anthropologists are well aware of the desirability of producing models and typologies which, as far as possible, have been stripped of temporal and spatial markings.

A model is an organizational framework by which the implications of new ideas and insights can be seen, and through it new ideas are set out in relation to one another and to the older ideas which they displace.[66] Since a model organizes, profiles and interprets an accumulation of data, it provides a basic proposition through which the variety of observations and statements become explicable. In any analysis it is not a question of whether or not models will be used; rather, it is a question of whether they will be used consciously or unconsciously.

Max Black has some illuminating comments on the comparison between scientific models and literary metaphors. Metaphors cause one situation to be construed in terms of another. In the same way, scientific models can be defined as systematically developed metaphors, in that a model suggests new ways of looking at problematic situations by transferring some of the features of another situation which is better understood. This 'may help us to notice what would otherwise be overlooked and the shift in relative emphasis attached to details—in short, to see new connections'.[67]

In the social sciences, models are employed to analyze and interpret the properties of social behaviour, social structure and social process.

64. Esler, *Community*, pp. 13-14.
65. Esler, *Community*, p. 15.
66. T.F. Carney, *The Shape of the Past: Models and Antiquity* (Lawrence, KS: Coronado Press, 1975), pp. 3-4.
67. Black, *Models and Metaphors*, p. 237.

There are different kinds of models, and they perform a diversity of functions.[68] Carney argues that what he calls homomorphic models are most useful to those who seek to understand antiquity.[69] Cross-cultural models, a subset of this category, are used by anthropologists.[70] These cross-cultural models have two features which make them attractive to biblical scholars: (1) their formats are relatively precise and there is an abundance of literature, what these models involve is easily taught; (2) their structures and assumptions are available for inspection, in that the logic of the analytical procedure can be systematically checked.[71]

Cultural Anthropology and Biblical Studies

In its use of cross-cultural models, anthropology comes well-suited for tackling the issue of hermeneutics. Anthropologists are required to enter into a unique world view and comprehend a whole interrelated system of meaning and interpretation, and then translate their discoveries into the language and thought patterns of their contemporary

68. In his list Ian Barbour includes: experimental, logical and mathematical models, as well as theoretical models. See Ian Barbour, *Myths, Models and Paradigms: A Comparative Study in Science and Religion* (New York: Harper & Row, 1974), pp. 29-31 for definitions.

69. Homomorphic models are defined against isomorphic models. The latter are scale models or replicas in which there is a one-to-one relationship between the features of the model and the thing modelled. A homomorphic model is one in which only the gross similarities, and not all the details of the thing modelled are replicated. They are cast in abstract terms. He lists five main types: ideal, cross-cultural, comparative, postulational and multivariate. See Carney, *Shape of the Past*, pp. 9-10.

70. A cross-cultural model is constructed in the following way: (a) culture areas are established as historical evidence dictates; (b) there is a uniform, methodical and detailed comparison of the forms of the particular problem which occur in these culture areas; (c) the secondary literature—modern scholarship interpreting the object of concern in each of the culture areas, and observations on the functioning of the object of concern in general—is reviewed and incorporated into the study. According to Carney *(Shape of the Past*, p. 16), 'this kind of model puts us into the right ball park. We now know the sorts of things we may expect to find. We have some idea of how much variation we will find in each of them. We have some notion of the meaning of such things for their contemporaries. And we can spot anachronisms when they crop up, whether these anachronisms involve assumptions about or interpretations of data.' Carney uses the concept of bureaucracy in the ancient world to explain this particular type of model.

71. Carney, *Shape of the Past*, p. 20.

society. The critical results of contemporary research bear striking resemblance to the operations and goals of the anthropological enterprise. George Worgul states,

> With the advent of form criticism and redaction criticism attention has been turned to the cultural and community life as the fabric which forms the basis for the composition of the biblical record. Culture and community are the very foundation for anthropology as a science and specify its field of enquiry. . . The New Testament writings express the world view of the communities from which they emerged. Consequently, they are potentially primary data for anthropological analysis.[72]

Within the social sciences, anthropologists have asked whether their theories and methods can be applied to historical societies for which there is no face-to-face evidence. The conclusion reached states that, while historical data may be limited, contemporary data are not substantially different. Any 'document is a witness and like most witnesses, it does not say much except under cross-examination. The real difficulty lies in putting the right questions'.[73] Mary Douglas's study of food laws in Leviticus[74] and Gillian Feeley-Harnik's study of Philemon and her longer study on the Lord's Supper[75] provide positive examples of anthropology's investigation of biblical texts. Victor Turner moves into the area of Icelandic legend, and applies his anthropological experience and thinking to literature in an effort to determine a people's mentality from texts. His starting point is a statement made by Evans-Pritchard:

> An anthropological training, including fieldwork, would be especially valuable in the investigation of earlier periods of history in which institutions and modes of thought resemble in many respects those of the simpler people we study. For such periods the historian struggles to determine a people's mentality from a few texts, and anthropologists cannot

72. George Worgul, Jr, 'Anthropological Consciousness and Biblical Theology', *BTB* 9 (1974), pp. 3-12 (4).

73. Gillian Feeley-Harnik, 'Is Historical Anthropology Possible? The Case of the Runaway Slave', in Gene M. Tucker and Douglas A. Knight (eds.), *Humanizing America's Iconic Book* (SBL Centennial Addresses; Chico, CA: Scholars Press, 1980), pp. 95-126 (95-98), quotation on p. 98.

74. Mary Douglas, 'The Abomination of Leviticus', in *idem*, *Purity and Danger*, pp. 41-58.

75. Feeley-Harnik, 'Historical Anthropology', pp. 95-126 and Gillian Feeley-Harnik, *The Lord's Table: Eucharist and Passover in Early Christianity* (Philadelphia: University of Pennsylvania Press, 1981).

help wondering whether the conclusions he draws from them truly represent their thought.[76]

Symbolic anthropology is that branch of anthropology which relates
most positively to religion, and is the one about which 'religionists'
are also enthusiastic.[77] Anthropologists representative of this approach
include Clifford Geertz, Mary Douglas, and Victor Turner. Clifford
Geertz's concept of culture situates this group:

> The concept of culture I espouse. . . is essentially a semiotic one. Believ-
> ing, with Max Weber, that man is an animal suspended in webs of sig-
> nificance he himself has spun, I take culture to be those webs, and the
> analysis of it to be therefore not an experimental science in search of law
> but an interpretative one in search of meaning.[78]

Symbols are primary in this branch of anthropology. They make
statements about human beings, society and the world, and especially
about humans' relationships to all three. They not only describe these
relationships but also create relationships which they simultaneously
convey. In these settings symbols give order, if not purpose, to
humans' lives. Symbols fuse these same relationships

> by at once granting cosmic sanctions to social norms and evincing those
> cosmic convictions through social practices. On the one hand society
> becomes part of the cosmos, which thereby both explains and justifies it.
> On the other hand, the cosmos gets manifested through society, which
> thereby verifies it.[79]

Geertz defines cultural analysis as 'sorting out the structures of
signification. . . and determining their social ground and import'.[80] He
concentrates on the richness and complexity of the symbol systems as
seen in action, and his interest is in what he calls a 'thick description'
of culture. He describes this in terms of the antics of two boys who
are engaged in rapidly contracting the eyelids of their right eyes. One
is an involuntary twitch, while the other is a conspiratorial signal to a
friend. In terms of actual activity, 'one could not tell which was twitch
and which was wink'. Yet, according to Geertz, the difference is vast:

76. Victor Turner, 'An Anthropological Approach to the Icelandic Saga', in *idem*,
On the Edge of the Bush (Tucson: University of Arizona Press, 1985), p. 75.

77. Segal, 'Application', p. 217.

78. Clifford Geertz, 'Thick Description: Toward an Interpretive Theory of Culture', in *idem*, *The Interpretation of Culture* (New York: Basic Books, 1973) p. 5.

79. Segal, 'Application', p. 218.

80. Geertz, 'Thick Description', p. 9.

> The winker is communicating, and indeed, communicating in a quite
> precise and special way: (1) deliberately, (2) to someone in particular,
> (3) to impart a particular message, (4) according to a socially established
> code, (5) without cognizance of the rest of the company. . . Contracting
> your eyelids on purpose when there exists a public code in which so
> doing counts as a conspiratorial sign is winking.[81]

He continues by drawing out further possibilities in this kind of
description: 'Suppose there is a third boy, who, "to give malicious
amusement to his cronies parodies the first boy's winks as amateurish,
clumsy, obvious, and so on"'. This also is part of a socially established code which gives a particular message.[82]

The object of symbolic anthropology is a 'thick description' of what
is happening, and it is the difference between seeing this scene as
winking and twitching, and seeing it as a parodist practicing a bur-
lesque on a friend faking a wink to deceive an innocent into thinking a
conspiracy is in motion. At a later point Geertz compares this to

> trying to read (in the sense of constructing a reading of) a manuscript,
> foreign, faded, full of ellipses, incoherencies, suspicious emendations,
> and tendentious commentaries, but written not in conventionalized graphs
> of sound but in transient examples of shaped behaviour.[83]

Models from the field of cultural anthropology provide another lens
by which to view the text, a set of questions which can produce new
insights or even new answers to exegetical dilemmas. A number of
studies have appeared over the past few years which have applied
Victor Turner's model of social drama[84] and Mary Douglas's model
of grid and group[85] to a particular text or aspect of the Bible.

---

81. Geertz, 'Thick Description', p. 9.
82. Geertz, 'Thick Description', pp. 6-7.
83. Geertz, 'Thick Description', p. 10.
84. Worgul, 'Anthropological', pp. 3-12; James W. Flanagan, *David's Social Drama: A Hologram of Israel's Early Iron Age* (JSOTSup, 73; Sheffield: Almond Press, 1988).
85. John Gager, 'Body Symbols and Social Reality: Resurrection, Incarnation and Asceticism in Early Christianity', *Religion* 12 (1982) pp. 345-63; Sheldon R. Isenberg and Dennis E. Owen, 'Bodies, Natural and Contrived: The Work of Mary Douglas', *RelSRev* 3 (1977), pp. 1-17; Leland J. White, 'Grid and Group in Matt-hew's Community: The Righteousness/Honor Code in the Sermon on the Mount', *Semeia* 35 (1986), pp. 61-90; Jerome H. Neyrey, 'Body Language in 1 Corinthians: The Use of Anthropological Models for Understanding Paul and his Opponents', *Semeia* 35 (1986), pp. 129-70; Jerome H. Neyrey, 'Witchcraft Accusations in

Conclusions

At the present time those who attempt to use a social-scientific methodology can do so with a certain amount of confidence because of the careful analysis and exegesis that has already been undertaken. Guidelines will be extrapolated from these studies to guide the present inquiry.

Previous studies emphasize the importance of both description and explanation in any social-scientific study. Victor Turner's analysis of Icelandic myth is preceded by a social history of Iceland during that particular period. In his study John Elliott includes a social profile of the addressees of 1 Peter and their situation, and from Wayne Meeks explicit direction is given as to how social history should be undertaken. He states that one should 'begin with the wider view, the ecology, of the Pauline groups and work in towards patterns of meaningful action by which their lives were shaped'.[86] His instruction, to move from the wider society to what is specifically relevant for the situation of the Pauline churches, will be followed in Chapter 2 of this book.

Since the issues in 1 Corinthians 7, marriage/sexual intercourse, singleness/celibacy, are the concerns of kinship, this description will

2 Cor. 10-13: Paul in Social Science Perspective', *Listening* 21 (1986), pp. 160-70; Jerome H. Neyrey, 'Bewitched in Galatia: Paul and Cultural Anthropology', *CBQ* 50 (1988), pp. 72-100; Jerome H. Neyrey and Bruce Malina, *Calling Jesus Names: The Social Value of Labels in Matthew* (Sonoma, CA: Polebridge Press, 1988). A recent thesis (Robert Atkins, 'The Integrating Function of Adoption Terminology Used by the Apostle Paul: A Grid-Group Analysis' [PhD dissertation; Northwestern University, 1987]) is important for its attempt to gain greater precision in using Mary Douglas's model. It is based on a study by Gross and Rayner (Jonathan L. Gross and Steve Rayner, *Measuring Cultures: A Paradigm for the Analysis of Social Organization* [New York: Columbia University Press, 1985]) which measures mathematically strengths of grid and group as they existed in a particular conflict situation within a given community. Refining their predicates of measurement, Robert Atkins plots the Pauline church to provide a framework for his conclusions on Paul's use of the concept of adoption. The task is a difficult one because much of the information required by the Gross/Rayner analysis is unavailable at a distance of two thousand years. The potential, however, of this type of measurement is that it provides verification of the evidence which is uncovered in a 'thick description' of conflict situations.

86. Meeks, *Urban Christians*, p. 8.

concentrate on male/female relationships prevalent in the kinship patterns existing in the Graeco-Roman world of the first century. Conclusions will then be drawn as to what is particularly applicable to the Pauline community at Corinth.

Anthropologists have asked questions about the appropriateness of using historical and literary texts to provide anthropological data. Since many compare this kind of evidence favourably with that obtained from personal interviews and field work observations,[87] this thesis will work from that premise and describe kinship patterns primarily through the use of legal and literary texts.

Explanation follows upon description, and again the work of previous scholarship suggests the most appropriate way of proceeding. The models of cultural anthropology are a convenient place to begin because a relationship has already been established between this discipline and biblical studies. The similarities in intent and the overlapping interests between these two disciplines have been noted.[88] In addition, because a vast amount of secondary literature exists, the models used by cultural anthropology are accessible to the biblical scholar and are reasonably easy to understand.

In anthropology the use of a model in a particular situation is a question of fit. A model is not a social law but a research tool which provides a basic proposition through which a variety of observations and statements become explicable.[89] A researcher begins with a conceptual model or an organizing image of the phenomena to be studied, that is with a set of ideas about the nature of the phenomena to be investigated. It is this conceptual model that determines what questions are to be asked by the researcher and how the information and observations are to be organized.

At the interpretative phase, the research findings are set into the context of ideas proposed by the model. There is often no straightforward execution of a clear cut plan, but instead a working back and forth between theory and research.[90] In other words, the text and the

87. In 'Icelandic Saga', p. 73, Victor Turner states that 'the texts here [Icelandic Legend] arc many and full of the very materials that anthropologists rejoice in when vouchsafed to them by informants in the field'.

88. See pp. 53-56.

89. See pp. 51-53.

90. Matilda Riley, *Sociological Research: A Case Approach* (New York: Harcourt, Brace & World, 1963), pp. 6-7, 27.

model are to interact; the exegesis and the explanatory information are to be held in tension. Again Turner, in his study of Icelandic legend, provides an example. He integrates his explanatory information about the model, social drama, with the evidence from *Njal's Saga*, moving from one to the other as he interprets the conflict. In this study there will be a working back and forth between explanation and research as the models of Victor Turner and Mary Douglas and the exegesis of 1 Corinthians 7 are held in tension.

In using anthropological theory to interpret 1 Corinthians 7, description will precede explanation. The factionalism involves conflicting views about whether marriage and sexual intercourse or singleness and celibacy are more appropriate to the Christian calling. The language used, husband/wife and brother/sister, is kinship terminology, and kinship is the study of these basic social bonds and the proper patterns of behaviour associated with various statuses and roles.[91] Before proceeding to the explanatory models of Victor Turner and Mary Douglas, a description of the relevant kinship patterns which informed first century Corinth will situate the social context of the theological and ethical discussions in ch. 7.

91. Fox, *Kinship and Marriage*, p. 27.

Chapter 2

THE SOCIAL CONTEXT OF 1 CORINTHIANS 7:
MARRIAGE, A DESCRIPTION

> To understand the documents of the Bible is to understand the meanings
> and feelings of an alien culture.[1]

Throughout 1 Corinthians 7 Paul refers to the Corinthians in marital language: γυνή, ἀνήρ, ἄγαμος, χήρα and παρθένος. Another set of terms is also used. In vv. 12-15, ἀδελφός and ἀδελφή refer to those who are also ἀνήρ and γυνή, and in v. 29 those who are married men are addressed as ἀδελφοί. In v. 16 Paul addresses directly those who are γυνή/ἀδελφή and ἀνήρ/ἀδελφός as γύναι and ἄνερ.

These terms are a part of the language of kinship, and concern the arrangement by which people are enabled to live together and co-operate with one another in an orderly social life. Kinship involves the allocation of rights and their transmission from one generation to another. These rights include group membership, succession to office, inheritance of property, locality of residence, and type of occupation.[2] In this chapter not only will the anthropological category of kinship provide a framework for understanding the patterns of marriage in the Graeco-Roman world of the first century, but it will also serve to situate the conflict in ch. 7.

Kinship as an Anthropological Category

In its social function, kinship links people together by a convergence of interest and sentiment, and controls and limits those conflicts which occur because of a divergence of such sentiment or interest. The

1. Malina, *Christian Origins*, p. 12.
2. Rodney Needham, 'Remarks on the Analysis of Kinship and Marriage', in Rodney Needham (ed.), *Rethinking Kinship and Marriage* (London: Tavistock Publications, 1971), pp. 3-4. Fox, *Kinship and Marriage*, especially pp. 13-53.

proper functioning of societies depends upon the presence of an orderly sequence for reciprocal behaviour. The orderly sequence and the expected patterns of behaviour associated with it are called statuses and roles. The terms used to describe these various statuses signal behavioural expectations.[3]

In primitive societies the most important statuses and status terms are those defined in terms of kinship position. According to Burton Pasternak, the particular combination of kinship terms that people employ is not accidental. Rather, nomenclature systems exhibit an internal logic and consistency such that, given certain bits of information, it is possible to predict other attributes of the system as well as features of cultural behaviour and social organization. He explains,

> Where we find a system of kinship terms that seems out of place, where some aspects of usage appear to violate a prevailing model, or where the model itself seems to have changed, such discoveries may indicate that earlier conditions and social characteristics have changed or that society is in the process of transformation.[4]

Anthropologists have distinguished two sets of kin terms: terms of reference and terms of address. The first set is used in talking about a relative, whereas the second set is used in directly addressing a relative. It is important to discover in what social contexts and for what social purposes these alternative sets are used. Frequently, a kinship relation is used in situations when an individual is violating the norms of kinship, or when there is an attempt to manipulate him/her. According to Keesing, the 'use of kin terms often turns out to be a political strategy, not an everyday social nicety'.[5]

Marriage is that institution which has moulded the terminology of kinship, and from it arise those primary relationships by which people in any society relate as male and female. In most cultures the distinction between the sexes is the primary social distinction, and some important institutions always rest on the difference of gender.[6] This distinction is not simply behavioural, but is imbued with moral,

3.   Pasternak, *Kinship and Social Organization*, pp. 124-26. For example, when an individual adopts a particular role, (s)he adopts a demeanour and behaviour that is both appropriate and expectable.

4.   Pasternak, *Kinship and Social Organization*, pp. 125-26.

5.   Roger Keesing, *Kin Groups and Social Structure* (New York: Holt, Rinehart & Winston, 1975), p. 126.

6.   Douglas, *Purity and Danger*, p. 140.

attitudinal and emotional attributes. P.G. Rivière states that in all societies there is a structuring principle based on the differences between the genders, and almost by definition it will manifest itself in marital institutions. He calls upon anthropologists to analyze marriage, not in terms of its function, but as one of many possible forms of relationships between the sexes that exist in society. He defends his approach:

> The categories of male and female do not exist in isolation; they have empirical referents in the form of men and women, and the behaviour, activities, and relationships between men and women adapt themselves in accordance with other changes in the social and natural environment. Such changes bring about changes in the notions of the ideal male and female categories... The argument here is that factors which bring about changes at one level will bring about changes at another, and furthermore that changes in one category will bring about changes in a complementary category and influence the nature of the relationship between them.[7]

Modifications and alterations in the relationships between men and women have widespread ramifications for other aspects of society. For example, Robin Fox presents four rules of kinship as being at the heart of any society: (1) Women have children; (2) men impregnate women; (3) men usually exercise control; (4) primary kin do not mate. He explains: 'gestation, impregnation, domination and the avoidance of incest lie at the root of all social organization'.[8] These rules are closely tied to the institution of marriage. However, if singleness and celibacy were to become the ideal form of male/female relationships, the structure of any society would be radically altered. Victor Turner, commenting on how marriage comes under attack in many religious movements, states: 'celibacy becomes the rule and the relationship between the sexes becomes a massive extension of the sibling bond'.[9] Sexual continence neutralizes marriage and family, and, in turn, the statuses and behaviours that specifically pertain to that institution are dramatically altered.[10]

---

7.   P.G. Rivière, 'Marriage: A Reassessment', in Needham, *Rethinking Marriage and Kinship*, p. 67. He cites the changes in the status of women in the last one hundred years as an example of change in the notion of the ideal male and female categories.

8.   Fox, *Kinship and Marriage*, p. 31.

9.   Turner, *Dramas*, p. 246,

10.   In 'Ecstatics and Ascetics: Studies in the Functions of Religious Activities for Women in the Greco-Roman World' (PhD dissertation; Princeton University, 1976), p. 138, Ross Kraemer states, 'In traditional societies, the rejection of sexuality

A cultural analysis of kinship has taken anthropologists in a slightly different direction. Those who are concerned with symbolic systems—that is, 'with the ways people conceptualize the cosmos and use key symbols as models or paradigms of their social and natural world'[11]—have increasingly been exploring the realm of kinship. These scholars have attempted to analyze cultures as symbolic systems independent of the social systems in which they are embedded, and have recognized that kinship provides symbols central in a people's orientation to their world. As the vital relationships of natural connection and shared essence, whether physical or spiritual, kinship provides a model of relatedness.

The point these anthropologists make is that there exist two kinds of relatedness: that which is culturally conceived and that which is of symbolic import. The latter is the model used to conceptualize relations with deities as well as fictive and adoptive kin relationships. Those investigating symbolic relatedness warn the observer not to conclude too quickly that the culturally conceived model is primary, and have pointed to many examples where people are classified by a kin term according to their role vis-à-vis a particular individual rather than their genealogical relationship, where the two do not coincide.[12]

Four things emerge from this discussion of kinship: where it occurs, kinship terminology needs to be investigated as to its social context and function; an investigation of both culturally conceived and symbolic models of kinship is vital in understanding social roles and behaviour in a particular society or group; marriage is an aspect of social organization and social structure; and a description of marriage needs to take into consideration changes in the notions of the ideal male and female categories.

This framework situates any discussion of marriage patterns within the context of societal structure. Within Graeco-Roman society it suggests that any change in marriage patterns could pose a challenge to

---

usually entails the rejection of roles associated with one's sex and with sexuality, namely reproduction, child-raising and often the associated tasks of domesticity. Since, in most cases, all of these tasks fall to women. . . , the rejection of sexuality carries with it the potential release of women from obligations and roles which are almost always linked to sex and sexuality.'

11. Keesing, *Kin Groups*, p. 127.
12. Keesing, *Kin Groups*, p. 128.

the ordering of political structures.[13] Within the Corinthian church a debate over marriage would posit a range of choices concerning status, roles and behaviour within the group, and more broadly the arrangement of the social structures of that group. In essence, the anthropological category of kinship moves a discussion of marriage and marriage strategies from a theology of sexual asceticism, to a framework of social structure and organization.

Although the conclusions that anthropologists draw about the society they study are normally based on personal observations and a cataloguing of information, recently certain anthropologists have begun to analyze societies from the evidence available in historical and literary texts.[14] On the basis of this data they proceed to investigate the social dynamics operating within the social unit.[15] Likewise, in a study of Corinth, a description of marriage and marriage patterns in the Graeco-Roman world will precede an analysis of the social dynamics in ch. 7.[16]

This description, in seeking to explore changes in marriage and

13.   In 'Marriage in Ancient Greece', in Georges Duby and Michelle Perrot (eds), *A History of Women in the West*. I. *From Ancient Goddess to Christian Saints* (ed. Pauline Schmitt Pantel; trans. Arthur Goldhammer; Cambridge, MA: Harvard Press, 1992), p. 235, Claudine Leduc discusses marriage and the condition of the wife in light of Greek polity. Using an anthropological framework, she argues that the manner in which marriage was arranged is indicative of the evolution of political structures in different city states, that women and matrimonial strategies are central issues for understanding how city states came to be.

14.   Turner ('Icelandic Saga', pp. 71-75) discusses his own decision to study texts as data and evidence for social dramas at other times and places. He also provides an example of the proper manner of proceeding. He begins his discussion of a social drama with 'something of the salient Icelandic settings in space and time' (p. 75), that is social history. Examples of social dramas in history studied by Turner include Beckett and Hidalgo. See Turner, *Dramas*, pp. 60-156.

15.   The relationship between data and dynamics is situated by Turner in *Schism and Continuity in An African Society*, p. xvii. He describes how, while working with the Ndembu, he sought a measure and a metaphor that would enable him to gauge and to describe the transformations in that society. For the former he settled on censuses and genealogies. Through these descriptions he documented the social changes in a way that offered him controls over the interpretations. The social drama provided the metaphor.

16.   Norman Petersen is criticized for his failure to describe the institution of slavery before proceeding to analyze Philemon. See Tannehill, 'Exploring Paul in New Ways', p. 77.

marriage patterns in first century society, will be suggestive rather than exhaustive. At the outset the study recognizes the limitations of the evidence available. Jo-Ann Shelton identifies this difficulty succinctly:

> The literary works used as source material for ancient civilization were written by upper class men, therefore there is more information about men than women and more information about upper class women than lower class women. Of the latter little is known about their daily lives.[17]

In spite of this limitation, an understanding of 1 Corinthians 7 demands that the models and paradigms for behaving and thinking about marriage which were part of the primary socialization of members of the church at Corinth be presented. A first step identifies the inhabitants of Corinth. A second step collects the data about the patterns of marriage operating in that society, and moves from the larger culture to what may be specifically relevant for the social context of the Corinthian correspondence.[18] A final step relates these findings to the church at Corinth.

The Inhabitants of Corinth

In 146 BCE Corinth was destroyed by the Romans, and although it is probable that the city was plundered and burned, references to total destruction and to the city having been abandoned occur in late texts

---

17.   Jo-Ann Shelton, *As the Romans Did: A Sourcebook in Roman Social History* (New York: Oxford University Press, 1988), p. 306. Paul Veyne ([ed.], *From Pagan Rome to Byzantium* I, in Philippe Aries and George Duby [gen. eds.], *A History of Private Life* [trans. Arthur Goldhammer; Cambridge: Belknap Press of Harvard University Press, 1987], p. 36), states in introduction to his discussion of marriage: 'Note, however, that everything I am about to say applies to only a tenth or a twentieth of the free population, to the class of the wealthy who also considered themselves cultivated'.

18.   This manner of proceeding, from the larger society to the Christian community, is that outlined by Wayne Meeks. He states (*Urban Christians*, p. 8) that '[the social world of early Christianity] has a double meaning, referring not only to the environment of the early Christian groups but also to the world as they perceived it and to which they gave form and significance through their special language and other meaningful actions. One is the world they shared with other people who lived in the Roman Empire; the other, the world they constructed. We will begin with the outside view, the ecology of the Pauline groups, and work in toward the patterns of meaningful action by which their lives were shaped.'

or in contexts where poetical or rhetorical exaggeration might be expected.[19] After the conquest the Romans confiscated the civic territory of Corinth and kept it under public ownership as state domain. The senate took no immediate steps to colonize and, in effect, frustrated the later proposals of tribunes to do so. The Roman policy of colonization was a deliberate step, usually carried out for reasons of defense. When it was undertaken, a colony was established as a fully organized, self-governing community with an elaborate urban centre and a functioning administrative apparatus for its corporate existence.[20]

Roman Residents

In 44 BCE, shortly before his assassination, Julius Caesar issued a directive refounding both Corinth and Carthage.[21] His policy was strictly practical, and since his interest was in the urban proletariat of Rome, colonists who proceeded to Corinth were primarily freedmen.[22] In addition to Roman settlers, a number of emancipated Greeks

---

19.   The (1) primary ancient sources and the (2) archaeological evidence are as follows: (1) a. Polybius: An eyewitness to the destruction but too fragmentary to be of much help. b. Strabo: states that Polybius wrote that he himself saw Roman soldiers displaying contempt for works of art and dedications to the gods. c. Antipater of Sidon: A Greek poet who states that the destruction was total and that not a trace of the city was left. d. Cicero: He visited Corinth in 79–77 BCE. There he saw and spoke with people he called *Corinthii*, who were less moved than he by the ruins about them. This passage is important because it was written by a person who visited Corinth during the years of supposed abandonment. (2) Few of the buildings excavated seem to have been subjected to the great violence customarily associated with the plundering of Corinth in 146 BCE. See James Wiseman, 'Corinth and Rome. 1. 228 BC–AD 267', in H. Temporini and W. Haase (eds.), *ANRW*, 7.1, II, pp. 436-548 (491-94).

20.   E.T. Salmon, *Roman Colonization Under the Republic* (Ithaca, NY: Cornell University Press, 1970), p. 19.

21.   Appian (*History* 8:136 in Murphy-O'Connor, *St Paul's Corinth: Texts and Archaeology* [Good News Studies 6; Wilmington: Michael Glazier, 1983], p. 113) states: 'But at a still later time it is said that Caesar, who afterwards became dictator for life. . . when he was encamped near the site of Carthage, he was troubled by a dream in which he saw a whole army weeping, and that he immediately made a memorandum in writing that Carthage should be colonized. Returning to Rome not long after, and the poor asking him for land, he arranged to send some of them to Carthage and some to Corinth.'

22.   Strabo, *Geography* 8.6.23c in Murphy-O'Connor, *St Paul's Corinth*, p. 66.

from Rome were given land in Corinth or were encouraged to settle
there. Because of Corinth's strategic position economically, several
tradesmen, seamen and businessmen from the East, especially from
Egypt, also came as settlers.[23] Common to such cities were persons
formerly enslaved and displaced by war and piracy, political exiles
and soldiers of fortune.

In the decades which followed its incorporation as a colony, Corinth
built up a peculiarly intimate connection in trade and culture with
Rome. Excavations have made clear exactly how Corinth tried to
mimic Rome in its sculpture, architecture, organization and even its
names.[24]

Greek Residents

The formation of Roman colonies often created a subject class and a
situation in which the old city continued to exist side by side with the
colony.[25] Since the use of places of cult, building activities and trade
between 146 BCE and 44 BCE[26] are attested, a reconstruction of events
proposes that some of those who fled after the defeat in 146 BCE
returned when the Roman army departed.

The dynamics of such continuity are hard to measure especially
since the percentage of Greek population to the Roman settlers is unknown.[27] Therefore the caution of Barbara Levick, speaking of the

Another reference to the colonists of Corinth is the poet Crinagoras (Greek *Anthol-
ogy* 9.284, in Murphy-O'Connor, *St Paul's Corinth*, p. 51): 'What inhabitants, O
luckless city, have you received, and in place of whom? Alas for the great calamity to
Greece! Would, Corinth, that you be lower than the ground and more desert than the
Libyan sands, rather than wholly abandoned to such a crowd of scoundrelly slaves,
you should vex the bones of the ancient Bacchiadae.' This statement seems to reflect
more a Greek's lament for past glories than an accurate report of reality. These
freedmen are identified as small shopkeepers, artisans, teachers and secretaries. See
Murphy-O'Connor, *St Paul's Corinth*, pp. 66-67.

23.   Wiseman, 'Corinth and Rome 1', p. 495.

24.   Cyril C. Richardson (ed.), *Early Christian Fathers* (LCC 1; London: SCM
Press, 1953), p. 35. For example, Corinth had symbolic representations in public
places of the seven hills of Rome.

25.   A.H.M. Jones, *The Greek City: From Alexander to Justinian* (repr.; Oxford:
Clarendon Press, 1979 [1940]), p. 173.

26.   Wiseman, 'Corinth and Rome 1', p. 495.

27.   Salmon (*Roman Colonization*, p. 25) states that various official actions
might occur to the natives. They might be expelled *en masse* or they might be permitted to remain as inferior inhabitants, or they might be allowed to maintain their

Pisidian colonies of Galatia is important: 'No consistent pattern... can be discerned in the relations between Roman settlers and native populations, they were strictly *ad hoc*, and... they might be radically affected by reasons of discipline or expediency'.[28] If the inscriptions are an indication, at the time of Paul the official language of the city was Latin.[29] Murphy-O'Connor, referring to the structure and administration of Corinth, calls it a Roman city.[30]

Jewish Residents
In addition to the native Greeks and Roman settlers, another group inhabiting the colony was the Jews. There are many general statements in a number of sources which locate Jews virtually everywhere in the inhabited world.[31] The most specific reference occurs in Philo, writing about 40 CE:

political existence in a separate community of their own. Some might even be admitted to the *colonia* with burgess rights. No evidence is given for Corinth.

28. Barbara Levick, *Roman Colonies in Southern Asia Minor* (Oxford: Clarendon Press, 1967), p. 71.

29. 'Of the 104 texts which are prior to the reign of Hadrian (AD 117-138) 101 are in Latin and only three in Greek, a virtual monopoly for the Latin language'. See John Harvey Kent, *Corinth viii/3: The Inscriptions 1926-1950* (Princeton: American School of Classical Studies at Athens, 1966), p. 19. This use of Latin indicates the strength of the Roman influence at Corinth. It is, however, recognized that Greek was used, even among the Romans, as the language of literature.

30. Murphy-O'Connor, *St Paul's Corinth*, pp. 6-7. According to Kent (*Corinth viii/3*, p. 23), '(t)he colony was organized on a tri-partite basis of an assembly of citizen voters, a city council, and annual magistrates; her civic government, which continued to function without any major changes until early Byzantine times, thus conformed to a pattern typical of the great majority of Roman colonies, and was in effect a miniature replica of the government of Republican Rome'. The city council functioned locally in much the same manner as the Senate at Rome. A property qualification was established for councillors and jurors, thus the Romans controlled Corinth by placing power in the hands of the well-to-do.

31. In 'Judaism on the World Scene', in Stephen Benko and John J. O'Rourke (eds.), *The Catacombs and the Colosseum: The Roman Empire as the Setting of Primitive Christianity* (Pennsylvania: Judson, 1971), p. 83, Robert Kraft cites, 'Sibylline Oracle—"Every land and sea shall be full of (Jews)"; Strabo, as quoted by Josephus—"It is not easy to find a place in the inhabited world which this tribe has not penetrated and which has not been occupied by it"; Agrippa 1 to Gaius in A.D. 39 or 40 gives a detailed list of places where Jewish "colonies" have been established—"in every region of the inhabited world—in Europe, Asia, Libya, on mainlands, on islands, both on the coast and inland"; Speech of Agrippa II to dissuade

> As for the Holy City, I must say what befits me to say. While she, as I
> have said, is my native city she is also the mother city, not of one country
> Judaea, but of most of the others in virtue of the colonies sent out at
> divers times to the neighbouring lands Egypt, Phoenicia, and Syria (the
> so-called Coele Syria as well as Syria proper), to lands lying far away,
> Pamphylia, Cilicia, most of Asia up to Bithynia and the corners of
> Pontus, similarly also into Europe, Thessaly, Boetia, Macedonia, Aetolia,
> Attica, Argos, Corinth, and most of the best parts of the Peloponnese.[32]

Murphy-O'Connor notes how in the midst of cataloguing geographic
regions, Philo has given prominence to two cities, Argos and Corinth.
The fact that these are singled out, particularly since the Peloponnese
as a region is listed, leads him to conclude that they had 'particularly
large and vital Jewish communities'.[33]

The most comprehensive statement of Jewish legal rights in the
Diaspora is the decree of Augustus (2-3 CE). According to it Jews
were allowed to follow their own customs, to assemble in synagogues,
to send money to Jerusalem, and to be exempt from any civic activity
that would violate the Sabbath or their consciences.[34] Specific information on Greek Jewry, however, is virtually non-existent, and a
knowledge of the Jewish community of Corinth is frequently extrapolated from what is known elsewhere in the Diaspora, particularly
Egypt. Although the Jews in Egypt enjoyed a certain degree of home
rule and laws, they would do so only with the consent of the Roman
prefect, and in an uneasy balance with the other inhabitants of the city.
Economically and socially they were a microcosm of the whole
empire.[35]

Jews from revolting in 66 CE, as reported by Josephus—"There is no people in the
inhabited world which does not hold our fate in its hands"; Philo—"One single
country cannot support the Jews because they are so numerous"; Josephus—"The
Jewish race is scattered widely over the entire inhabited world among the local
inhabitants, especially in Syria".'

32.   Philo, *Legatio ad Gaium*, p. 281, cited in Murphy-O'Connor, *St Paul's
Corinth*, pp. 77-78.

33.   Murphy-O'Connor, *St Paul's Corinth*, p. 78; also Richardson, 'Absence'
pp. 60-63.

34.   Josephus, *Antiquitates Judaicae*, XVI, pp. 162-65. E. Mary Smallwood,
The Jews Under Roman Rule: From Pompey to Diocletian (Leiden: Brill, 1976),
p. 143.

35.   See Murphy-O'Connor, *St Paul's Corinth*, pp. 79-80; Naphtali Lewis, *Life
in Egypt Under Roman Rule* (Oxford: Clarendon Press, 1983).

Conclusion

By the time of the writing of 1 Corinthians, Corinth had been resettled for almost a century. Its primary settlers were displaced Romans who came to a colony that, while not completely in ruins, was beginning again.[36] Although Jews, Greeks and Romans made up its population, Corinth was a Roman city. From the start its structure and adminis-tration were Roman and it maintained a particularly close relationship with Rome. Not only did Corinth not take part in the Greek opposi-tion which confronted Augustus and continued after his death,[37] but the isthmus became a centre for emperor worship.[38]

Because of its relationship to Rome and its tendency to copy that city in other areas of its life, a description of marriage patterns in Corinth will begin with the place of marriage in Roman law.[39] A second step will explore how the law was expressed in practice. A final section will situate marriage in terms of the debate over mar-riage and its desirability which was taking place within the philo-sophical schools of the first century.

Marriage and Roman Law

The Familia[40]

In the first centuries of its history, Roman law reflected a rigidly patriarchal and hierarchical society. The only people with full rights

36. G.W. Bowerstock, *Augustus and the Greek World* (Oxford: Clarendon Press, 1965), p. 94; Murphy-O'Connor (*St Paul's Corinth*, p. 5) cites Pausanius: 'Corinth is no longer inhabited by any of the old Corinthians but by colonists sent out by the Romans'.

37. Bowerstock (*Augustus*, pp. 103-108) recounts in detail the opposition to Augustus and nowhere is Corinth mentioned.

38. Oscar Broneer, 'Paul and the Pagan Cults at Isthmia', *HTR* 64 (1971), pp. 169-84 (185). While Broneer recognizes that this practice would not likely reach the indigenous population of Greece with the same impact as in Italy, he continues: 'But Corinth was at that time essentially a Roman city. . . '

39. Distinct differences between these structures and the laws of Greece and of Hellenistic Judaism will be noted.

40. Beryl Rawson in 'The Roman Family', in *idem* (ed.), *The Family in Ancient Rome: New Perspectives* (Ithaca, NY: Cornell University Press, 1986), p. 15 states, 'The various relationships within the Roman family (husband-wife, father-son, father-daughter, mother-son, mother-daughter, between brothers and sisters and between all of these other dependents) have received unequal attention from Roman historians, and we need to know much more about all of them'.

were male citizen heads of family groups. Women had no political rights and could exercise civil rights only with the consent of a tutor or guardian. In law, the *familia* was a group of persons subject to the power of the *paterfamilias* for reasons deriving from nature (children and descendants) or from law (wives and slaves). The *pater* was an undisputed and absolute lord.[41] His power had various designations according to the relationship between parties: *patria potestas* was power over his descendants both male and female; *manus* was the power of the *pater* over his wife.[42]

A child was from birth subject to the control of the father either as *filiusfamilias* or *filiafamilias*. Depending on his life-span, the *pater* could be the grandfather or even great-grandfather of someone in his *potestas*. At the death of the *pater*, each adult son became a *paterfamilias*. The *pater's* power included that of life and death[43] which, in the case of a daughter, allowed the death penalty as the punishment for unchastity.[44]

41.   The Romans believed that the *patria potestas* had been defined by Romulus. FIRA 1, p. 8 (Dionysius of Halicarnassus 2.26-27). See Shelton, *As the Romans*, p. 18.

42.   Jane F. Gardner, *Women in Roman Law and Society* (Bloomington: Indiana University Press, 1986), pp. 5-6. Descriptions of the household in classical Greece focus on Athens. Here the οἶκος constituted the basic socio-political unit and conformed closely to that of the Roman *familia*. See David Verner, *The Household of God: The Social World of the Pastoral Epistles* (Chico, CA: Scholars Press, 1983), pp. 27-32. Like the households of Greece and Rome, the traditional Jewish household was a patriarchal structure. In some ways the authority of its head was even more pronounced than in the other two. See Verner, *Household*, pp. 44-45.

43.   Seneca, *De Clementia* 1.15, tells of a Roman equestrian who flogged his son to death. There is no suggestion he was brought to trial for any crime. Livy 39.18 speaks of the execution of people involved in the Bacchanalian excesses of 186 BCE. Women who were found guilty of involvement were handed over to family councils for infliction of the death penalty. Those women who were not loyal dependents of anyone were executed by the state. See Rawson, 'Family', pp. 16, 49.

44.   Valerius Maximus reports two instances. Pontius Aufidianus killed both his daughter, who had lost her virtue, and her seducer. A certain Atilius, himself a prostitute in his youth, killed his daughter because she was engaged in sexual immorality. See Gardner, *Women in Roman Law*, p. 7. Two stories from the history of early Rome give further examples of this power. One tale concerns Horatia, who was engaged to one of the Curiatii. When her three brothers fought the Curiatii killing all three of them at the expense of two of their own, Horatia grieved at the death of her fiancé. Hearing this, her surviving brother stabbed her. Though the brother was

The law stated that persons *in potestate* could own no property. Anything given or bequeathed to them belonged to the *pater*;[45] however, in the case of sons, guardianship only remained in effect until age fourteen. Daughters, as established in the Twelve Tables, were under guardianship for life. Roman brothers and sisters were equal heirs on intestacy,[46] and in spite of various attempts to limit the amount a woman might inherit, the opportunities for Roman women to acquire wealth could be substantial.[47]

Betrothal
The Roman girl was betrothed when quite young in a solemn ceremony called *sponsalia*.[48] According to law, from that moment on she

forced to do penance for his impulsive act, his father affirmed that if his son had not killed Horatia, he would have killed her himself by the authority allowed fathers. In another story Appius Claudius wanted a young woman named Verginia. After exhausting all efforts to keep her from Claudius, Verginia's father killed her announcing that he had provided her with an honourable death. See Sarah Pomeroy, *Goddesses, Whores, Wives and Slaves: Women in Classical Antiquity* (New York: Schocken, 1975), pp. 152-53. Neither the guardian nor the husband had this authority. The *lex Iulia de adulteris* (18 BCE) specifically allowed a father to impose summary justice on a daughter caught in the act of adultery in his or his son-in-law's house; but it must be imposed immediately and he must kill the adulterer as well.

45.   For the influence of the Roman *patria potestas* on the Hellenistic Jewish household, see G. Schrenk, 'The Father Concept in Later Judaism', *TDNT*, pp. 974-75.

46.   In early Roman society, where intestate succession was the norm, the claims of the *familia* were paramount. The rules governing such were framed primarily with reference to a deceased *paterfamilias*. The order of priority of claim was (a) *sui heredes*, (b) *agnatae*, (c) *gentiles*. The first included all children of both sexes, including adopted children and a wife *in manu*. Agnates meant all those who together with the deceased were descended from the same male relative and would be in the latter's *patria potestas* were he alive. Both male and female agnates counted, but at some unknown date the eligibility of women was restricted with only the sister of the deceased being permitted succession. Succession between generations went through the male line only. See Gardner, *Women in Roman Law*, pp. 191-92.

47.   The *lex Voconia* in 196 BCE established that women could inherit as *agnatae* only within the second grade, that is, of lateral relatives only sisters, and limited the amount a woman might inherit to 200,000 asses. E. Cantarella, *Pandora's Daughters: The Role and Status of Women in Greek and Roman Antiquity* (trans. M.B. Fant; Baltimore: The Johns Hopkins University Press, 1981), p. 122.

48.   Sponsalia were promises which amounted to a verbal contract, *stipulatio*. By the first century BCE, *stipulatio* had ceased to be used in betrothal, and

was bound to her betrothed by a bond that, although not marital, gave her precise social standing and imposed fidelity. Marriage could take place only if both parties had reached puberty. For girls, from at least the time of Augustus, puberty was set at age twelve.[49] As marriage without *manu* became more common, betrothal developed into a matter of simple consent. This lessening of the contractual element did not, however, erase the penalties prescribed if the engagement were broken.

To encourage marriage, Augustus exempted betrothed men from the penalties attached to bachelors. Because many were abusing the privilege by betrothing themselves to infants, Augustus ordered that no betrothal should be valid unless the man married within two years.[50]

Marriage

When marriage took place, the woman, married with *manus*, passed from the power of her father to that of her husband, where the content and extent of control was not very different from that she had just left. In the eyes of the law, marriage merely gave a woman a new master.[51] A unique institution of matrimonial law, *usus*, points out her category as a 'thing'.

arrangements for dowry were made separately. The elements of binding contract which sometimes accompany betrothal (marriage contracts, penalty clauses, etc.) were not strictly part of the betrothal itself. See Cantarella, *Pandora's Daughters*, p. 116.

49.   In the sample of funerary inscriptions examined by Keith Hopkins, eight per cent of Roman girls were married at age ten or twelve. See Keith Hopkins, 'The Age of Roman Girls at Marriage', *Population Studies*, 19 (1965), pp. 309-27 (321).

50.   Suetonius, *Life of Augustus*, ch. 34 states that 'when he [Augustus] noticed that the effect of the law was being circumvented by engagements to pre-puberty girls and by frequent changes in marriage partners, he curtailed long engagements and set a limit upon divorces'. Quoted in Meyer Reinhold, *The Golden Age of Augustus* (Toronto: Samuel Stevens, 1978), p. 47.

51.   *Coemptio*, the most widely used of the ceremonies that transferred a woman to a new family was an application of the old form of sale and purchase. The woman, as if she were an object, was sold to the buyer in the presence of a person who held a scale on which the buyer put down the price of the object or woman. Although symbolic later on, its origin was an actual purchase. See Cantarella, *Pandora's Daughters*, p. 117.

In the Roman world (and even today) one of the ways property could be acquired was by *usucapion*, that is the use of a thing over a period of time. According to the laws of the Twelve Tables, use for a year in the case of movable goods, and two years in the case of immovable property, conferred ownership. *Usus* was simply *usucapion* of a woman. In cases when *coemptio* was not celebrated, in fact, or if technically unsuccessful, the husband (or his father) acquired *manus* over the woman after she had been 'used' for a year, the same time period established for movable goods.[52]

However, if the wife, at the end of each year, had spent three nights away from the conjugal home, the husband would not acquire this right. This existed, not to allow the wife increased independence, but to permit her family continued control and jurisdiction over her. By comparison, in a Jewish household, although the woman at marriage was transferred from her father's authority to that of her husband, she did possess certain legal rights: the right to sue at law without the assistance of a guardian and the right to retain property over which her husband had no control.[53]

Divorce

Divorce was a private act, and, basically, subject to no limitation by law. In the situation of a *manus* marriage, the wife could not take the initiative and obtain release. The husband had the right of divorce, but only if his wife poisoned the children, substituted or stole the keys, or drank wine.[54] If he divorced her for any other reason, he was liable to forfeit his property, paying half to his ex-wife and half to the goddess Ceres. A legal precedent was created when Spurius Carvilius Ruga, without surrendering any property, divorced his wife because she failed to produce any children. As a direct result, in later Republican law there were no fixed grounds for divorce. After divorce, the father retained his *potestas* and with it the right to keep the children with him.

Although according to Jewish law, a wife could not divorce her husband, she could bring charges against him, and the court could force him to divorce her. In Hellenistic Egypt, the evidence of papyri

52. Cantarella, *Pandora's Daughters*, p. 117.
53. Verner, *Household*, p. 45.
54. The absence of punctuation in the classical texts makes this difficult to read. See Gardner, *Women in Roman Law*, p. 83.

tells of one Jewish woman who did take an active role in dissolving her marriage.[55]

Augustan Marriage Legislation

Two important pieces of legislation, the *lex Julia de maritandis de ordinibus* (18 BCE) and the *lex Papia Poppaea nuptialis* (9 BCE), were passed to reconfirm the fundamental importance of marriage and the marital ethic, and to increase the birthrate.[56] These laws were later merged into a single text (*lex Iulia et Papia*). In it, marriage was viewed as a duty incumbent upon all Roman men between the ages of twenty-five and sixty and upon women between twenty and fifty. Women could wait for two years after the death of a husband and eighteen months after a divorce to remarry. Marriages which were fertile brought rewards, while sanctions were applied to those in which there were no children. Freeborn women with three children and freedwomen who had four children were no longer subject to guardianship.[57]

Under this legislation, a husband and wife could inherit the whole of each other's property if both or either were below the age at which children could, in the eyes of the law properly be required (25 years for men and 20 years for women). Also, if the husband exceeded the age of sixty and the wife fifty, or if they had one child living, or had lost one child above the age of puberty or two above the age of three or three after their name-day, full inheritance was allowed.[58] If none

55.   *CPJ* 146 as cited in Kraemer, *Ecstatics*, p. 214.

56.   Concern over a low birth rate in Greece is addressed by Polybius: 'In our own time the whole of Greece has been subject to a low birth rate and a general decrease of population, owing to which cities have become deserted and the land ceased to yield fruit, although there have neither been continuous wars or epidemics... For as men had fallen into such a state of pretentiousness, avarice and indolence that they did not wish to marry, or if they married, to rear children born to them, or at most as a rule but one or two of them, so as to leave these in affluence and to bring them up to waste their substance, the evil rapidly and insensibly grew.' Polybius, *Hist.* 36.17, pp. 5-10; trans. Paton; ed. LCB; cited in Yarborough, 'Elitist', p. 18.

57.   Gaius, *Institutes*, 1.145. The agnatic guardianship of women was abolished entirely by Claudius (Gaius, *Institutes*, 1.147, 171). See S. Dixon, 'Family Finances: Terentia and Tullia', in Rawson (ed.), *Family*, p. 99.

58.   P.A. Brunt, *Italian Manpower 225 BC–AD 14* (Oxford: Clarendon Press, 1971), p. 564.

of these qualifications were fulfilled, either spouse could take only one-tenth of the other's property. In general *caelibes* were debarred from receiving under wills and *orbi*, married men aged 25-60 and married women aged 20-50 who had no children, could take only half of what they were left in wills other than that of their spouse.[59]

Preference was given to candidates for political and bureaucratic office who had three legitimate children. These men would be given first choice when governorships of provinces were distributed to ex-magistrates. Even young men just starting a career were anxious to have the privilege that fatherhood brought.[60]

Other laws were passed which limited the husband's power to dispose of the dowry, and gave to the woman the right to control the goods that constituted it. If divorce occurred, the dowry was fully recovered.[61] Guardianship also underwent certain modifications. By means of a complex mechanism called *coemptio fiduciae causa*, women could replace legitimate tutors with persons they trusted, and frequently a widow became free to choose her own tutor. Under the principate, a woman whose guardian had denied her authorization to do something could take action against him, and under Claudius, legitimate guardianship of freeborn women was abolished.

At the end of the Republic a series of provisions set in motion a revision of the principles of the agnate line, and allowed kinship of the female line for the first time.[62] Children were now obliged to respect

---

59. Brunt, *Italian Manpower*, p. 564.

60. Richard I. Frank, 'Augustus' Legislation on Marriage and Children', in Ronald Stroud and Joan Palvel (eds.), *California Studies in Classical Antiquity* (Berkeley: University of California Press, 1976), 8, pp. 41-52 (44-46). The ingenuity that was taken to circumvent these laws is further evidence that they were taken seriously. See Rawson, *Family*, p. 10 n. 18.

61. In Hellenistic Judaism, widows and divorcees, in most circumstances were able to recover at least a portion of their dowries. Similarly, in Greek households, the dowry was to be used for the woman's support in the event of divorce or the death of her husband. See Verner, *Household*, pp. 45, 32.

62. Although daughters could not pass on the family name to their offspring, in the imperial period there was a growing tendency for children to incorporate their mother's name as well as their father's into their own name or to adopt the maternal name. See Rawson, *Family*, p. 18 and Cantarella, *Pandora's Daughters*, p. 140; Peter Garnsey and Richard Saller, *The Roman Empire: Economy, Society and Culture* (Berkeley: University of California Press, 1987) pp. 141-42. The use of a family name indicates membership in a particular family. Kinship theory calls it jural exclusiveness or jural non-exclusiveness. The former states that an individual cannot

mother and father equally, and, in the case of a husband's shameful
conduct, a woman, with the intervention of the praetor, would obtain
custody of the children. Consequently, between the middle of the last
century BCE and the middle of the second century CE, the Romans
whittled away the legal rights of male relatives over their kinswomen.
In effect, the sphere of effective kinship became narrower.[63]

Marriage in Roman Practice

Desirability of Marriage
There is evidence that the rigour of the law concerning marriage was
mitigated by a more elastic practice. In some circles it was no longer
obligatory or even desirable to marry and produce children. Laments
over the infertility of old Roman stock are found in the writings of
the late first century BCE.[64] In 46 BCE Cicero called upon Caesar to
remedy this evil:

> It is for you alone, Gaius Caesar, to reanimate all that you see lying shat-
> tered, as was inevitable, by the shock of war itself: courts of law must be
> set on foot, licentiousness must be checked, and the growth of population
> fostered; all. . . must be knit together by stringent regulations.[65]

In that same year Caesar responded to this falling off in population by
offering prizes for large families.

In two odes published in 23 BCE, Horace echoes Cicero's complaint
when he affirms that the decay of the family is the root of all evil:

---

hold membership in more than one kin group, thus the kin group of one parent
determines the individual's legal and social status. This exclusiveness promotes the
development of clearly distinct social classes while its opposite inhibits this development. See Bernard Farber, *Comparative Kinship Systems: A Method of Analysis*
(New York: John Wiley & Sons, 1968), pp. 5-7.

63. Keith Hopkins in *Death and Renewal* (Cambridge: Cambridge University
Press, 1983), p. 91 concludes that whatever the risk to tradition and to morals, the
Romans preferred to leave control over fortunes directly to their daughters, wives
and widows rather than to distant kinsmen.

64. Keith Hopkins (*Death and Renewal*, pp. 79-81) lists four reasons for this
reduction in fertility: the increased competition for status; individuation; secularization
and the higher status of women. Frank ('Augustus' Legislation', p. 50) cites 'the
profound psychological conflicts between upper class men and women as the reason
why marriage and children were avoided'.

65. Cicero, *Pro Marc.* pp. 8, 23 quoted in James Field, 'The Purpose of the *Lex
Iulia et Papia Poppaea*', *Classical Journal*, 40 (1944–45), pp. 398-416 (400).

Whoe'er will banish impious slaughter and intestine fury, whoe'er shall seek to have inscribed upon his statues 'Father of Cities', let such have the courage to curb our lawless licence, and so win fame among men of after-times; since we—alas the same!—with envy filled, hate virtue while it lives and mourn it only when snatched from sight. Of what avail are dismal lamentations if wrong is not repressed by penalties.[66]

Augustus made his first attempt to curb childlessness in 27 BCE by ordaining that the governors of the senatorial provinces should be annual magistrates chosen by lot, except when a senator enjoyed a special privilege because he had a large number of children, or because of his marriage.[67] The failure of this law is celebrated by Propertius in an elegy written not later than 26 BCE.

In very truth Cynthia rejoiced when that law was swept away, at the making of which we both wept for many an hour, for fear it should divide us... How should I furnish children to swell our country's triumphs? From my blood shall no soldier ever spring.[68]

In 18 BCE Augustus passed the *lex Julia de maritandibus ordinibus*. Included in its enactments were a series of rewards and penalties, inheritance of bequests and precedence of entry into public office which were dependent upon marriage and number of children. Those who continued to refuse marriage were barred from attending state plays and festivals.

Another law, *lex Julia caducaria*, passed in 4 BCE, attached these same penalties to those married but childless, and extended the sanctions to include the equestrian order. This move was received with violent opposition. Demands for its repeal are described by Dio:

And when the knights were very urgent in seeking repeal of the law regarding the unmarried and the childless, he (Augustus) assembled... the unmarried men of their number... and those that were married... Then perceiving that the latter were fewer in number... he was filled with grief.[69]

Augustus suspended this law twice and then in 9 CE introduced the less stringent *lex Papia Poppaea*. It dealt with the problem of equestrian celibacy and childlessness; however, its penalties differentiated the

---

66. Horace, *Odes* III.24.25-34 as quoted in Field, 'Purpose of *Lex*', p. 401.
67. Dio LIII.13.2. See Field, 'Purpose of *Lex*', p. 401.
68. Propertius, *Elegies*, II.7. See Field, 'Purpose of *Lex*', p. 402.
69. Dio LVI.1.2 as quoted in Field, 'Purpose of *Lex*', p. 406.

treatment accorded those married and childless and *caelibatus*.

The effect of Augustus's laws was felt not only in Rome but also in the provinces. Tacitus, writing of informers who were rewarded for reporting violations of Augustus's laws states,

> . . . sentries were set over us, and under the *lex Papia Poppaea* lured on by rewards; so that if a man shirked the privileges of paternity, the state as universal parent might step into the inheritance. But they pressed their activities too far: the capital, Italy, every corner of the Roman world had suffered from their attacks, and the position of many had been wholly ruined.[70]

The search for ways around the Augustan measures continued after Augustus's death, and Dio Cassius attributes to Tiberius a speech given to the men of Rome who were attempting to revoke this legislation. In it Tiberius castigated the large number of men who had not married and produced children, and indicated that he was increasing both the penalties and rewards established by Augustus.[71] Therefore, a century after Horace first wrote about the moral laxity exemplified by a rejection of marriage and children, there is evidence that this rejection continued to cultivate a following in Graeco-Roman society.

Independence of Roman Women
Other evidence that the rigour of the law was mitigated by a more elastic practice points to the degree of economic and social independence a Roman woman actually possessed. Opinions vary, however, as to the extent of this independence. In a provocative essay of some years ago, M.I. Finley, representing one side of this discussion, describes Roman women through to the end of the Republic by speaking of 'the silence of the women of Rome'. According to him, upper class Roman women, with a few scandalous exceptions, led passive, repressed lives in the shadow of their fathers, husbands and sons to a degree unparalleled in subsequent periods.[72] This picture of social reality is questioned by Sarah Pomeroy. She states that 'the momentum of social change in the Hellenistic world combined with Roman elements to

70.   Tacitus, *Ann.* III.28 as quoted in Field, 'Purpose of *Lex*', p. 411. *Ann.* written c. 116–18 CE, in sixteen books cover 14–68 CE.
71.   Dio Cassius, *Roman History*, 56:1-10 quoted in Yarborough, 'Elitist', p. 18.
72.   M.I. Finley, 'The Silent Women of Rome', *Horizon* 7 (1965) pp. 57-64. He admits that changes took place during the Empire.

produce an emancipated, but respected, upper class woman'.[73] She argues that Roman matrons had a range of choices in their roles and life styles as well as a demonstrable influence on the cultural and political life of the time.[74]

The conclusions depend on how the evidence is interpreted. The law, although changing, was specific about restrictions under which women should live. Other evidence, including history, moral anecdote and rhetorical *exempla*, slander and satire, as well as funerary inscriptions, is at times at variance with the legal perspective.[75] There are, however, difficulties in interpreting this data: the reconciling of conflicting descriptions, and the reading of evidence which unanimously reflects a male perspective.

By the end of the Republic many of the laws concerning marriage, dowry and guardianship were becoming less rigid. Because marriage with *manus* was viewed with increasing disfavour, a situation was created in which a wife was connected to her father's family for life as daughter or sister. Since the latter could not oversee her in the same way as her husband, and since, through inheritance, she could accumulate her own financial resources, a wife could gain greater independence.[76]

The status of the Greek woman and her Jewish counterpart was also undergoing change. In Hellenistic Egypt, Greek women bought and sold real estate as well as moveable property. They borrowed and loaned and were able to make wills. Generally their economic responsibilities outstripped their legal competence.[77] Similarly, evidence from the Egyptian Jewish community attests to Alexandrian Jews contracting marriage according to the Greek form of ὁμολογία.[78] They adjudicated divorces in Greek courts according to Greek laws, so that

73. Pomeroy, *Goddesses*, p. 189.

74. Pomeroy, *Goddesses*, p. 149.

75. Amy Richlin, 'Approaches to the Sources on Adultery at Rome', in Helena P. Foley (ed.), *Reflections of Women in Antiquity* (New York: Gordon and Breech Science Publishers, 1981), pp. 379-404. Richlin outlines five categories of evidence on Roman attitudes toward adultery (they include the ones listed, with the exception of funerary inscriptions). Her suggestions as to how the conflicting data can be reconciled form the basis for what follows on women's emancipation.

76. Hopkins, *Death and Renewal*, pp. 77-78.

77. Verner, *Household*, pp. 35-36.

78. ὁμολογία reflects the increasing tendency of the bride herself to become an active party to the marriage contract.

Jewish women, with the assistance of their guardians could divorce their husbands by mutual agreement.[79]

In Rome, from the time of the Republic, certain women provide examples of the distinction between law and reality. One of these, Terentia the wife of Cicero,[80] in three areas in particular, exercised considerable discretion: finance, politics and matchmaking. In her financial dealings Terentia appears to have been free from Cicero's control, proceeding quite independently in the management of her properties with the assistance of her freedman Philotimus.[81] About her involvement in politics, Plutarch comments,

> . . . for she was otherwise by nature neither at all meek nor timorous but an ambitious woman, and as Cicero himself says, taking a larger role in his political affairs than she shared with him in domestic matters.[82]

In the third area, that of matchmaking, for example, Cicero, scouting prospects for the third marriage of his daughter Tullia, discovers that by the time he writes approving a certain suitor, she is already married to one who could have compromised him politically.

Evidence is not limited to Terentia. In spite of the prohibition on women pleading on behalf of others, there is mention of a woman lawyer, Afrania, wife of a senator. Another woman, Hortensia, daughter of a famous orator, delivered an oration before the triumvirs.[83] The political influence of Servilia, mother of Brutus, is taken for granted, while Caerellia, an intimate friend of Cicero's, is portrayed as a woman who is independently wealthy and an intellectual.[84] In Pompeii a woman named Eumachia, who made her money in a brick

---

79.   See Verner, *Household*, p. 46.

80.   A study of this woman has to deal with two layers of bias. First there is the generalized cultural bias, resulting from the fact that we see Terentia through the eyes of men, Cicero and Plutarch. The more specific bias is the attitude of these two main literary sources. Cicero, in his correspondence from the period leading up to and including his divorce, villified Terentia in order to elicit pity and sympathy from his friends. Plutarch shared this bias. The hostile depiction of Terentia in these sources is more than adequately balanced by the earlier correspondence in which Cicero portrayed his family without rancour. Teresa Carp, 'Two Matrons of the Late Republic' in Foley (ed.), *Reflections*, pp. 344-45.

81.   Cicero, *Ad Familiares*, 14.2.2.3, 14.1.5. See Dixon, 'Finances', p. 100.

82.   *Cic.* 20, cited in Carp, 'Matrons', p. 349.

83.   Cantarella, *Pandora's Daughters*, p. 141.

84.   Carp, 'Matrons', pp. 343-44.

manufacturing concern, paid for one of the major buildings and do-
nated it to a workman's association. She held the title *sacerdos
publica*.[85]

Inscriptional evidence draws attention to the accomplishments of
other women not important or influential enough to be mentioned by
historical writers. One inscription from Corinth, dated 43 CE, acclaims
the accomplishments of a Junia Theodora who bestowed monetary
gifts to the city and to its citizens. A good example of this new type of
Graeco-Roman woman, she is praised in decrees of the Lycian Con-
federation for exerting her influence to gain the favour of Roman
governors for various Lycians and for aiding Lycian exiles.[86] Another
inscription speaks of Hedea racing her war chariot and winning at the
Isthmian games in 43 CE.[87]

Furthermore, a number of inscriptions ranging in date from the
first to the third centuries CE attest to the prominent role played in the
life of Asia Minor by wealthy Greek women, a number of whom held
Roman citizenship. These women not only held distinguished civic and
federal magistracies and priesthoods, but discharged liturgies which
required lavish expenditure on various ceremonies, games, banquets
and on civic buildings such as baths and colonnades. According to
A.J. Marshall this was actual power because it secured effective influence. He does recognize, however, that in a man this kind of influence
would lead into the Roman hierarchy. In a woman it did not.[88]

Women were asked to serve as founders or patrons of men's clubs.
In this role they provided a meeting place, often in their own homes,
and endowments for other expenses of the association such as banquets

85.   Meeks (*Urban Christians*, p. 24) states that women with estates and in
businesses of all sorts are attested in Pompeii.

86.   See A.J. Marshall, 'Roman Women and the Provinces', *Ancient Society* 6
(1975), pp. 109-28 (123). Also Mary R. Lefkowitz and Maureen B. Fant, *Women's
Life in Greece and Rome: A Source Book in Translation* (Baltimore: The Johns Hopkins University Press, 1982), p. 157, 'The people of Patara have decreed: Whereas
Junia Theodora, a Roman resident in Corinth, a woman held in highest honour. . .
who copiously supplied from her own means many of our citizens with generos-
ity. . . ' (Pleket 8 excerpt Tr.M.R.L.)

87.   Kent, *Corinth viii/3*, p. 29. 'Hedea, at the Isthmian Games with Cornelius
Pulcher as judge, won the race in armour and the chariot race. . . She was first in
her age group. . . citizen. . . girl!' Delphi, c. 45 CE (Pleket 9 Tr.M.R.L.). In
Lefkowitz, *Women's Life*, p. 160.

88.   Marshall, 'Roman Women', pp. 123, 125-26.

and the funerary expenses of its members. Other inscriptional evidence recounts the successes of women athletes, philosophers and physicians.[89] While these activities are not presented as abnormal, other examples point out the vulnerability of women who chose a lifestyle which could be considered different.[90]

With these instances of independent activity and freedom, the examples of other, more traditional, women compete. Because of their virtuous actions or characteristics, certain women are held up as models by men to help their own women order their lives. The tales of Lucretia and Verginia describe the extremes to which chaste women have gone in defence of their honour. The syntactic structure of the two legends is almost identical. Object of illicit desire, a woman dies to affirm the supreme value of conjugal fidelity and virginity. Equally predictable and instructive are the stories of Veturia, Volumnia[91] and Cornelia.[92] It was women like these who provided the model of *matrona* and *univira*, women, dedicated to one husband, wives and mothers who, in the fulfilment of family duties, forgot themselves.

The satires of Martial and Juvenal condemn women whose

---

89.   One such funerary inscription to a woman physician reads: 'Farewell, lady Panthia, from your husband. After your departure, I keep up my lasting grief for your cruel death. Hera, goddess of marriage, never saw such a wife: your beauty, your wisdom, your chastity. You bore me children completely like myself; you cared for your bridegroom and your children; you guided straight the rudder of life in our home and *you raised high our common fame in healing—although you were a woman you were not behind me in skill* [italics mine]. In recognition of this your bridegroom Glycon built this tomb for you.' See Lefkowitz, *Women's Life*, p. 162. Other evidence is given on pp. 157-62.

90.   Clodia, a woman who lived in the first century, chose an independent lifestyle. When she accuses one of her lovers of theft and attempted poison, Cicero, defending her lover, dwells on the fact that she is a woman whose conduct alone makes her accusations unreliable. Cantarella, *Pandora's Daughters*, pp. 131-32.

91.   Veturia and Volumnia, one the wife, one the mother of Coriolanus went to his camp as he was leading the Volscians against Rome. They persuaded him to lay down arms, a course of action all others had failed to persuade him to follow.

92.   Among the Roman matrons, Cornelia was a paragon. A widow, she remained faithful to the memory of her husband to whom she had borne twelve children. She continued to manage her household and was praised for her devotion to her children's education. Through two of her sons, Tiberius and Gaius Gracchus, she exercised a profound influence on Roman politics. A bronze portrait statue was erected in her honour by the Romans and restored by the Emperor Augustus. See Cantarella, *Pandora's Daughters*, p. 130.

behaviour and ideology are at odds with the old models. Their poetry speaks of a contagion of corruption which affects even the lowliest woman. In one of his satires, written in the form of advice to a friend to dissuade him from marriage, Juvenal focuses on the vice of lascivi-ousness in women. He describes women as amusing themselves with eunuchs, imposing lovers on their husbands, buying and selling as they wish, and behaving in a despotic manner.[93] While Juvenal's hatred for women bears the marks of an individual misogyny, and therefore ought not to be the object of generalizations, Martial was of a differ-ent order. The fact that the same themes and accusations appear in the two poets suggests that they echo commonplaces of an era.[94]

In another literary form, the romantic novel, women who are beau-tiful, chaste and faithful-unto-death,[95] are presented as the ideal. In the novel, the hero and heroine undertake a journey during which they are isolated and alienated from society. Their ultimate goal, however, is to return home to the social world of the family and community, and above all, marriage, reaffirming the value of the traditional social order.[96]

Men found it hard to accept that their daughters, wives and mothers were different from Verginia and Lucretia. Aria who killed herself,[97] and a certain unnamed wife who threw herself into Lake Como with an incurably ill husband, were set forth by men of this era as models of proper feminine behaviour and devotion. Tacitus, in praising the Germans, gives one of the best expressions of this attitude:

93.   Satire 6. 161-69, 245-67, 398-412 as cited in Marcia Colish, *The Stoic Tradition from Antiquity to the Early Middle Ages*. I. *Stoicism in Classical Latin Literature* (Leiden: Brill, 1985), pp. 213-14.

94.   Satire is intended to amuse; however, it is unlikely that any humorous genre could have amused its audience without being recognizable, even if exaggerated.

95.   Tomas Hagg, *The Novel in Antiquity* (Berkeley: University of California Press, 1983), p. 96.

96.   Virginia Burrus, 'Chastity as Autonomy: Women in the Stories of the Apocryphal Acts', *Semeia* 38 (1986), p. 106.

97.   Martial speaks of Aria as a person to be emulated as do both Tacitus (*Ann.* 6.29 and 16.70) and Pliny (*Letters* 3.16). She kept the death of her son a secret from her husband in order not to grieve him while he was recovering from an illness. In 42 CE when her husband was condemned to death for having taken part in the con-spiracy of Scribonianus against Claudius, she, before her husband's eyes, encour-aging him to do the same, thrust the dagger into her own breast, withdrew it and said, 'Paetus, it does not hurt'. Cantarella, *Pandora's Daughters*, p. 150.

... marriage is very strict there, nor would you give more praise to any part of their *mores*... By these means the women live their lives with their chastity firmly girded, corrupted by no lures of extravaganzas, no unsettling excitements at dinner parties. Men as well as women know nothing of secrets in letters. Adulteries are very rare in such a numerous people, for which the penalty is to hand, given over to their husbands: the husband drives the wife naked from home, her hair cut off, in the presence of her relatives, and drives her through the whole village with a crop; for there is no mercy for a virtue that has become public property; she will win a husband not by looks, youth, or money. For no one there laughs at vices, nor are corruption and being corrupted called 'the times'... And good *mores* have more force there than good laws elsewhere.[98]

In Roman practice the categories of male and female were in transition. Increasing pressure on the traditional roles of women and men created new opportunities for women to act independently, and this, in turn, had an effect upon the way people thought and lived out the established models of male/female relationships. The identification of what was properly feminine and masculine became the object of controversy. In some circles this brought about a bitter reaction in the form of misogyny; in others an emphasis on a sense of order and a preservation of the status quo became primary.[99]

Marriage and its Desirability in Philosophical Debate

The evidence from Roman law and practice suggests that within the Graeco-Roman world in the first century CE marriage was not taken for granted but was openly discussed as an issue. A similar debate, focusing on the desirability of marriage, was taking place within the philosophical schools. This section will not be exhaustive, but will focus on marriage discussions within the Stoic and Cynic schools, for the purpose of situating their arguments within an anthropological framework which, in turn, seeks to understand the relationship between matrimonial strategies and political structures.

Claudine Leduc's discussion of marriage and the condition of the wife in the light of Greek polity concludes that women and matrimonial strategies are central issues for understanding how city-states

98. Richlin, *Sources*, p. 388.
99. Meeks, 'Androgyne', p. 207.

came to be.[100] Similarly, Will Deming, in his research into the Hellenistic background of 1 Corinthians 7, relates discussions on marriage to the Stoic dedication to a traditional Greek life in the city-state and a Cynic calling to the philosophical life. He concludes,

> One could even say that marriage became the central issue in the debate unwittingly, due to the claims it made on an individual regarding one of these two causes, for no participant in the debate ever evaluates marriage solely on its own merits.[101]

Plato and Aristotle situate the first century debate. Plato treats marriage and family as a concern of the city state. Affirming marriage to be a civic duty, he writes,

> Regarding marriage as a whole, there shall be one general rule: each man must seek to form such a marriage as shall benefit the state rather than such as pleases himself.[102]

Since the purpose of marriage is to provide the city state with the next generation of citizens, Plato would require all men to marry by a certain age and he would allow divorce where those married longer than ten years were without children. Those refusing to marry should be punished by the state.[103] Aristotle presumes a progression from marriage to households to city states, insisting this is the work of nature, a part of the divine plan.[104] In effect, 'those household matters which we normally consider private, individual matters are here part of a social-political, philosophic ethic'.[105]

The Stoics situate marriage as one component in a larger system of morality. They begin with the structure of the universe and the place of marriage within it, that all men form a natural moral community of rational beings, and that community is a cosmopolis transcending all social and political configuration.[106] This *cosmos* consists of a plurality of city-states within which citizens are organized into households. Integral to the creation of the household is the marriage union.

100. Leduc, 'Marriage', pp. 235-95.
101. Will Deming, *Paul on Marriage and Celibacy: The Hellenistic Background of 1 Corinthians 7* (Cambridge: Cambridge University Press, 1995), p. 61.
102. Plato, *Laws* 6.773B as quoted in Verner, *Household*, p. 71.
103. Plato, *Laws* 4.721 AB and 6.784 CE in Verner, *Household*, p. 71.
104. Aristotle, *Politics* 1.1252a17-1253a39 cited in Deming, *Paul*, pp. 54-55.
105. David Balch, *Let Wives Be Submissive: The Domestic Code in 1 Peter* (Chico, CA: Scholars Press, 1981), p. 26.
106. Colish, *Stoicism*, p. 38.

Marriage, thus, becomes a central part of the divine plan and without it the future of the city-state would be in doubt.[107] In turn, the desirability of marriage becomes part of a larger discussion in this period as to whether the moral code of the Greek city-state should continue as the social, economic and political centre of an individual's life.[108]

The Cynic movement[109] affirmed individualism and self-sufficiency in place of the social structures of marriage and the city-state. This system, which valued the pursuit of philosophy as a full-time profession, argued for freedom from house, home, marriage and children, a 'freedom from all ties which morality, law, state and community life in general may put upon the individual'.[110] Whereas the Stoic generally did not criticize existing institutions, the Cynic carried out a rigorous and practical critique of social traditions.

The differences between these two positions are seen in the issues treated in *topoi* on marriage. Four issues stand out because of the frequency with which they recur: (1) whether marriage is desirable (especially for the wise man); (2) whom one should marry; (3) relations between husbands and wives; (4) the significance of providing children.

In the earlier period of Stoic-Cynic debate Antipater of Tarsus (mid-second century BCE) allows no exception. Whether a male wishes or not, he should marry in order to fulfil his obligation to the gods. In *On Marriage*, he begins with the conviction that men are political beings who are destined to play a part in a cosmic order composed of households and city-states. The institution of marriage is the foundation of this order, all morally upright youth are to ally themselves to the divine plan by considering marriage

> to be among the primary and most necessary of those things which are
> fitting, being eager to complete every task laid upon them by nature, most

---

107. Deming, *Paul*, pp. 54-55.

108. Deming, *Paul*, p. 57.

109. Two notes of importance: (1) the Cynic school of the first century CE is known for the most part through Stoic interpreters; (2) differences existed within Cynicism. These are described by Meeks as 'mild' and 'austere'. An austere Cynic gives up finding any good within settled society; a mild Cynic takes the common institutions of the *polis* for granted and justifies his own disengagement from them by the benefit he would render if people would heed him. See Wayne Meeks, *The Moral World of the First Christians* (Philadelphia: Westminster Press, 1986), p. 55.

110. Deming, *Paul*, p. 61.

especially the duty that concerns the safekeeping and growth of the father-land, and even more so, the honor of the gods...[111]

The Cynic author of the *Epistles of Diogenes* 47 stands in direct opposition to Antipater. He argues that a wife and children are a burden and that the philosopher should live self-sufficiently. He then challenges the Stoic position that marriage is necessary because it guarantees the future of the human race:

> One should not wed nor raise children, since our race is weak and marriage and children burden human weakness with troubles. Therefore those who move toward wedlock and the rearing of children on account of the support these promise, later experience a change of heart when they come to know that they are characterized by even greater hardship.[112]

In Epictetus both positions are expressed clearly. Describing the ideal Cynic from a Stoic viewpoint, he says that the Cynic should be 'free from distraction, wholly devoted to the service of God'.[113] In another voice, Epictetus the Stoic reasons,

> In the name of God, I ask you, can you imagine an Epicurean state: One man says, 'I do not marry', 'Neither do I', says another, 'For people ought not to marry'. 'No, nor have children, nor perform the duties of citizens.' And what do you suppose will happen then? Where are the citizens to come from? Who will educate them?[114]

Musonius Rufus (circa 30 CE-end of century) describes marriage, the basis of social life, as taught by nature. Households should be considered as a wall around the city, and the beginning of that wall is marriage. No-one lives for himself, but for all humankind.[115] Musonius devotes an entire treatise to refuting the Cynic claim that the philosopher cannot marry. Accordingly, the philosopher is an example of what is in accord with the divine will, and since marriage is in accordance with that will, the philosopher must marry.[116]

---

111. Antipater of Tarsus, *On Marriage*, 3.255.5.6 (Stob. 4.508.2-4 W.-H.) trans. in Deming, *Paul*, Appendix A, p. 227.

112. *The Epistles of Diogenes* 47; J. Malherbe, *The Cynic Epistles: A Study Edition* (trans. Abraham; Missoula, MT: Scholars Press, 1977), p. 179.

113. Epictetus, *Discourses*, 3.22,69; 3.22,76 and 81 as cited in Balch, *Wives*, p. 146.

114. Epictetus, *Discourses*, 3.7,19-20 cited in Verner, *Household*, p.78.

115. Epictetus, *Discourses*, 3.22, 23, 46, 81-82 cited in Meeks, *Moral World*, p. 51.

116. Musonius, *Fragment* 14, 'Is Marriage an Impediment to the Pursuit of

The debate is complex in that, the differences between the Stoic and Cynic philosophies can sometimes be seen within the writings of those philosophers who represent a Stoic position. Seneca's (4 BCE–65 CE) *On Marriage* and other writings portray a negative attitude to marriage: the wise man should be free from the affairs of a single city-state, free to study philosophy. Yet in his ninth *Epistle* he argues that the self-sufficiency needed to study philosophy does not preclude marriage and the raising of children.[117]

Epictetus's thinking on marriage concerns the obligations of citizenship, and embraces the Stoic vision of city-states, households and marriages. Because human existence as ordained by nature derives its meaning from citizenship within the city-state, marriage and having children are primary. However he does recognize that certain conditions made it impossible for an individual to marry. Present circumstances, for example, make it difficult for a married man with children to find leisure for the public interest. It would seem that the ideal philosopher can refrain from marriage and children, but it is not to be made into a general principle.

Hierocles's treatise *On Marriage* best illustrates the scope of the Stoic position. Marriage is important for the survival of the city-state: 'for our whole race is naturally adapted to partnership' and marriage is 'the first and most elementary of partnerships'.[118] He continues,

> Our country especially urges us to do so [marry and have children]. For I dare say that we raise children not so much for ourselves as for our country by planning for the constitution of the state that follows us and supplying the community with our successors.[119]

In spite of his extensive arguments concerning the desirability of marriage,[120] he also allows for an avoidance of marriage if particular circumstances require it:

Philosophy?', 14.92.6-9; 94.32–96.8 cited in Deming, *Paul*, p. 78.

117. Seneca, *Epistles*, 9.17-19 cited in Deming, *Paul*, p. 77.

118. Hierocles, *On Duties. On Marriage* 4.22.21-24, *Moral Exhortation, A Greco-Roman Sourcebook* (trans. Malherbe; Philadelphia: Westminster Press, 1986), p. 104.

119. Hierocles, *On Duties. On Marriage* 24.14; *Moral Exhortation* (trans. Malherbe), p. 104.

120. He argues that marriage is a matter of prime importance for the wise man; marriage is advantageous; married life is beautiful, neither burdensome nor grievous. See *On Duties*, 4.22.21-24; *Moral Exhortation* (trans. Malherbe), pp. 101-104.

So, since we should imitate the man of intellect in those things we can, and marriage is preferred by him, it is evident that it would also be fitting to us except some circumstances prevent us.[121]

This discussion has been selective rather than exhaustive, seeking merely to point out that a difference of opinion existed in the first century Graeco-Roman world concerning marriage and its desirability, and that this difference would be part of the Corinthians' socialization. In his analysis of life in the Graeco-Roman world of the first century CE, Paul Veyne draws attention to the profound changes in the understanding of marriage that emerged during the first century CE:

In the first century BCE a man was supposed to think of himself as a citizen who had fulfilled all his civic duties. A century later he was supposed to consider himself a good husband. . . At some point people began to internalize, as a moral code, what had been a civic and dotal institution; monogamous marriage.[122]

In attempting to account for this shift, Veyne identifies the transition from Republic and independent city-states to Empire. The essence of this transformation was the way in which people perceived themselves: as citizens for whom marriage is a duty or as responsible moral individuals.[123] With this change in emphasis citizens could now ask themselves whether or not they would fulfil the obligation to marry. According to Veyne, the resulting ambiguity created anxiety over whether a marriage crisis existed and whether celibacy was spreading.[124]

An anthropological perspective posits that such modifications and alterations in the relationships between men and women have widespread ramifications for other aspects of society. A change or ambiguity in the pattern of relating between the genders, particularly in the area of marriage, results in changes in the accepted arrangement of social organization. In effect, the structure of any society could be radically altered.

---

121. Hierocles, *On Duties. On Marriage*, 22.21-24; *Moral Exhortations* (trans. Malherbe), p. 100.

122. Veyne, *From Pagan Rome*, p. 36.

123. Veyne, *From Pagan Rome*, p. 37. The new moral code said: 'Here are the duties of the married man'. The old moral code said: 'Marriage is one of the duties of the citizen'.

124. Veyne, *From Pagan Rome*, p. 38.

Kinship and Status Dissonance

This discussion of marriage in the context of Roman law and practice and philosophical debate identifies the tensions that existed within the patriarchal,[125] social and political structures of Graeco-Roman society. Roman law allowed a limited kinship of the female line. Marriage *sine manu* was becoming more popular; thus, a wife related more directly to her father's household than to her husband's. Women could reclaim their dowry if divorce occurred, and held the right to inherit. By the time of Claudius, guardianship laws had become ineffective. Only succession to rank remained unavailable to the Roman matron.

Peter Garnsey, addressing the situation in the Roman Empire, speaks of the fact of change within the family and the complexity of its actual practice:

> On the one hand the emperors and jurists did move with the current of changing attitudes and practices in their legal innovations, though rather belatedly in cases like the recognition of the mother's legal relationship with her children and the limitation of father's power of life and death. On the other hand, a fundamental conservatism in regard to basic legal principles did lead to a substantial disjunction between those principles and wide-spread *mores*.[126]

According to anthropologists, any kind of modification and alteration in the kinship system, and particularly within marriage patterns, will have widespread ramifications for other aspects of that society. For example, if there is a change in the residence pattern; that is, a change in where the male and female live or have their primary reference point, eventually the ideological 'rules' are changed. In this process of change, social structures are more or less stable, and more or less well integrated depending on whether the adjustments resulting from a shift in residence rules have been worked out. The adjustment to new

---

125. A.R. Radcliffe-Brown defines patriarchy: 'A society may be called patriarchal when descent is patrilineal (i.e. the children belong to the group of the father), marriage is patrilocal (i.e. the wife removes to the local group of husband), inheritance (of property) and succession (to rank) are in the male line, and the family is patripotestal (i.e. the authority over the members of the family is in the hands of the father or his relative)'. See A.R. Radcliffe-Brown, 'On Rules of Descent and Inter-Kin Behaviour', in Nelson Graburn (ed.), *Readings in Kinship and Social Structure* (New York: Harper & Row, 1971), p. 91.

126. Garnsey, *Roman Empire*, p. 147.

patterns includes changes in kinship terminology and rules for kin behaviour, but often these lag behind.[127]

Social reality in the cities of the Graeco-Roman empire was measured according to one's juridical standing and one's social status. Juridical standing included categories of citizen and non-citizen, senator or equestrian or plebian, freeborn, freedman or slave. These had an influence on an individual's life, establishing a consciousness which was reinforced by legislation and economic reality as well as by overt symbols such as distinctive dress.[128]

Social status was measured in many ways. Tony Reekmans has extracted from Juvenal's satires seven social categories in which there is a traditional hierarchy of ranks: language and place of origin, formal *ordo*, personal liberty or servitude, wealth, occupation, age and sex.[129] It was possible for an individual to be low according to one or more measures yet high on others. This phenomenon is called 'status discrepancy' or 'status dissonance', and is a basic term by which Roman mobility both up and down is explained.[130]

Status ambiguity creates stress, causing those in this position to attempt to change the social structures and redefine the situation to gain consistency. Wayne Meeks states,

> Depending on the number of categories in conflict, the relative importance of those categories in widely held attitudes, the distance traversed in each category from one level to the next, and so on, such criss-crossing produces feelings and reactions of varying power, both within the mobile person or group and in others, especially actual or potential competitors.[131]

127. Keesing, *Kin Groups*, pp. 135-36.

128. John E. Stambaugh, 'Social Relations in the City of the Early Principate: State of Research', in P.J. Achtemeier (ed.), *SBLSP* (Missoula, MT: Scholars Press, 1980), pp. 75-90 (75).

129. Tony Reekmans, 'Juvenal's Views on Social Change', *Ancient Society* 2 (1971), pp. 117-61, esp. 124.

130. Stambaugh, 'Social Relations', pp. 75-76. A member of the senatorial aristocracy might choose to behave in a way appropriate to a slave, while a freedman might gain great wealth and imitate the prerogatives of the upper ranks. A slave in the imperial household might enjoy considerable administrative responsibility and, in turn, political power. A woman might enjoy the prestige or at least the financial resources usually reserved for the *paterfamilias*. These are examples of status dissonance.

131. Meeks, *Urban Christians*, p. 22-23.

In Graeco-Roman society, because the patriarchal structure of society
was in transition, some women and men were status dissonants. Junia
Theodora, a woman with considerable effective power whose upward
mobility was hindered by her sex, is a specific example of a woman
at Corinth who might be considered a status dissonant. Therefore,
depending on whether or not adjustments to changing patterns were
being made, they would be open to programs of social change. If a
relatively large proportion of persons in a society or in a group have
ambiguous status or view the rules as ambiguous, that society/group is
in an unstable condition.[132]

Kinship and the Christian Community at Corinth

The Church and Changing Patterns in Society

The Corinthian church existed in a city which was developing rapidly
as a major economic force within the Roman Empire. Corinth's ties
with Rome were strong both politically and economically, and within
it there existed all the variety and diversity that could be found in any
city of the first century. Corinthian society, as part of the Graeco-
Roman world, would be influenced by the changes taking place in the
marriage patterns within this world. The ambiguities which existed
within those patterns of relationships would be part of the experience
of Corinth's inhabitants. The question as to whether the church would
be affected by this diversity in marriage patterns and role expectations
is related to a wider debate over the status of the early Christians at
Corinth.

Deissmann's analysis of the papyrus documents laid the groundwork
for a consensus which concluded that Christianity was the achievement
of the noble proletariat who fought against the corruption of imperial
Rome and triumphed.[133] This conclusion remained an assumption of
exegesis until the 1960s and one which Judge, writing at this time,
contradicts:

> Far from being a socially depressed group, then, if the Corinthians are at
> all typical, the Christians were dominated by a socially pretentious section
> of the population of the big cities. Beyond that they seem to have drawn

132. Gerhard Lenski, 'Status Crystallization: A Non-Vertical Dimension of
Social Status', *American Sociological Review* 19 (1954), pp. 405-13 (411).

133. Edwin A. Judge, 'The Early Christians as a Scholastic Community, Part I',
JRH 1 (1960), p. 4.

on a broad constituency, probably representing the household dependents of the leading members. . . The interests brought together in this way probably marked the Christians off from the other unofficial associations, which were generally socially and economically as homogeneous a possible.[134]

A study by Gerd Theissen, confirming Judge's conclusion, describes a congregation that is highly diversified within itself.[135] These conclusions represent a shift in opinion which makes the status of the early Christians in Corinth higher and more diversified than earlier thought.[136] Meeks agrees and continues,

> . . . those persons prominent enough in the mission or in the local community for their names to be mentioned or to be identifiable in some other way usually—when we have evidence to make any judgment at all about them—exhibit signs of a high ranking in one or more dimensions of status. But that is typically accompanied by low rankings in other dimensions. Although the evidence is not abundant, we may venture the generalization that the most active and prominent members of Paul's circle (including Paul himself) are people of high status inconsistency (low

---

134. Judge, 'Social Identity', p. 202.

135. Theissen, *Social Setting*, pp. 69-120. Theissen begins his discussion of social stratification in Corinth with Paul's description of the congregation in 1 Cor. 1.26-29. From an analysis of these verses, he moves to a reading of Paul's response to the conflicts at Corinth in light of various sociological theories regarding conflict and its management. Applying these theories he finds evidence that the Corinthian community comprised groups of widely divergent social backgrounds: both the socially disadvantaged and those of privileged social position were members of the Church. Theissen sets forth criteria indicating elevated social status. These include statements about holding office, about 'houses', about assistance rendered to the congregation and about travel (p. 73). He concludes: 'of the seventeen persons (including one group) listed, nine belong to the upper classes according to the criteria discussed above. In three instances, three of the criteria apply: houses, services rendered and travel for Aquila, Priscilla and Stephanas. In four cases, two criteria apply: offices and travel for Erastus and Sosthenes; office and "house" for Crispus; service rendered and travel for Phoebe. In two cases, one criterion fits: services rendered for Gaius and Titius Justus, on the basis of whose character, a certain position in life seems a perfectly reasonable conclusion. . . The result is clear. The great majority of the Corinthians known to us by name probably enjoyed high social status' (p. 94).

136. Gager (*Kingdom*, p. 96) is an exception to this shift in opinion about the composition of early Christian groups.

status crystallization). They are upwardly mobile, their achieved status is
higher than their attributed status.[137]

The evidence increasingly supports the view that the church contained
all the variety and ambiguity which was found in Corinthian society.
Consequently, the changing patterns of marriage within the Graeco-
Roman world and the debate within that world concerning its desirability would influence the Corinthian church as it sought to define its
social structure and organization.

Paul's Kinship Terminology
At this point, three conclusions which arose out of the discussion of
kinship earlier in this chapter need to be recalled: (1) where it occurs,
kinship terminology needs to be investigated in terms of its social
context and function; (2) the use of kinship terminology often reflects
a situation in which an individual is violating certain norms of kinship
or when there is an attempt being made to manipulate the individual;
(3) both culturally conceived and symbolic models of kinship are
equally important in understanding social roles and behaviour in a
particular group.[138]

The anthropologist considers it is important to analyze the kinship
terminology used by a social unit:

> In short, kinship terminology can reflect and reveal many aspects of social
> behaviour and social organization and, for these same reasons, the study
> of nomenclature systems can also be of practical value to those interested
> in problems of cultural change.[139]

In 1 Corinthians Paul indicates that believers relate to God, the
Father, as children and to one another as brothers and sisters.[140] In
8.1-7a the fatherhood of God is referred to as a matter of communal
knowledge which Paul contrasts with popular belief in the world
outside the church. The Corinthians are God's children through an
adoption process which takes place in baptism. Thus, to know God as
Father and Christ as the Son and themselves as adoptive siblings is a

137. Meeks, *Urban Christians*, p. 73.
138. See discussion, pp. 59-62.
139. Pasternak, *Kinship*, p. 126.
140. The references to God as Father are found at 1.3, 9 ('his son and Jesus');
8.6, 15.4, 28 ('the Son'). The references to Christians as brothers occurs 37 times
throughout 1 Cor. The word sister occurs twice, 7.15 and 9.5. In the latter Paul
refers to the same woman as both sister and wife.

reference point for the Corinthian Christians' understanding of themselves. According to Norman Petersen these are 'organizing metaphors', for they provide an image in relation to which the organization of behaviour can take place.[141]

In 1 Corinthians 7 kinship terminology is extensive. Paul speaks of husband, wife, children, widower, brother(s), sister and, in vv. 25-40, a male/female bond of an uncertain nature. In vv. 12-16 Paul mixes two sets of kinship terminology. In effect, when speaking about the same group of people, he refers to them as husband/wife and brother/ sister. In v. 16, when he refers directly to this group, he addresses them as γύναι and ἄνερ. In the following excerpt, one solid line indicates brother/sister terminology or its pronoun; two lines, husband/ wife terminology or its pronoun.

v. 12: εἴ τις ἀδελφὸς γυναῖκα ἔχει ἄπιστον,
καὶ αὕτη συνευδοκεῖ οἰκεῖν μετ᾽ αὐτοῦ
μὴ ἀφιέτω αὐτήν

v. 13: καὶ γυνὴ εἴ τις ἔχει ἄνδρα ἄπιστον
καὶ οὗτος συνευδοκεῖ οἰκεῖν μετ᾽ αὐτῆς
μὴ ἀφιέτω τὸν ἄνδρα

v. 14: ἡγίασται γὰρ ὁ ἀνὴρ ὁ ἄπιστος ἐν τῇ γυναικὶ
καὶ ἡγίασται ἡ γυνὴ ἡ ἄπιστος ἐν τῷ ἀδελφῷ

v. 15: εἰ δὲ ὁ ἄπιστος χωρίζεται, χωριζέσθω
οὐ δεδούλωται ὁ ἀδελφὸς ἢ ἡ ἀδελφὴ ἐν τοῖς τοιούτοις
ἐν δὲ εἰρήνῃ κέκληκεν ὑμᾶς ὁ θεός

v. 16: τί γὰρ οἶδας, γύναι, εἰ τὸν ἄνδρα σώσεις;
ἢ τί οἶδας, ἄνερ, εἰ τὴν γυναῖκα σώσεις;

Since kinship terminology is part of a community's common knowledge and affirms specific patterns of relating and the behaviour associated with them, it is important to focus on the terminology used, and more particularly, on Paul's mixing of kinship language in these verses. One set of terms, ἀνήρ and γυνή, represents a culturally conceived model of relating; whereas, the second set, ἀδελφός and ἀδελφή, represents a symbolic model.[142] In other words, the people addressed in vv. 12-16 fill two roles, husband or wife and brother or sister. Culturally, they are husband and wife to unbelievers or to each other as

141. Petersen, *Narrative*, p. 206.
142. See p. 62.

believers. Symbolically, they are brother and sister to each other. Since the marriage relationship has been investigated at length in terms of the changing patterns of marriage in that society, it will not be discussed here. The latter form of relating, however, is less obvious and demands attention.

In their study of kinship, cultural anthropologists concentrate on a symbolic model of relating which serves to conceptualize relations with deities as well as adoptive or fictive kin relationships. In this model, the symbolic extensions of kinship serve to broaden the range of social ties or readjust local groups according to pressures of demography and ecology.[143] In other words, this form of kinship functions to create alliances. One example of a symbolic pattern of kin relationships studied by anthropologists is found in the *compadrazgo* (co-parenthood) in Mesoamerica which derives from the Catholic institution of baptism: a 'godfather/godmother' sponsors a child ritually in baptism. The elements in the ritual of baptism important in *compadrazgo* include the notion of spiritual rebirth and of sponsorship, as well as the establishment of a spiritual affinity between the participants. An analogy is drawn between the sponsor's special role in the ritual and the parent's role in conception.

The language of kinship is used to describe this relationship. The Spanish terms for mother and father are *padre* and *madre*; for co-parents, *padrino* and *madrina*. The child is to show absolute respect and obedience to his/her *padrino*. Although the *compadrazgo* are non-kin, the complex of relationships created 'is much like the family in that it has religious sanction, shares the same incest prohibitions, and once established is indissoluble'.[144] G.P. Murdock's cross-cultural comparison of incest regulations has revealed a tendency to extend incest taboos to all relatives referred to by a kinship term appropriate

143. Keesing, *Kin Groups*, p. 130.
144. Mario Davilá, 'Compadrazgo: Fictive Kinship in Latin America', in Graburn (ed.), *Readings in Kinship*, p. 397. A kin group is considered intimate when sets of relatives are considered so close that marriage cannot increase their closeness. The criterion of membership is the recognition that the particular relatives share a common kinship identity which cannot be modified by marrying one another or other individuals. If one function of marriage is to create closer bonds between kinship groups, then there are certain situations in which marital ties are not desirable. Marriage would be proscribed where individuals are already considered part of the same intimate kin group. Not only would marriage be superfluous but it might foster internal conflict. See Farber, *Comparative Kinship*, p. 14.

to a primary relative. For example, if a certain woman is referred to as 'sister' she is likely to be sexually taboo even if she is not a biological sister.[145]

It seems clear from Paul's use of kinship language that members of the church at Corinth found themselves belonging at the same time to two kinship patterns. In some ways this is not unusual, in that anthropologists describe how people in a society often move easily from one social situation to another. The roles that individuals enact in a particular situation determine the parts they will play. Confusion and conflict of interest are avoided because the individual's status is defined by context. One day the individual behaves as a member of one group, another day as a member of a different group. Most times, membership in a group does not demand an exclusive allegiance.

> It merely includes ego (the individual) in a social category from which groups are crystallized in certain defined contexts. What is required to make such a system work is a situational sorting out, or clear labelling, of statuses, and a set of principles for making decisions in those situations where two allegiances conflict or where presence is required in two different places at once.[146]

Keesing does admit that the key to conflict resolution is the exclusivity of the allegiance demanded in each situation.

Cultural anthropologists would agree with his conclusion, and they would add that it must not be assumed too quickly that in a situation of conflict the culturally conceived model is primary. In other words, the natural kinship structure into which the person has been born or married, and which previously defined his/her place and connections within society may be challenged by a new set of relationships which also demand allegiance, and present new definitions of place and connections. In a situation where the two patterns of relating do not coincide, the complex articulation between the system of labels and the system of roles needs to be untangled carefully in each case.

When a husband and wife attempt to relate as brother and sister, the potential for conflict is great. The duties and obligations demanded by the marital relationship are in opposition to those expected in a brother and sister fictive kinship relationship. The intensity of the conflict becomes clear when these two understandings of kinship terms are

145. Pasternak, *Kinship*, p. 29.
146. Keesing, *Kin Groups*, pp. 124-25.

seen as reflecting different patterns of social structure and organization. In effect, resolution of this conflict will determine structures within the church, and the roles and behavioural obligations among its members will be set accordingly.

Conclusion

To set the factionalism at Corinth about marriage and sexual intercourse against singleness and celibacy within this broader perspective of a society's changing understanding of marriage, and the conflicting statuses and roles which differing viewpoints create, situates the conflict in 1 Corinthians 7. In addition, when the terminology which Paul uses to address the Corinthians is investigated in terms of the anthropological category of kinship, the intensity of the conflict and the care needed in its resolution become clear. The description of the social context having been completed, the social dynamics of the tensions in 1 Corinthians 7 will be uncovered using Victor Turner's model of social drama.

Chapter 3

A SOCIAL DRAMA UNFOLDS:
THE SOCIAL DYNAMICS OF A CONFLICT

> In Christ there is neither male nor female. The trouble is, everywhere else there is![1]

In this chapter, Victor Turner's model of social drama will provide a method for investigating the dynamics of the conflict in 1 Corinthians 7. Its format will be used to uncover information about the forces of dissension within the community and their rhetoric. This will be complemented by Mary Douglas's model of grid and group. In it she charts people's social experiences according to those aspects of their life based on group involvement and individual-oriented aspects of social structure, such as kinship ties. Her model will be used to situate the opposing elements in ch. 7.

Victor Turner's Model of Social Drama

Victor Turner's model of social drama arises out of his detailed studies of situations of crisis which arose regularly in Ndembu village life. He presents his model as a way of uncovering the social dynamics of conflict:

> Through the social drama one can sometimes look beneath the surface of social regularities into the hidden contradictions and conflicts in the social system. The kinds of redressive mechanism deployed to handle conflict, the pattern of factional struggle, and the sources of initiatives to end crisis which are all clearly manifest in the social drama, provide valuable clues to the character of the social system.[2]

In the early 1970s Turner began to explore ways in which this model

---

1.   Mary Daly quoted in Osiek, *Social Setting*, p. 6.
2.   Turner, *Schism and Continuity*, p. xvii.

might be used more generally to analyze social patterns. He compares
the culture of a society at any moment to debris, or 'fall-out' of past
ideological systems. Order or coherence is achieved out of conflicting
or concurring wills.[3] Important to the social process and the achievement of order are the models, patterns and paradigms for behaviour
and thinking that arise out of what individuals have been explicitly
taught and what they have learned from social experience. Turner's
concern is to probe the ways in which social actions of various kinds
acquire form through the metaphors and paradigms for behaving and
thinking which individuals absorb, and in certain intensive circumstances generate unique forms and, in turn, new metaphors and paradigms.

Turner speaks of this process of cultural life as a dialectic of structure and anti-structure expressing the social drama:

> When one surveys large spans of social processes, one sees an almost
> endless variety of limited and provisional outcomes. Some seem to fall on
> the programmatic side of the scale, others eschew precise structural articu-
> lation. But the besetting quality of human society seen processually, is the
> capacity of individuals to stand at times aside from the models, patterns
> and paradigms for behaviour and thinking, which as children they are
> conditioned into accepting, and in rare cases, to innovate new patterns
> themselves or to assent to innovation.[4]

To provide examples of how his model works, he analyzes various
situations of conflict from information available in historical and literary documents.[5]

Social Drama at Corinth

The evidence for conflict within the community at Corinth begins with
Paul's statement about internal discord and reports of factionalism
which he has received from Chloe's people (1.11). One scholar associates the vocabulary used in this section (vv. 10-16) to that of political intrigue and civil strife. He argues that the word σχίσματα is

---

3.   Turner, *Dramas*, p. 14.

4.   Turner, *Dramas*, pp. 14-15.

5.   These include the conflict between Thomas Beckett and Henry II, that lived
out by Hidalgo and the Mexican Revolution of Independence (1810) and the local
feuds of medieval Iceland as described in Icelandic legend. See Turner, *Dramas*,
pp. 60-155; Turner, 'Icelandic Saga', pp. 71-118.

usually associated with neither heresy nor a harmless clique, but 'factions engaged in a struggle for power'.[6]

The reports given to Paul speak also of ἔριδες in the church (1.11). ἔρις signals a 'hot dispute', and appears in accounts of political life at the moment when the pressure of circumstances 'draws the citizens into confused knots'.[7] In 3.3 Paul combines ἔρις with ζῆλος to describe the source of the Corinthians' divisive behaviour. The verb μεμέρισται (1.13) has as its root the meaning 'party', and is used to speak of 'being split into parties',[8] and, according to one scholar, ἐγὼ μέν εἰμι is to be viewed as a case of a simple declaration of allegiance.[9]

A number of scholars conclude that a struggle for power motivates the writing of 1 Corinthians 1–4, and that factionalism is the opponent Paul combats throughout the letter.[10] In light of this conclusion, Paul's object in writing to the Corinthians is to prevent στάσις (revolt, disunion).[11]

To start with the fact that there is more than one point of view on

6. The word σχίσματα which occurs again in 11.18 and 12.25 has caused sharp disagreement among scholars. Those who want to minimize the rigidity of the divisions within the church understand it to mean cliques rather than parties. See Munck, *Paul*, ch. 5. In 'On the Discord in Corinth: 1 Corinthians 1–4 and Ancient Politics', *JBL* 106 (1987), pp. 85-111 (87), J.L. Wellborn, as a result of his investigation of political language as it would be understood and used in the first century, argues for the strong sense of σχίσματα as parties engaged in a power struggle.

7. Wellborn, 'On the Discord', p. 87.

8. Wellborn, 'On the Discord', p. 87.

9. Conzelmann, *1 Corinthians*, p. 33.

10. Debates about the existence of a party or parties opposing Paul have had a long history. Gunther (*St Paul's Opponents*, p. 1) has isolated thirteen different hypotheses. Although some scholars have tried to find evidence for three parties in 1 Cor. 7–16, the majority begin by reconstructing one opponent which was opposed to Paul and assign it to one of the three names mentioned in 1.12. For a history of interpretation see Hurd, *Origin*, pp. 96-107. More recently scholars have begun again to explore the evidence for more than one viewpoint within the congregation. While some recognize that it would be unusual for the congregation to agree on all the issues in chs. 7-16, few make a deliberate attempt to situate opposing viewpoints within the congregation through a detailed exegesis. Exceptions include Richardson, 'Absence', pp. 59-74; Theissen, *Social Setting*, Chapters 3-4; Yarborough, 'Elitist', pp. 1-31.

11. Robertson and Plummer (*First Epistle*, p. 100) states that Paul is urging them to give up not erroneous beliefs, but party spirit.

the issue of marriage/sexual intercourse and singleness/celibacy within the Christian community involves asking questions which are specifically designed to probe the conflicts and contradictions in that social system and to unearth the patterns for behaving and thinking about marriage and singleness that are operative within the church at Corinth. Turner's model of social drama provides the investigative tool and the text of 1 Corinthians 7, evidence of a social system in conflict.

Root Metaphor in the Social Drama

The first point that Turner makes about the social drama is that in a conflict situation what divides the actors are differing viewpoints on an explanatory paradigm. He uses Stephen Pepper's concept of root metaphor to label this explanatory paradigm:

> The method in principle seems to be this: A man desiring to understand the world looks about for a clue to its comprehension. He pitches upon some area of common sense fact and tries if he cannot understand other areas in terms of this one. The original idea then becomes his *basic analogy* or *root metaphor*. He describes as best he can the characteristics of this area, or if you will, 'discriminates its structure'. A list of its structural characteristics become his basic concepts of explanation and description (e.g., the gen words, the kin words, the nature words). . . In terms of these categories he proceeds to study all other areas of fact whether uncriticized or previously criticized. He undertakes to interpret all facts in terms of these categories.[12]

According to Turner, root metaphors pervade a culture's whole system, finding expression in its myths, rituals and social institutions. They go beyond social relationships to include outlooks, patterns of belief and goals of humankind that inform these relationships. They are cultural models existing in the minds of the actors, but they also 'reach down to the irreducible life stances of individuals', emerge in life crises, and are held as axiomatic, matters of life and death.[13]

During any process of enculturation, the individual orders new experiences and brings them into conformity with those already

12.   Stephen Pepper, *World Hypotheses*, p. 91 as quoted in Turner, *Dramas*, p. 26. Turner adds the words in brackets to Pepper's definition and the quotation marks in the eighth line.
13.   Turner, *Dramas*, p. 64.

absorbed. That individual is also interacting with other members of the community and striving to reduce dissonance between his/her structure of assumptions and theirs. While a certain ambiguity can be tolerated, intolerance to ambiguity is expressed in various ways, not the least of which is a pressure to conform.[14]

A Root Metaphor in 1 Corinthians 7

In 7.17-24, Paul sets forth two pairs of opposites: uncircumcision/ circumcision and slave/free. These follow the order of a declaration found in Gal. 3.26-28.[15] While there are several differences between vv. 17-24 and the formula in Galatians, the most probable reason why Paul chooses these pairs of opposites is because the conflict in ch. 7 is related to the male/ female pair of opposites in the baptismal formula of Gal. 3.26-28.[16] This conclusion receives confirmation from the fact that there is no obvious reason why Paul would mention circumcision/ uncircumcision or slave/free in the Corinthian context. In other words, there is no specific evidence of circumcision/uncircumcision or slave/ free unrest within the congregation, nor is there any evidence that the Corinthians' questions encouraged Paul to mention the contrasting pairs. Further, a consideration of Paul's careful balance of male/ female obligations and debts within marriage in vv. 2-4 suggests that the third pair in this formula, male/female, is at the heart of the controversy in ch. 7.

14.   Douglas, *Implicit Meanings: Essays in Anthropology* (London: Routledge & Kegan Paul, 1975), pp. 52-53.

15.   In *There is No Male and Female: The Fate of a Dominical Saying in Paul and Gnosticism* (Philadelphia: Fortress Press, 1987), pp. 7-9, Dennis MacDonald cites a growing consensus among scholars concerning Gal. 3: (a) Paul is quoting from early baptismal liturgy; (b) that the original setting of this saying is baptism; (c) that the breaking of the pattern, 'there is no. . . or. . . ' is an allusion to Gen. indicated by the apparent influence of Gen. 1.27 (LXX) on male and female. Scholars, in locating this saying, can be grouped into three categories: (1) Paul's own circle; (2) Pauline communities; (3) parties opposed to Paul. Questions also remain as to the extent of the revolutionary social programme proposed by Gal. 3.26-28.

16.   The direct reference to baptism is eliminated and the Jew/Greek reference is changed to read circumcision/uncircumcision. Because of these differences between vv. 17-24 and the formula in Gal. 3.26-28, a number of scholars are cautious in associating the two. Those who do make this association include Bartchy, *Slavery*, pp. 129-31; Scroggs, 'Eschatological' p. 293; Fiorenza, *Memory*, pp. 220-21.

According to its definition a root metaphor is described and explained in terms of structural characteristics which become the categories by which the metaphor is understood and lived. In order to explain what is meant by structural characteristics, Turner adds the words 'the gen words, the kin words, and nature words' to Stephen Pepper's definition. For him these are the 'possible exhaustive set of classes among which all things might be distributed'.[17] Since the formula in Gal. 3.26-28 is related to the conflict in ch. 7, its formulation as a root metaphor would affirm that 'in Christ, all are children of God'. In an effort to 'discriminate its structure', a list of the structural characteristics by which people identified themselves in the first century, Jew/Greek slave/free and male/female, become the basic concepts of explanation and description.

To view the world in terms of race, nature and kin was a popular pattern of expression in the first century, in that the opposition of social roles was an important means whereby a Hellenistic man established his identity. A common phrase asserted gratitude 'that I was born a human being and not a beast, a man and not a woman... a Greek and not a barbarian'.[18] This pattern was adopted by the Jewish Tannaim, and found its way into the synagogue liturgy: 'Three blessings one must say daily: Blessed (art thou) who did not make me a Gentile; Blessed (art thou) who did not make me a woman; Blessed (art thou) who did not make me a boor.'[19] The discussion in the previous chapter suggests that this sharp differentiation between men and women was being reduced, and that the traditional roles were no longer taken for granted but vigorously debated.

A social drama occurs when conflicting understandings of the structural characteristics of a root metaphor face each other. In baptism all believers had become children of God. The formula in Galatians suggests that they had been taught about this new life in Christ in terms of the contrasting social roles that were important in the first century. However, within first century society there were disagreements over how these roles were to be lived out, and, as a microcosm of that society, similar differences could be expected within the Christian community. According to Turner's description of a root metaphor

17. See Turner, *Dramas*, p. 26.
18. Meeks, 'Image' pp. 167-68.
19. In one version 'boor' is changed to 'slave'. See Meeks, 'Image', pp. 157-58.

and how it functions in conflict situations, it seems clear that the factionalism in ch. 7 involves different understandings of the final pair of structural characteristics: what did it mean to live as children of God, 'no male and female'.

Structure and Anti-structure in a Social Drama

Turner's understanding of structure and anti-structure helps to define the manner in which the conflict over 'no male and female' would manifest itself within the community. He argues that root metaphors always engender two responses, a structural presentation and an anti-structural one:

> In human history, I see a continuous tension between structure and communitas, at all levels of scale and complexity. Structure, or all that holds people apart, defines their differences, and constrains their actions, is one pole in a charged field for which the opposite pole is communitas, or anti-structure, the egalitarian 'sentiment for humanity'. . . representing the desire for total, unmediated relationship between person and person, a relationship which nevertheless does not submerge one in the other but safeguards their uniqueness in the very act of realizing their commonness. Communitas does not merge identities, it liberates them from conformity to general norms. . . [20]

In order to define structure and anti-structure, Turner has concentrated on ritual as it is found in rites of passage, particularly in initiation rites.[21] This is marked by three stages: separation, limen and aggregation. In the first stage, the individual is detached from an earlier fixed point in the social structure, from a set of cultural conditions or from both. In the final state, aggregation, the rite of passage is consummated, and the ritual subject has reached a relatively stable state. The subject now has clearly defined rights and obligations in relation to others, and is expected to behave in accordance with

20. Turner, *Dramas*, p. 274.
21. Turner defines rites of passage as 'rites which accompany every change of place, state, social position and age'. See Victor Turner, *The Ritual Process: Structure and Anti-structure* (Chicago: Aldine Publishing, 1969), p. 94. These initiation rites, whether into social maturity or cult membership, best exemplify transition since they have well-marked and protracted marginal or liminal phases. See Victor Turner, 'Betwixt and Between: The Liminal Period in *Rites de Passage*', in June Helm (ed.), *Symposium on New Approaches to the Study of Religion* (Seattle: University of Washington Press, 1964), pp. 4-20 (5).

certain customary norms and ethical standards. It is on the middle state, that of limen, which is defined by anti-structure and *communitas*, that Turner focuses his attention.

Qualities of Anti-structure

People in a liminal state are in transition, and cannot be situated according to 'the network of classification that normally locates states and position in cultural space'.[22] They are between positions that are assigned by law, custom, convention and ceremony, and their present ambiguous and indeterminate attributes are expressed by a rich variety of symbols such as death, being in the womb, invisibility, or bisexuality. Many people in this transitional state go naked or wear only a strip of clothing to demonstrate in their physical situation, their liminal state of being persons with no status, property, insignia, or secular clothing of rank, role or position in the kinship system.

In societies dominated by kinship institutions, gender distinctions have great structural importance. In liminal situations, however, neophytes are treated, or are symbolically represented, as being neither male nor female. Turner argues that the peculiar unity of the liminal consists in its embracing in one representation opposite processes and notions: that which is neither this nor that, and yet is both.[23] Of the long list of qualities[24] which adhere to liminal state, one which has particular relevance for an analysis of 1 Corinthians 7 is the theme of sexual continence. Just as the undifferentiated character of liminality is marked by the discontinuance of sexual relations and the absence of sexual polarity, the return to society as a structure of statuses is marked ceremonially by the resumption of sexual relations.[25]

What emerges in the liminal period is society as an unstructured or rudimentarily structured and relatively undifferentiated *communitas*.

22.   Turner, *Ritual*, p. 95.
23.   Turner, 'Betwixt', p. 9.
24.   Turner (*Ritual*, p. 106) lists the following as properties of liminality: transition, totality, homogeneity, communitas, equality, anonymity, absence of property, absence of status, nakedness or uniform clothing, sexual continence, minimization of sex distinctions, absence of rank, humility, disregard for personal appearance, no distinctions of wealth, unselfishness, total obedience, sacredness, sacred instruction, silence, suspension of kinship rights and obligations, continuous reference to mystical powers, foolishness.
25.   Turner, *Ritual*, p. 104.

This results in a community of equal individuals who submit together to the general authority of the ritual elders. The social structure is of a highly specific type: between instructors and neophytes there is complete authority and complete submission; among neophytes there is complete equality.

During this liminal period, a transformation takes place. Knowledge (*gnosis*) is obtained which endows the neophytes with the characteristics of their new state.[26] It is a period of deconstruction and reconstruction in which the neophytes receive additional powers to enable them to cope with their new situation in life.[27] This acquisition of *gnosis* is the heart of the liminal experience. It includes the main outlines of the theogony, cosmogony and mythical history of the group, and great importance is attached to keeping secret the nature of this new knowledge.

Liminality is by definition a transitional state, and the neophytes return to the secular with more alert faculties and an enhanced knowledge of 'how things work', while at the same time becoming subject to law and custom.[28] Yet there are situations in which the liminal state can become permanent.[29]

In his discussion of pilgrimages, Turner distinguishes between three types of *communitas*. The first, a spontaneous *communitas*, is described as the 'direct, immediate and total confrontation of human identities which tends to make those experiencing it think of mankind as a homogeneous, unstructured and free community'.[30] The third is an ideological *communitas* which is a label applied to a variety of utopian models of societies. It is the second, a normative *communitas*, which has implications for 1 Corinthians 7. In it, under the influence of time, the original existential *communitas* or anti-structure is organized into a permanent social system. This structure arises out of the need to mobilize and organize resources to keep the group growing and to bring about social control in order to pursue collective goals. It is not the same as a structural system, in that it tries to preserve in its

26.   Turner, 'Betwixt', p. 11.
27.   Turner, 'Betwixt', pp. 8-9.
28.   Turner, 'Betwixt', p. 15.
29.   Turner cites the monastic and mendicant states of the great world religions and millenarian movements. See Turner, *Ritual*, pp. 97-102, 107.
30.   Turner, *Dramas*, p. 169.

religious and ethical codes and its other regulations, the original experience of brotherhood/sisterhood.[31]

Qualities of Anti-structure (communitas) at Corinth

The qualities of *communitas* in comparison with structure can be clearly seen in the community at Corinth. According to Peter Richardson, the quarrelling among the factions triggers Paul's recollection of two issues: baptism and wisdom.[32] Each of these is integrally related to conditions of anti-structure.

Baptism, the community's rite of initiation, is directly related to the factionalism in 1.10-17. Baptism is a central motif throughout the letter, and Gal. 3.26-28 which is referred to in chs. 7 and 12 is a part of early baptismal liturgy. In 6.11 Paul indicates that the Corinthians derive their particular charter of freedom from this source. The warning in 10.1-22 suggests the danger of misrepresentation and misappropriation, and the peculiar custom referred to in 15.29, whatever its meaning,[33] displays the centrality of baptism in the Corinthians' thinking.

According to Turner's description, the cry 'I am of Paul', 'I am of Apollos', 'I am of Peter', is a clear example of people in a liminal state. Paul's own disclaimer about his baptismal activity in 1.14 and his reluctance to name people he had baptized (1.14, 16) is an attempt to redefine the controversy, to move it away from factions gathered around ritual leaders and their initiands:

> He has reduced the Corinthian problem to this central core, the origin of which lies in the Corinthian conception of baptism. Thus it is Paul who equates the party spirit with the baptism motif in 1.2ff., thereby suggesting that a dispute about apostolic authority is tied to this pervasive Corinthian concern.[34]

Concern for wisdom is another quality of anti-structure and *communitas*, and some of the Corinthians understand themselves to be wise (1.21-2.16; 3.18-23 and 8.1), perfect (2.6), spiritual (2.15; 3.1; 12.1 and 14.37). To put it in Turner's terms, they understand that the

31. Turner, *Dramas*, p. 169.
32. Richardson, 'Absence', pp. 65-66.
33. See Conzelmann, *1 Corinthians*, pp. 275-77.
34. J.H. Schütz, *Paul and the Anatomy of Apostolic Authority* (SNTSMS, 36; London: Cambridge University Press, 1975), p. 189.

gnosis obtained at baptism has given them superiority within the community, and access to secret wisdom which allows them to become the interpreters of the community's axiomatic principles.

The vocabulary in 1 Cor. 2.6–3.4 refers to distinct levels of religious status or achievement. πνευματικὸς-ψυχικός designates the stages along the process leading to spiritual perfection. Since the higher religious ideal is to become perfect or wise, the merely infantile and milk-like teachings need to be left behind to feed on *gnosis*. In doing so, the wise person possesses perfect good and immortality.[35] For the Corinthians who are betwixt and between the positions assigned by law, custom, convention and ceremony, all things are lawful (6.12; 10.23),[36] all things are theirs (3.21).

A number of the issues within the congregation relate to Turner's presentation of the qualities of liminality against those of the final state, aggregation (anti-structure in opposition to structure). Liminality includes the wearing of uniform apparel by both sexes, and, although an interpretation of Paul's advice in 1 Cor. 11.2-16 has had a long history, what does seem clear is that this passage represents a blurring of the distinction between the sexes.[37] The conflict over a secret or esoteric mode of expression in ch. 14 also relates to the liminal state.

The prominence of 'body' issues throughout 1 Corinthians offers collaborating evidence that the conflicts involve structure and order and their opposite, anti-structure and *communitas*. Mary Douglas writes that 'the human body is never seen as a body without at the same time being treated as an image of society'.[38] Issues in 1 Corinthians involve bodily orifices such as the genitals (chs. 5–7), the mouth for eating (chs. 8–10, 11) and the mouth for speaking (chs. 12–14). Bodily surface is discussed in 11.2-16 and the body as an image for the church is found in ch. 12. The question of whether there will

35. Richard Horsley, 'How Can Some of you Say that there is no Resurrection of the Dead?: Spiritual Elitism in Corinth', *NovT* 20 (1978), pp. 203-31 (207-10).

36. These are identified as Corinthian slogans which Paul quotes. See Hurd, *Origin*, p. 67.

37. MacDonald, *Male and Female*, pp. 72-111.

38. Mary Douglas, 'Social Preconditions of Enthusiasm and Heterodoxy', in Robert F. Spencer (ed.), *Forms of Symbolic Action: Proceedings of the 1969 Annual Spring Meeting of the American Ethnological Society*, (Seattle: University of Washington, 1969), p. 69.

be a body in the resurrection, and what that body will be like orders ch. 15. Observations on the physical body and how it should be controlled imply many things about membership, roles, structure, order and authority in the societal body.

Structure and Anti-structure in 1 Corinthians 7

Verses 17-24 suggest that a living out of the root metaphor, 'in Christ all are children of God', in its third set of opposites, 'no male and female' is at the heart of the conflict in ch. 7. Turner's model of social drama directs the exegete to look in the text for evidence of an anti-structural and a structural presentation of this paradigm.

Turner regards sexuality as the expression, in its various modalities, either of anti-structure (*communitas*) or structure. He sees,

> sexuality, as a biological drive (being), culturally and hence symbolically manipulated to express one or the other of these major dimensions of sociality. It thus becomes a means to social ends, quite as much as an end to which social means are contrived. Whereas structure emphasizes, and even exaggerates, the biological differences between the sexes, in matters of dress, decoration, and behaviour, communitas tends to diminish these differences.[39]

Therefore, an anti-structural expression of the metaphor 'no male and female' would explain itself in ways that stress the similarities between males and females while a structural presentation would demand that those things that emphasize the differences between males and females become primary. The most obvious pattern of inequality in the area of male/female relationships, and one already subject to much discussion in the first century, was that of the marriage relationship with its unequal roles and functions.

The evidence from the first century Graeco-Roman world shows that marriage was being discussed and questioned. In various writings concern is expressed over the failure to marry and the decline in the birth rate. The numerous treatises on marriage suggest that the debate over whether one should marry reflects a tension in that society. This observation finds confirmation in the comments of historians and the marriage laws promulgated by Augustus and his successors.[40] Yet statuses and roles based on a patrilineal kinship structure were still

39. Turner, *Dramas*, p. 247.
40. Rawson, 'Family', p. 16.

important, and the laws of Augustus regulating family life, whether or not they were rigorously upheld, declared it illegal not to marry. Therefore, the living out of the symbol 'no male and female' in an anti-structural form as singleness/celibacy is consonant with the writings of the first century, with the moralists' *topoi* and with the Corinthians' immediate social experience.[41]

To apply Turner's explanation of sexuality to the root metaphor in ch. 7 leads to the conclusion that singleness and abolition of sexual relationships between married persons would be a way of living *communitas* while marriage and a sexually-active existence would affirm structure. According to v. 1b some of the believers in Corinth have asserted that Christians should not have sexual intercourse.[42] They speak of abstinence as an absolute moral good.[43]

41. Evidence from within 1 Cor. points to the possibility that non-sexual relationships between men and women were a part of Christian practice in Corinth. See Richard Horsley, 'Spiritual Marriage With Sophia', *VC* 33 (1979), pp. 30-54 and MacDonald *Male and Female*, p. 67.

42. Two things are important here: (1) that ἅπτομαι plus the genitive means sexual intercourse. This idiom occurs at least seven times in the extant literature of antiquity from the fourth century BCE to the second century CE. In all these occurrences, it is a euphemism for sexual intercourse, and in none of them does the idiom extend to something like 'take a wife' or 'marry'. The evidence includes: Plato *Leges* 8.840a: 'During all the period of his training (as the story goes) he never touched a woman, nor yet a boy' (LCLii.162-3); Aristotle (*Politica* 7.14.12): 'As to intercourse with another woman or men, in general it must be dishonourable (μὴ καλόν) to be known to take any part in it (ἁπτομενον) in any circumstances whatsoever as long as one is a husband' (LCL 21.625-5); Genesis 20.6 LXX (of Abimelech with Sarah): 'That is why I did not let you touch her (ἅφασθαι ἀυτης)' (NIV) cf. Ruth 2.9 LXX: 'I have told the men not to touch you (ἁφασθαι σοῦ)' (NIV). See Gordon Fee, '1 Corinthians 7.1 in NIV', *JETS* 23 (1980), pp. 307-14 (308-309). (2) that this statement is part of the Corinthians' letter to Paul. See Hurd's (*Origin*, p. 68) chart cataloguing scholarly opinion concerning this quotation in 1 Cor. Of the twenty-four works listed fourteen regard 7.1b as Pauline. However, an interpretation which began with Origen finds an increasing number of biblical scholars affirming that 1b originated within the Corinthian community. The evidence includes certain stylistic and contextual considerations, and the fact that Paul responds to this maxim in the same manner as he responds to sayings in 6.12, 8.1, and 10.23, all of which are commonly regarded as Corinthian slogans.

43. The word καλὸν has various meanings. Some scholars give it a purely utilitarian and pragmatic meaning, while others interpret the term to refer to moral 'good' but as one 'good' among several 'goods'. For others it was the goal of morality, the highest member of a series of lesser 'goods', while for a few of the

In response to this slogan Paul states that, because of immorality, each man or woman should have his or her own spouse and married couples should engage in sexual relations. The pattern of his argument in vv. 1-7 and the vocabulary used support the view that there are two expressions of the root metaphor coming from within the community. The pattern of his argument can be outlined in the following way:

General Principle: καλὸν ἀνθρώπῳ γυναικὸς μὴ ἄπτεσθαι

Reason for Concession: διὰ δὲ τὰς πορνείας

Concession: ἕκαστος τὴν ἑαυτοῦ γυναῖκα ἐχέτω, καὶ ἑκάστη τὸν ἴδιον ἄνδρα ἐχέτω

Explication of Concession: τῇ γυναικὶ ὁ ἀνὴρ τὴν ὀφειλὴν ἀποδιδότω, ὁμοίως δὲ... (vv. 3-4)

Restatement of Concession: μὴ ἀποστερεῖτε ἀλλήλους

Concession to Concession: εἰ μήτι ἂν ἐκ συμφώνου πρὸς καιρόν

Rationale: ἵνα σχολάσητε τῇ προσευχῇ

Restatement of First Concession: καὶ πάλιν ἐπὶ τὸ αὐτὸ ἦτε

Rationale: ἵνα μὴ πειράζῃ ὑμᾶς ὁ Σατανᾶς διὰ τὴν ἀκρασίαν ὑμῶν

Limitation on First Concession: τοῦτο δὲ λέγω κατὰ συγγνώμην, οὐ κατ' ἐπιταγήν

Restatement of General Principle: θέλω δὲ πάντας ἀνθρώπους εἶναι ὡς καὶ ἐμαυτόν

Limitation on General Principle: ἀλλὰ

Verse 1b affirms a state of absolute celibacy. In response, Paul, in 7.2-5a, makes certain statements which argue that the avoidance of the debts and obligations of the marriage relationship constitutes fraud. While some of the vocabulary used, ἀποστερέω, ἐξουσιάζω, ἀποδίδωμι, ὀφειλή is unusual for Paul,[44] it does relate to the thought and practice of the patrilineal kinship system which defines the rights and duties within the marriage relationship.[45] In a kinship system, certain

Fathers it was understood to mean here the absolute of ethical conduct. See Hurd (*Origin*, pp. 158-61) for how each of these meanings would affect the interpretation of this phrase.

44. The word ἀποστερέω is used three times in Paul, and all are in 1 Cor. (6.7, 8; 7.5). ἐξουσιάζω is used at 6.12 and 7.4; ἀποδίδωμι is used five times and ὀφειλή is used ten times.

45. The possibilities that Peter Richardson ('Judgment in Sexual Matters in 1 Corinthians 6.1-11', *NovT* 25 [1983], pp. 37-58 [44-46]) outlines about the nature of the lawsuit in ch. 6 supports the conclusion reached here about the relationship between the vocabulary used and the marital debts and obligations owed within the patriarchal model. In *Dirt, Greed and Sex: Sexual Ethics in the New Testament and their Implications for Today* (Philadelphia: Fortress Press, 1988), p. 198,

rights and obligations are transferred at marriage from the kin group of one spouse to that of the other. In a patrilineal system, these are transferred to the kin group of the husband. One of the rights the kin have over a woman is her sexuality.[46] It seems reasonable to suggest that in its arguments, one group is calling upon the community and, more particularly, the anti-structural adherents to honour those debts and obligations which have been transferred to the husband's kin group through marriage.

In his argument Paul recognizes these debts; however, the command is to both husbands and wives not to defraud each other. This is followed by a concession in which fraud is redefined: some abstinence from sexual intercourse is not fraud. Paul then reminds married couples that they are to come together again because of incontinence/desire,[47] yet in the next verse he tells them that this is not a command but a concession.[48] In these verses Paul's argument recognizes two positions:

v. 1b   Pro-singleness/celibacy
vv. 2-5a Pro-marriage/sexual intercourse
v. 5b   Paul limits the absoluteness of marriage and sexual intercourse
v. 5c, d   Pro-marriage/sexual intercourse
v. 6   Paul limits the absoluteness of marriage and sexual intercourse
v. 7a   Pro-singleness/celibacy
v. 7b   Paul qualifies the preference for singleness/celibacy

Therefore, the initial statement (v. 1b), καλὸν... ἅπτεσθαι, in conjunction with the language of marital rights and duties (vv. 2-5) and the oscillation in Paul's statements supports the conclusion that the clash in this chapter involves different understandings of kinship

---

William Countryman concludes that 5.1-8 is concerned with a violation of family hierarchy and the rights owed to the *pater*.

46.   Louise Lamphere, 'Strategies, Cooperation and Conflict Among Women in Domestic Groups', in Rosaldo and Lamphere, *Women*, p. 98.

47.   Conzelmann (*1 Corinthians*, p. 114) gives both translations for ἀκρασία: incontinence, unrestrained desire.

48.   How vv. 6-7 relate to vv. 1-5 has been variously debated. John Hurd affirms that Paul's meaning is that marital intercourse is his concession not his command. See Hurd, *Origin*, pp. 161-63 for a discussion of the main points.

which arise out of the root metaphor, 'in Christ all are children of God, no male and female'.

Two expressions of the root metaphor confront each other. Single-ness and celibacy are at the heart of the anti-structural response while their opposite, marriage and sexual expression, are demanded by the exponents of structure. According to Turner's model, as arguments are developed to support each position, the opposition intensifies and positions become entrenched.

When celibacy is made absolute, 'the relationship between the sexes becomes a massive extension of the sibling bond'.[49] As this response to the root metaphor develops into an organized anti-structure (nor-mative *communitas*[50]), it seeks to maintain the original experience of brotherhood/sisterhood by opposing any laws or regulations or insti-tutions which stand in opposition to this emphasis[51] and by making its views the basis of organization and of social statuses and roles within the church:

> The *ekklesia* itself, not just the initiates during their period of induction, is supposed to be marked by sacredness, homogeneity, unity, love, equal-ity, humility, and so on—as Turner would say, by *communitas*.[52]

Because ideology exists in symbolism,[53] their anti-structural declara-tion would carry the power to shape the symbolic universe by which the group distinguished itself from the outside world. Through it, the group could make a factual claim about an objective change in reality that would fundamentally modify social roles:

> New attitudes and altered behaviour would follow—but only if the group succeeds in clothing the novel declaration with an air of factuality.[54]

However, those who supported marriage and a system of hierarchical relationships would also develop arguments to support their position as the proper basis of organization within the church. For them, the baptismal formula, 'no male and female', does not negate the rights and debts of the patrilineal kinship structure as it was reflected in

49. Turner, *Dramas*, p. 246.
50. See pp. 107-108.
51. Turner, *Dramas*, p. 169.
52. Meeks, *First Urban*, p. 157.
53. Turner states that because symbols teach people to accept their own place in society, ideology exists in symbolism. See Flanagan, *David's Social Drama*, p. 108.
54. Meeks, 'Androgyne', p. 188.

marriage.[55] This social system, with its unequal roles and patterns of behaviour, should remain the same both within and outside the church. As a result, the metaphor, 'in Christ all are children of God, no male and female', would be more a baptismal-ecclesiological statement than a theological statement directed against the order of creation.[56]

Once two expressions of a root metaphor come into being, each begins to develop a set of rules which define in detail what is appropriate and what is inappropriate behaviour.[57] In Corinth conflict arises when 'no male and female' is interpreted exclusively in terms of singleness and celibacy or marriage and the expression of sexual relationships. It is, therefore, plausible to suggest that both groups gave some indication as to how their understanding of the root metaphor should apply in specific situations and why it should be understood in this particular way. To take this one step further, it is likely that the anti-structure group argued that in order to remove any temptation, married couples should divorce.[58] This action would be vigorously opposed by the pro-structure group.

When the interests and attitudes of groups stand in obvious opposition, a social drama begins. Such conflict brings

> fundamental aspects of society, normally overlaid by custom and habits of daily intercourse into frightening prominence. People have to take sides in terms of deeply entrenched moral imperatives and constraints, often against their own personal preferences.[59]

A social drama, arising in this kind of conflict situation, has four main phases of public action accessible to observation: breach, crisis, redressive action, reintegration. In 1 Corinthians 7 Paul attempts to redress the situation. In this chapter, the first two phases of the social drama, breach and crisis, will be analyzed from an exegesis of his arguments.

55. Turner, *Dramas*, p. 247.
56. See Madeleine Boucher, 'Some Unexplored Parallels to 1 Cor. 11, 11-12 and Gal. 3, 28: The NT on the Role of Women', *CBQ* 31 (1969), pp. 50-58 (57). Boucher parallels this formula with similar statements in Judaism. She states, 'it is possible that the two religions were alike in teaching at once the religious equality and the social subordination of women. . . ' (p. 55).
57. Turner, *Dramas*, p. 17.
58. L.O. Yarborough, *Not Like the Gentiles: Marriage Rules in the Letters of Paul* (Atlanta: Scholars Press, 1985), pp. 95-96.
59. Turner, *Dramas*, p. 35.

The Breach Phase in the Social Drama

Since Paul responds to a crisis situation, it is difficult to identify what specific action might have formed the breach phase of the social drama. According to Turner, it is in this stage that the normal patterns of social integration break down because of a deliberate non-fulfilment of some crucial norm regulating social action.[60]

Many commentators conclude that vv. 10-11 refer to an actual situation that has already taken place or was about to take place within the community when the Corinthians wrote their letter to Paul.[61] In these verses Paul cites a word of the Lord, orders obedience to it, and then makes an exception which allows the exact opposite of what the Lord says.[62]

Two reconstructions of the social situation addressed by these verses have been given. First, it has been suggested that a husband has denied his wife her conjugal rights because he belongs to the ascetic party. Since the marriage is no longer a full marriage, the wife desires to be free from him and possibly wishes to marry another.[63] A second suggestion presents the woman as the one who has divorced or is about to divorce her husband.[64] A comparison of the structure of these verses with the pattern in vv. 8-9 indicates the more probable situation.

Pattern	vv. 8-9	vv. 10-11
Verb of Saying:	λέγω	παραγγέλλω, οὐκ ἐγὼ ἀλλὰ ὁ κύριος
Dative of those addressed:	τοῖς ἀγάμοις καὶ ταῖς χήραις	τοῖς γεγαμηκόσιν
General Principle:	καλὸν αὐτοῖς ἐὰν μείνωσιν ὡς κἀγώ	γυναῖκα ἀπὸ ἀνδρὸς μὴ χωρισθῆναι...

60. Turner, *Dramas*, p. 38.

61. The use of ἐάν plus the subjunctive can indicate a conceding of exceptions ('if she separates herself after all') or an already existing situation ('if she has separated herself'). Despite the linguistic difficulties of the latter, Conzelmann (*1 Corinthians*, p. 120), Robertson and Plummer (*First Epistle*, p. 140), Talbert (*Reading Corinthians*, p. 44) and Victor Furnish (*The Moral Teaching of Paul* [Nashville: Abingdon Press, 2nd edn, 1985], p. 40) decide for an already existing situation rather than a hypothetical possibility.

62. This occurs in only one other place, 1 Cor. 9.14.

63. Murphy-O'Connor, *1 Corinthians*, pp. 63-64.

64. Moffatt (*First Epistle*, p. 78) and Robertson and Plummer (*First Epistle*, p. 140) provide examples of this opinion.

καὶ ἄνδρα γυναῖκα μὴ
ἀφιέναι

Concession: εἰ δὲ οὐκ ἐγκρατεύονται —ἐὰν δὲ καὶ χωρισθῇ,
γαμησάτωσαν μενέτω ἄγαμος ἢ τῷ
ἀνδρὶ καταλλαγήτω—

Reason for Concession: κρεῖττον γάρ ἐστιν
γαμῆσαι ἢ πυροῦσθαι

There are two awkward features in vv. 10-11: Paul's reference to a dominical saying and the separation of the two halves of the general statement by the concession. The modern Greek text indicates this separation by using dashes. Unlike v. 9, no reason is given in v. 11 why the general principle, which is a command of the Lord, should need a concession.

In vv. 10-11 Paul uses two words for divorce, χωρισθῆναι and ἀφιέναι. χωρίζω, which means 'to separate' and not specifically 'to divorce', is used in connection with the woman.[65] However, the word χωρισθῆναι is found in marriage contracts in the papyri.[66] There the passive (or middle form) means to separate (oneself), be separated by divorce.[67] Therefore, in v. 10, the legal dissolution of a marriage has taken place or is taking place. If these verses are related to 7.1b and to an anti-structural understanding of the root metaphor, then clearly

65. How this verb is interpreted is central to how the social situation reflected in vv. 10-11 is understood. For example, the fact that χωρίζω means 'to separate' and is used in the passive has led Murphy-O'Connor ('Divorced Woman', pp. 601-606) to argue for a Jewish milieu in which a woman was less likely to initiate divorce proceedings. It also leads him to argue that the husband was the one who belonged to the ascetic party.

66. R.L. Roberts, Jr, 'The Meaning of *Chorizo* and *Douloö* in 1 Corinthians 7.10-17', *ResQ* 8 (1965), pp. 179-84 (179), cites references to this use: (1) a second century BCE papyrus (PS1 166, 11); (2) three references to first century BCE papyri (BGU 1101, 5; 1102, 8; 1103, 61).

67. James Moulton and George Milligan (*The Vocabulary of the Greek New Testament: Illustrated from the Papyri and Other Non-Literary Sources* [5 Parts; London: Hodder & Stoughton, 1924], V, p. 696) state that the word had almost become a technical term in connection with divorce, as in 1 Cor. 7.10, 11, 15. Henry George Liddell and Robert Scott (*A Greek English Lexicon* [Oxford: Clarendon Press, 8th edn, 1901], p. 1750) show its use in the passive—κεχωρισμένη ἀπο τοῦ ἀνδρὸς Polyb. 32.12,6. Adolf Deissmann states that in marriage contracts there are usually conditions for the possibility of separation. These are introduced by the formula ἐὰν δὲ (οἱ γαμοῦντες) χωρίζονται ἀπ' ἀλλήλων. See Roberts, '*Chorizo*', p. 180.

someone in the church has understood divorce to be the only way to live an anti-structural life.[68]

The most plausible explanation is that a wife has divorced her husband. The reversal of the normal word order (woman-man rather than man-woman, as in vv. 2, 8, 12-13) indicates that Paul has in mind a particular case involving a woman.[69] The fact that the concession, even at the risk of awkwardness, is placed directly after the reference to her situation heightens this probability. In addition, in vv. 32-35 where Paul compares the single and married states as they relate to both men and women, there are breaks in the pattern in the comments that pertain to women. Paul says of the *man* that singleness leads to serving God while marriage leads to a division. He says neither of these things about the *woman*. If the married man was the one who belonged to the anti-structural party and who brought the conflict into the open, Paul would not have so easily made the statements in vv. 32-34a.

An important clue to the arguments of the contending factions is found in the saying of Jesus which is cited in v. 10. Here, Paul acknowledges the existence of a command prohibiting divorce; yet he allows the divorce to stand, thus appearing to judge anti-structure to be more important than a command of Jesus. It is, therefore, unlikely that Paul brought the injunction against divorce into his argument of his own accord.[70] More probably, Jesus' prohibition of divorce reflects the justification given by the structural group to defend its position. The breach has been made; a woman who is a member of the anti-structural party has divorced her husband, and has brought the issue of 'no male and female' into prominence within the community.[71]

68.   When each faction spells out, in terms of *its* understanding of the root metaphor, what was appropriate and what was inappropriate behaviour for males and females, the result is conflict. Consequently, what Paul says in these verses is thought to arise out of the opposing arguments, the details of which he has read in the Corinthians' letter to him.

69.   Conzelmann, *1 Corinthians*, p. 120; Furnish, *Moral Teaching* p. 40; Robertson and Plummer, *First Epistle*, p. 140.

70.   The same thing can be said of the reference to Paul's marital status in v. 7. See Hurd, *Origin*, p. 166-67.

71.   A breach may be made by an individual but s(he) acts or believes him/herself to be acting on behalf of other parties. See Turner, *Dramas*, p. 38. Peter Brown (*The Body and Society: Men, Women and Sexual Renunciation in Early*

The Crisis Phase

By the time Paul receives the Corinthians' letter, conflict within the community is intense. Chloe's people have brought news of ἔριδες (1.11); conflicting emotions have become intolerable.[72] In ch. 7 it seems evident that the breach stage in the social drama has taken place.

According to Turner, in the next stage, that of crisis, what was once a private matter becomes public, and consequently people have to take a position on it. In doing so, the 'normative patterns laid down in the course of deep regularities of conditioning, training and social experience' are revealed.[73] The deviant action cannot be ignored:

> Each public crisis has what I now call liminal characteristics, since it is a threshold between more or less stable phases of the social process, but it is not a sacred limen hedged about by taboos and thrust away from the centres of public life. On the contrary, it takes up its menacing stance in the forum itself and, as it were, dares the representatives of order to grapple with it. It cannot be ignored or wished away.[74]

The pattern and the language of Paul's argument in vv. 1-7 was noted earlier.[75] One other striking thing about these verses is the number of monotonously parallel statements in vv. 2-4 about the obligations respectively of men and women within marriage.

Since women were those to whom an anti-structural interpretation

Christianity [New York: Columbia University Press, 1988], pp. 403-404), gives an example of a woman in the time of Augustine who divorces her husband out of a desire for celibacy.

72. Wellborn ('On the Discord', p. 87) defines ἔρις as a 'hot dispute, the emotional flame that ignites whenever rivalry becomes intolerable. It invariably appears in accounts of ancient political life the moment the pressure of circumstances, that is, the approach of an enemy army or the election of mutually hostile consuls, draws the citizens into confused knots. For example, Plutarch describes the state into which Rome was thrown by the news that Caesar had crossed the Rubicon. The tempest swept the inhabitants of the country into the city, while the senators, seizing whatever possessions came to hand, abandoned Rome. Conflicting emotions prevailed everywhere, and throughout the city violent disturbances erupted. As was inevitable in such a large city, those who were pleased at Caesar's coming encountered those who were in fear and distress, and both giving voice to their opinions, "they began to quarrel with one another" (δι' ἔριδων ἦν, Plutarch *Caes.* 33)'.

73. Turner, *Dramas*, pp. 38-39.
74. Turner, *Dramas*, p. 39.
75. See this chapter, pp. 111-13.

of the root metaphor, 'no male and female', would have special appeal,[76] and since it was a married woman who seems to have brought the issue into prominence in the community (vv. 10-11), it is likely that at least some married women, as status dissonants, have refused sexual relations with their husbands on the grounds that it negated their newly found status as children of God and sisters to their husbands. In their argument, they appeal to Paul's singleness or celibacy (v. 7).[77] Others (male heads of households?) are insisting that the roles and obligations of the predominant kinship pattern should apply.

The address to the widowers[78] and widows in vv. 8-9 closely parallels vv. 1-2. Each passage opens with a statement beginning with καλὸν followed by the dative of the person(s) concerned. Each statement is qualified by a counter-statement. In each case the contrast is indicated by δέ.[79] Both passages begin with a statement in opposition to marriage and sexual relations. Then, a second statement follows advocating marriage and sexual relations as a means of avoiding immorality (πορνεία, v. 2) or loss of self-control (οὐκ ἐγκρατεύονται, v. 9). These alternative positions are further evidence for two opposing factions within the community. In vv. 2-5, immorality is cited as a possible consequence of prolonged sexual abstinence, while in vv. 8-9, marriage and sexual activity are judged preferable to a loss of self-control.[80]

---

76.   See Chapter 2, pp. 91-92 for information on the changing patterns of male/female relationships and on women as status dissonants.

77.   Hurd (*Origin*, pp. 166-67) states: 'It may also be that the Corinthians had made a direct reference to Paul's own marital status. . . It is unlikely that Paul would have independently reminded the Corinthians of his own celibacy, a topic that certainly did not further the practical goal which, we have suggested, Paul had in mind'.

78.   Orr ('Paul's Treatment', pp. 12-14) states that in v. 8 the unmarried are masculine and the widows, feminine. This allows a parallel or balance between widows and widowers. Since the word χῆρος is used neither in the NT nor in the LXX, the word ἄγαμος is an appropriate alternative, especially since the *alpha privative* in Greek may mean both one who has not been married and one who is out of marriage, or, as Orr puts it, 'demarried'. Liddell and Scott (*Greek-English Lexicon*, p. 5) define ἄγαμος as 'unmarried, single whether bachelor or widower'.

79.   Hurd, *Origin*, p. 166.

80.   Moulton and Milligan (*Vocabulary*, p. 529) point out that πορνεία is rare in classical Greek. Joseph Jensen ('Does Porneia Mean Fornication?', *NovT* 20 [1978], pp. 161-84 [181] relates πορνεία to self control and goes on to conclude: 'combining the contents of these vv. (vv. 5, 9), we end up with *porneia* and *egkrateia* as opposites. . . ' The same opposites appear in Gal. 5.19, 23 where *porneia* appears

A third group, forced by the two extreme positions to take sides, are those married to unbelievers. This section is addressed to τοῖς λοιποῖς (v. 12). The least complicated way to interpret these words is to understand them to refer to 'the others who are married', that is, married persons who have spouses who are non-Christian.[81]

Paul's pattern of response in vv. 12-16 is different from that of vv. 8-9-and 10-11.[82] If the previous pattern were followed, these verses should begin with 'to the rest I say, it is good to stay married (or to divorce), but if', or 'a brother/sister should (should not) divorce an unbelieving spouse, but if...' Instead Paul presents each alternative (stay married or divorce) in a conditional clause (εἰ) and then issues an imperative (μὴ ἀφιέτω αὐτήν/τὸν ἄνδρα χωριζέσθω). In these verses there is no general principle; the appropriate response depends on the situation in which individuals find themselves.

In his investigation of the meaning of the questions in v. 16, Kubo

---

among 'the works of the flesh' and *egkrateia* among 'the fruits of the Spirit'.

πυροῦσθαι is a middle passive infinitive which means 'to burn' either literally or figuratively. Barre ('To Marry or Burn', pp. 193-202) argues that the meaning is 'to be burned in the fires of judgment'. The biblical evidence for this (LXX or NT) is not convincing. For example, in the *T. Naph.* 8.8 πυροῦσθαι means 'self-control' particularly with reference to matters of sex (W. Bauer, W.F. Arndt, F.W. Gingrich and F.W. Danker [eds.], *A Greek–English Lexicon of the New Testament and Other Early Christian Literature* [Chicago: University of Chicago Press, 1979], p. 216). The figurative meaning 'to be inflamed with emotions', seems well supported and is preferable in this context: (1) Gerhard Kittel (TDNT; trans. G.W. Bromiley; Grand Rapids: Eerdmans, 1964, VI, pp. 949-50) attests to the existence of this meaning in the Greek world; (2) if, as seems probable, 9b can be seen, as 'a restatement of 9a then πυροῦσθαι can be equated with οὐκ ἐγκρατεύονται i.e. no self-control, therefore marriage; marriage, therefore no burning'.

81. Paul uses οἱ λοιπόι thirteen times as a substantive or an adjective: Rom. 1.13; 11.7; 1 Cor. 9.5; 11.34; 15.37; 2 Cor. 12.13; 13.2; Gal. 2.13; Phil. 1.13; 4.3; 1 Thess. 11.13; 5.60. 'The rest' is sometimes contrasted with 'we' but does not without exception refer to outsiders. In Phil. 1.13 the word contrasts those inside the Praetorium with those outside, while in 1 Cor. 15.37 τινος τῶν λοιπῶν occurs in the context of seeds or grains. When used as a noun, οἱ λοιποί is usually contrasted with what immediately precedes (Rom. 11.7; 1 Cor. 15.37; 2 Cor. 13.2; Phil. 1.13; 1 Thess. 5.6).

82. In the two previous sections, which begin with datives and verbs of saying, Paul states a principle and then a concession, εἰ... γαμησάτωσαν (v. 9), ἐὰν... καταλλαγήτω (v. 11). In vv. 12-16 there is no general principle, just the concession clause followed by the rationale for that concession.

argues that their sense is not determined by their structure but by the context in which they occur. After posing numerous possibilities, he states that vv. 12-14 and vv. 15-16 should be seen as two separate units, each of which encompasses Paul's advice to a particular group within the congregation. Kubo concludes that vv. 12-14 present Paul's instruction to a group that was uneasy about continuing a married relationship with unbelievers, while vv. 15-16 are addressed to a group which argues that marriages with unbelievers should continue. Kubo sets out his reconstruction as follows:

Group 1	vv. 12-13	Paul gives instruction
	v. 14	the reason
Group 2	vv. 15ab	Paul gives instruction
	vv. 15c-16	the reason[83]

Any reconstruction of the social situation of these verses must take note of the kinship vocabulary that Paul uses. In the following excerpt, one solid line indicates brother/sister terminology or equivalent pronoun; two lines, husband/wife terminology or equivalent pronoun.

v. 12: εἴ τις ἀδελφὸς γυναῖκα ἔχει ἄπιστον,
        καὶ αὕτη συνευδοκεῖ οἰκεῖν μετ᾽ αὐτοῦ
            μὴ ἀφιέτω αὐτήν

v. 13: καὶ γυνὴ εἴ τις ἔχει ἄνδρα ἄπιστον
        καὶ οὗτος συνευδοκεῖ οἰκεῖν μετ᾽ αὐτῆς
            μὴ ἀφιέτω τὸν ἄνδρα

v. 14: ἡγίασται γὰρ ὁ ἄπιστος ἐν τῇ γυναικί
        καὶ ἡγίασται ἡ γυνὴ ἡ ἄπιστος ἐν τῷ ἀδελφῷ

v. 15: εἰ δὲ ὁ ἄπιστος χωρίζεται, χωριζέσθω
        οὐ δεδούλωται ὁ ἀδελφὸς ἢ ἡ ἀδελφὴ ἐν τοῖς τοιούτοις
            ἐν δὲ εἰρήνῃ κέκληκεν ὑμᾶς ὁ θεός

v. 16: τί γὰρ οἶδας, γύναι, εἰ τὸν ἄνδρα σώσεις;
        ἢ τί οἶδας, ἄνερ, εἰ τὴν γυναῖκα σώσεις

Since kinship terminology provides information about aspects of culture and behaviour, anthropologists focus their inquiry on kinship terms which seem out of place, where some aspect of usage seems at odds with a prevailing model. Such discrepancies often indicate that earlier conditions and social characteristics have changed or that a society is in the process of transformation.[84]

In this section, where Paul addresses a specific problem concerning

---

83. Kubo, 'Optimistic', pp. 542-44.
84. Pasternak, *Kinship and Social Organization*, p. 126.

married relationships with unbelievers, he uses not only ἀνήρ-γυνή but also ἀδελφός-ἀδελφή. However, his use of this terminology is not uniform. While ἀδελφός is used throughout vv. 12-15 for the Christian partner in the relationship, ἀδελφή is found only in v. 15. In vv. 13-14 γυνή is used for the Christian wife.

If Kubo's proposal is followed, Paul does *not* use brother/sister language for the married *woman* when addressing the group that wants to *dissolve* marriage relationships with unbelievers (vv. 12-14). Husband/wife vocabulary is used consistently when the Christian *female* is addressed (v. 13), though not when the Christian *male* is addressed (v. 12). In addition, in v. 13 the noun ἄνδρα completes the prohibition; in v. 12 the pronoun αὐτήν is used even though γυναῖκα would have been stronger. Paul *does* use brother/sister language for *both* the man and the woman when addressing the group which urges that marriage relationships with unbelievers *continue* (v. 15).[85] His final appeal (v. 16) employs husband/wife terminology.

The confrontation in Corinth over marriage is reflected in two expressions of the root metaphor with their accompanying sets of vocabulary. Paul's avoidance of 'sister' in referring to the married woman when he addresses the group which urges divorcing an unbeliever supports the view that married women were involved. Implicit in these two sets of vocabulary are opposing views of social organization and of the statuses and roles which accompany each.

The words ἁγιάζω and ἀκάθαρτα serve to clarify the rhetoric of the schism. In v. 14, Paul speaks of the unbeliever being made holy by the believer. This is not Paul's usual understanding of holiness.[86] According to Wimbush, it reflects the arguments of the factions:

> They were probably thinking of marriage as that which could make the believer unclean or unholy and of the single, celibate life as holy. Holiness seems to have been regarded almost as a thing to be possessed. Paul

85. Relating as brother and sister would cause few difficulties in other areas of social interaction (widows, daughters, sisters), however, its problematic nature in the case of husbands and wives is obvious.

86. Conzelmann (*1 Corinthians*, p. 120) observes that 'it looks as if holiness is crassly regarded as a thing; it is transferable without faith (and even baptism) being necessary'. He asks, 'Is this kind of thinking a foreign body in the theology of Paul?' Paul's position 'would be thrown into specially sharp relief if in Corinth the ascetic demand had in fact been made: to annul mixed marriages in order to avoid the world and the powers of the world'. (p. 122)

plays along with the Corinthians in picking up their language but steers it
in a different direction.[87]

Verse 14 speaks of the children of mixed marriages being holy. It
seems to presume that the children were not themselves Christians and
would remain with the non-believing parent after the divorce.[88] In
Acts there are references to whole households being baptized on the
faith commitment of either a man or a woman (Acts 16.15, 33).
Whether Lydia or the Philippian jailer were married or had children
is not known; however, legally, in a patrilineal society, the children
belonged to the father, and only if he were declared unfit was custody
given to the wife.[89] Therefore, if a brother divorced his unbelieving
wife, the children would stay with him and remain clean. However, if
a sister divorced her non-believing husband, the likelihood is that the
children would remain with their father and therefore, become
unclean.

Both extremes in the social drama counter each other with claims
of pollution and holiness. One faction is arguing that to remain in a
mixed marriage conferred holiness on one's spouse and one's children. This argument sought to convince women married to unbelievers to stay married. The other faction has argued that a married
woman who wants to live a brother/sister existence should divorce her
husband (vv. 10-11). They now contend that mixed marriages would
be an even greater pollutant because, in the absence of a brother/sister
relationship, there is less likelihood of an agreement to remain
celibate. In v. 16 husband/wife vocabulary is used in direct address.
Neither a positive nor a negative response is expected,[90] which indi-

---

87. Wimbush, *Worldly Ascetic*, p. 19 n. 24. Wimbush refers to Procksch's
article on holiness. See Otto Procksch, 'ἁγιασμός', *TDNT* 1.113; Barrett, *First
Epistle*, p. 164; Murphy-O'Connor, *1 Corinthians*, p. 65.

88. Countryman, *Dirt,* p. 209.

89. See Chapter 2, p. 76.

90. Kubo ('Optimistic', pp. 537-44) cites the arguments on both sides. The
RSV is typical of a pessimistic translation ('wife, how do you know whether you
will save your husband'), while the NASB has an optimistic implication ('wife, how
do you know, perhaps you will save your husband'). The optimistic view was held
by all the Greek Fathers, and up until the fourteenth century it prevailed. Since then
the predominant view has been the pessimistic one. Jeremias's ('Missionarische
Aufgabe' pp. 255-60) presentation of new evidence in 1957 suggests that the type of
construction used in v. 16 is always understood in a positive way in contemporary
writings. The examples he cites from Epictetus are in the second person singular, as

cates that Paul does not unconditionally support either side in the controversy. Nevertheless, the use of the terminology of the pro-structure faction needs to be explored further.

In vv. 25-40[91] Paul considers another issue within the community.[92] Those who are bound by an oath with a virgin are being pressured to take sides in the dispute within the community. The Corinthian letter to Paul must have asked about a particular situation involving παρθένων.[93] When this word is used in the singular (vv. 28, 34, 36-38), it refers to a particular category of woman.[94] The distinction in v. 34 between the unmarried woman, ἡ γυνὴ ἡ ἄγαμος, and then παρθένος suggests that the latter is in a different category from either the married woman or the unmarried woman.[95]

As in other sections of this chapter, an investigation of breaks in pattern and of concessions helps to clarify what is taking place within the community. In vv. 26-28 a general statement (νομίζω οὖν τοῦτο καλὸν ὑπάρχειν, καλόν[96] ἀνθρώπῳ τὸ οὕτως εἶναι) is given a

is 1 Cor. 7.16. Kubo, however, questions whether any of Jeremias's examples are an exact duplicate of what is found in Paul—two double questions. His conclusion, that only an uncertain rendering makes sense of this passage ('wife, how do you know if you will save your husband or if you will not!') is the conclusion accepted here. See also Ben Witherington III, *Women in the Earliest Church*, (Cambridge: Cambridge University Press, 1988), pp. 32-33.

91. περὶ δέ (v. 25) separates vv. 25-40 from vv. 1-24. παρθένος which is prominent in vv. 25-40 does not appear in vv. 1-24. In spite of these considerations, vv. 1-16 and vv. 25-40 can be seen as a single unit consisting of two parts, with vv. 17-24 forming the bridge. See Hurd, *Origin*, p. 154.

92. The structure of these verses is as follows: in v. 25 Paul declares his authority; in vv. 26-27 he states the principles by which the matter should be judged; in v. 28, he makes a concession; vv. 29-31 and 32-34 give two arguments supporting and clarifying his statement in v. 28b concerning the afflictions of the married state; v. 35 provides a summary statement; vv. 36-40 address the specific situation.

93. Paul uses παρθένος only here in these verses and once in 2 Cor. 11.2 ('a pure virgin to Christ').

94. Elliott ('Paul's Teaching', pp. 220-21) argues that the plural τῶν παρθένων concerns engaged couples, and that, accordingly, ἡ παρθένος means an engaged woman. He points out that in the rest of the NT παρθένος means 'betrothed girl' (Lk. 1.27; Mt. 1.18, 23, Mt. 25.1-13).

95. The word ἄγαμος was taken to mean 'demarried', that is, 'widowers' (v. 8) or 'a divorced woman' (v. 11).

96. In *Paul's Literary Style: A Stylistic and Historical Comparison of II Corinthians 11.16-12.13, Romans 8.9-39, and Philippians 3.2-4.13* (Jackson: Evangelical

rationale (διὰ τὴν ἐνεστῶσαν ἀνάγκην[97]) and followed by specific examples (δέδεσαι γυναικί; μὴ ζήτει λύσιν. λέλυσαι ἀπὸ γυναικός; μὴ ζήτει γυναῖκα). A concession in v. 28a (ἐὰν δὲ καὶ γαμήσῃς, ουχ ἥμαρτες, καὶ ἐὰν γήμῃ ἡ παρθένος οὐκ ἥμαρτεν) is followed not by a rationale for the concession but by a reference to the afflictions of marriage (v. 28b). The situation in v. 27, although assuming some sort of obligation, must, nevertheless, involve an alternative to legal marriage.[98] Paul is addressing a man who is bound to a woman by some sort of bond or oath, and that person is contrasted to another who is in a state of freedom. The concession allows marriage: 'but if[99]

Theological Society, 1984), p. 305, Aida Spencer cites v. 26 as an example of pleonasm, which makes the sense stronger and more obvious.

97. Bauer, (*Greek-English Lexicon*, p. 52) gives the meaning of ἀνάγκη as 'necessity or compulsion of any kind, outer or inner brought about by the nature of things. . . ' In 2 Cor. 6.4; 12.10; 1 Thess. 3.7 ἀνάγκη is used to refer to external persecutions and difficulties. Because of the theological/eschatological argument in vv. 29-31 ἀνάγκη in v. 26 is often interpreted as an eschatological condition. Barrett (*First Epistle*, pp. 174-75) represents the view of a number of scholars: 'the necessity is probably to be interpreted in terms of v. 29 rather than v. 37; that is, Paul is thinking. . . of the eschatological woes that are impending over the world and are already anticipated in the sufferings of Christians'. However, since the eschatological statements serve primarily to provide a justification for Paul's arguments in vv. 29-31 (see J.G. Gager, Jr, 'Functional Diversity in Paul's Use of End-Time Language', *JBL* 89 [1970], pp. 325-37 [332]) ἀνάγκη should not necessarily he interpreted in terms of the eschatological influence. Further, if vv. 25-40 are considered as an a-b-a pattern (Hurd, *Origin*, p. 178), with vv. 25-28 and vv. 36-40 representing a and a, the meanings of ἀνάγκη in vv. 26 and 37 ought to be more closely associated. Ἐνεστῶσαν (Bauer, *Greek-English Lexicon* p. 382) used intransitively means 'being' or 'existing'.

98. In v. 27 difficulties surround the word γυναικί which can mean either 'wife' or 'woman', and the word δέδεσαι which can mean 'be bound in marriage' or 'be bound in a promise of marriage'. Elliott ('Paul's Teaching', p. 222) states that, throughout Paul's writings, γυνή is an ambiguous word. Since the context is clear in 7.3, 4, 10, 11, 12, 33, 39, he translates γυνή as 'wife'. However, in v. 1 he translates it 'woman' because the contrast is with ἄνθρωπος not ἀνήρ. Elliott concludes that γυνή means 'wife' only where the context is clear. In Rom. 7.2, δέδεται does mean 'be bound in marriage' but the context is clearly husband and wife. In v. 27 Elliott ('Paul's Teaching', p. 222) translates δέδεσαι as 'be bound in a promise of marriage', thus contrasting it with γαμέω in v. 28. Bauer *(Greek-English Lexicon*, p. 177) cites an example of this use in Achilles *Tat*. 1, 11 2 v. 1.

99. ἐὰν plus the subjunctive (v. 11) denotes what has occurred or is expected to occur, under certain circumstances, from a given standpoint in the present, either

you marry, you do not sin nor does the virgin'. Probably the anti-structure group is saying that, in this particular situation, it is a sin to marry.

Verses 29-31 and vv. 32-35 form an integral part of Paul's attempt to mediate the conflict and consequently will be addressed fully in the next chapter. However, these verses also shed light on the composition of the factions and their arguments.

Duncan Derrett relates all the statements in vv. 29b-31a to marriage and betrothal. He states,

> those that have wives may be as if they had none, (that is to say) those that weep (scil. the brides on leaving, or their female relatives in real or simulated grief at their departure?) as if they did not weep, those that rejoice (i.e. the bridegrooms and their families?) as though they did not rejoice, and those that buy (i.e. those that put up the cash) as if they had acquired no right.[100]

In a patrilineal society the marriage ceremony and the payment of bridewealth give certain rights to the husband and residually to his kin. Since Paul's use of the language of kinship rights and obligations in vv. 2-5 suggested the arguments of the pro-structure group, it is plausible to suggest that, in his use of kinship language in vv. 29b-31a, Paul is again using the words of the pro-structure group in his response. The pro-marriage/sexual intercourse faction may have argued that in marriage certain rights are purchased and that those individuals who do the buying have the right to their full use.

In vv. 32-34 Paul balances his statements concerning men and women with only two exceptions. As in the previous sections, a break in the pattern provides a clue as to the position of the contending factions.

θέλω δὲ ὑμᾶς ἀμερίμνους εἶναι.
    ὁ ἄγαμος μεριμνᾷ τὰ τοῦ κυρίου, πῶς ἀρέσῃ τῷ κυρίῳ
    ὁ δὲ γαμήσας μεριμνᾷ τὰ τοῦ κόσμου, πῶς ἀρέσῃ τῇ γυναικί,
    <u>καὶ μεμέρισται.</u>

general or specific. See Bauer, *Greek-English Lexicon*, p. 211. The occurrence of ἐάν here and in vv. 10-11 relates these two incidents, and suggests that vv. 25-40 may be part of the breach phase. However, these verses have been included in the crisis stage because vv. 36-40 seem to indicate that the decision has not been made.

100. J. Duncan Derrett, 'The Disposal of Virgins', in *idem*, *Studies in the New Testament*. I. *Glimpses of the Legal and Social Presuppositions of the Authors* (Leiden: Brill, 1977), pp. 189-90.

καὶ ἡ γυνὴ ἡ ἄγαμος <u>καὶ ἡ παρθένος</u> μεριμνᾷ τὰ τοῦ κυρίου,
    <u>ἵνα ᾖ ἁγία (καὶ) τῷ σώματι καὶ τῷ πνεύματι</u>
ἡ δὲ γαμήσασα μεριμνᾷ τὰ τοῦ κόσμου, πῶς ἀρέσῃ τῷ ἀνδρί.

Paul concludes his statement concerning the married man with the words καὶ μεμέρισται; there is no similar statement when he speaks of the married woman. In v. 13 he avoided brother/sister terminology for the believing wife; here he avoids saying that marriage causes divided loyalties (or a reason for splitting into parties[101]) for the married woman.

In v. 34 Paul writes καὶ ἡ γυνὴ ἡ ἄγαμος καὶ ἡ παρθένος μεριμνᾷ τὰ τοῦ κυρίου, ἵνα ᾖ ἁγία τῷ πνεύματι. Many questions arise concerning this verse, including a textual one.[102] If the United Bible Society reading is accepted, a problem of balance remains. The statement about ἡ γυνὴ ἡ ἄγαμος and ἡ παρθένος is followed by a purpose clause. These two types of women are concerned about the things of the Lord, but not so that they might serve the Lord (v. 33).[103] The purpose is rather that they might be holy both in body and in spirit.

Abstinence from sexual relations allows a woman to sanctify her body. In v. 14, as has been seen, the view of holiness was foreign to Paul. In v. 34 also the argument is inconsistent with Paul's teaching, since he believes that all Christians, married or unmarried, must be holy in body (1 Cor. 6.13, 15, 19, 20). In addition, v. 34 is inconsistent with v. 14. In v. 14 holiness came through *preserving* the

---

101. The noun μερίς means 'party', in a political sense. At 1.13 μεμέρισται can be translated 'split into parties'. See Wellborn, 'On the Discord', p. 87. ἐμέρισεν is also found in 7.17.

102. There are at least nine variant readings. The choice of the United Bible Society Committee coincides with the judgment of the Nestle text. Only the reading of Papyrus 46 has sufficient external support to rival the chosen text. It adds 'unmarried' to 'virgin'. Metzger describes this as a 'typical scribal conflation'. The United Bible Society reading as *lectio difficilior* is preferable to the retention of the adjective. See Bruce Metzger, *A Textual Commentary on the Greek New Testament: A Companion Volume to the United Bible Societies' Greek New Testament* (London: United Bible Societies, 3rd edn, 1971), pp. 555-56.

103. ἀρέσῃ is found nine times in Paul. With the dative it means 'to strive to please, accommodate (conduct, activity, oft. almost serve)'. See Bauer, *Greek-English Lexicon*, p. 105. D.L. Balch ('1 Cor. 7.32-35 and Stoic Debate About Marriage, Anxiety and Distraction', *JBL* 102 [1983], pp. 429-39 [430-31]) concludes that, in the sense that Epictetus describes the anxieties of a married man, 'to serve his wife is not too strong a rendering' for ἀρέσῃ.

marriage, since the marriage relationship made the unbeliever holy. In light of these inconsistencies, it seems likely that the 'holiness' statements point to arguments used within the community by the two extremes in order to gain support for their positions.[104]

The involvement of women in the controversy over marriage/ sexual intercourse versus singleness/celibacy is undeniable. Paul speaks of the single or 'demarried' man serving the Lord and of the married man serving his wife, but he does not make the corresponding statement concerning the woman in v. 34. His omission of καὶ μεμέρισται and the purpose clause (ἵνα... πνεύματι) are significant for his arguments: to say that married women are divided in their loyalties or that serving the Lord comes with the single state would have escalated the crisis, because wives who wanted to be treated as sisters would feel supported in their plea for absolute anti-structure. Further, those who supported marriage would be disturbed by the suggestion that marriage 'divided' wives in the same way that it did husbands.

In vv. 36-40 Paul turns to the specific question he had been asked to address.[105] Before he addresses the question itself he presents two arguments supporting the position he will take (vv. 29-31, 32-35).

A formal contract or vow has taken place between a man and a woman resulting in a state of affairs in which the woman and man are left in an ambiguous position, neither married nor unmarried. Throughout ch. 7 Paul has addressed specific situations within marriage: husband/wife, widower/widow, divorce, and mixed marriages. These categories are paralleled in Augustus's marriage law, where betrothal is also dealt with.[106]

The most probable reconstruction of the situation addressed in vv. 36-40 is that the man and woman are bound in an oath of betrothal.[107]

104. Barrett (*First Epistle*, p. 18) believes that Paul is either adopting antiquity's patriarchal view regarding the purity of women or is taking up the language and sentiment of some of the Corinthians, or, perhaps both.

105. Verses 39-40 are generally related to vv. 8-9 (Hurd, *Origin*, p. 154) and seen as an afterthought. However, similarities in vocabulary relate these verses to their immediate context: δέω vv. 27, 39; οὕτως vv. 26, 40; κρεῖσσον v. 38; μακαριωτέρα v. 40 and γνώμην vv. 25 and 40.

106. The understanding of mixed marriage in the Augustan laws is that of two people of unequal social status.

107. The interpretations of these three verses, in which there are no textual uncertainties, are divided into three groups. The passage concerns fathers and daughters, celibate marriage, or betrothal. The different interpretations are based on the different

According to the norms of the dominant society, as prescribed in the Augustan marriage reform, this should lead to a husband and wife relationship within two years, or else the man would be subject to legal penalties. Within the church the confrontation between two kinship systems complicates the promise to marry.

The statements found in vv. 36-38 are consistent with vv. 1-16. There a fear of immorality (v. 2) and loss of control (v. 9) led to certain concessions. In vv. 12-16 Paul took away from either extreme the right to decide the issue. Verses 36-38 also refer to sexual desire and contol (ἀσχημονεῖν, ὑπέρακμος, ὀφείλει, θέλημα, ἐξουσία).[108] Once

meanings that are possible for certain words in the passage. See Introduction, nn. 8-11 for details. The father/daughter theory seems the least probable of the three. In comparing the 'fathers and daughters' and 'spiritual marriage' theories, Hurd *(Origin*, pp. 171-75) presents seven points of exegesis. Of these only one favours the 'fathers and daughters' theory. As a result Hurd sets it aside as an explanation of vv. 36-38. The other two interpretations have similarities: in both the woman can be referred to as a virgin; in both there is a binding agreement which would allow the man to speak of ἡ ἑαυτοῦ παρθένος and others of ἡ παρθένος αὐτοῦ; in both cases celibacy is required; both situations could lead to certain aberrations if prolonged; in both cases the problem seems to have arisen because of the new found Christian 'calling'. Hurd *(Origin*, pp. 175-80) opts for the spiritual marriage theory with some hesitancy. Primarily, he argues that the number of Christians engaged to be married would not have constituted a significant proportion of the community. However, it can be asked why there needed to be a significant proportion of engaged couples in Corinth. As part of Augustus's attempt to control family life, those who were married and had children were given preferential treatment in public appointments, and those who were engaged were required to marry within two years or be subject to penalties. Because this was the law and because of the escalating crisis over conflicting kinship systems, even one instance within the congregation could have had widespread ramifications.

108. ἀσχημονεῖν: Paul uses ἀσχημοσύνη in Rom. 1.27 with reference to homosexual acts and ἀσχήμων in the neuter plural, in 1 Cor. 12.23 as an euphemism for genitalia. The relationship of this word to immorality or lack of control seems clear. ὑπέρακμος: two meanings are possible for this word, 'past the bloom of youth' (of the girl) or 'with strong passions' (of the man). Since the man is the subject of the previous verse, the latter translation is preferred. ὀφείλει: Paul uses ὀφείλην as a euphemism for marital intercourse in 7.3. θέλημα can mean both 'purpose' or 'desire'. The latter meaning occurs in Jn. 1.13. ἐξουσία means 'freedom of choice', 'authority' or 'power to do something'. The occurrence of ἐξουσίαν in 1 Cor. 11.10 speaks of the ability of women to protect themselves from the amorous glances of certain angels. See Bauer, *Greek-English Lexicon*, p. 278. See Hurd, *Origin*, pp. 172-74.

again Paul removes the right to decide from both the pro-marriage/sexual intercourse and the pro-singleness/celibacy factions. The young man is to marry if loss of control or immorality has become a problem for *him*.

In this reconstruction of the community situation, one faction is arguing that the marriage *must* take place because a permanent be-trothal will lead to immorality; the other group believes that it is a sin for children of God who are 'in Christ' to get married: the couple should relate to one another as brother and sister. Those in the anti-structure group are calling upon the man to break the Augustan law and thus provide a 'symbolic trigger'[109] to all in the church.[110] Those defending the normative pattern are pressing their case just as ur-gently. The fact that Paul must present arguments to convince his readers and the young man that the marriage should *not* take place (vv. 29-35) suggests the influence of the pro-marriage arguments. The man in v. 36 is a man caught in the middle, and he is being used by both sides in this confrontation over conflicting systems of social organization.

109. Turner (*Dramas*, p. 38) defines 'symbolic trigger' as a deliberate flouting of a social norm in order to create a confrontation.

110. In 'Background of 1 Cor. vii: Sayings of the Lord in Q; Moses as an Ascetic ΘΕΟΣ ΑΝΗΡ in II Cor. III', *NTS* 18 (1972), pp. 351-64 (357), David Balch concludes that the sayings of Jesus were at the heart of the Corinthian dispute over sexual asceticism. After commenting on the importance of γαμέω and γαμίζω to an interpretation of vv. 36-38, he continues: 'It is, then, extremely striking that these two verbs occur together in Q and that they appear together in the very passages in Luke which I suggest were being discussed in Corinth (Luke xx.35 = Matt. xxii.30 = Mark xii.25 and Luke xvii.27 = Matt. xxiv.38). To this must be added the fact that the rare form γαμίζω (causative?) does not appear anywhere else in the New Testament (or Old Testament) and is found only in Apollonius Dyscolus (*Syntax* 280.11) in extra-biblical Greek'. Against the anti-structure faction's use of the words of the Lord, Paul declares that marriage is not sinful. MacDonald (*Male and Female*, p. 71) points to Mk. 12.18-27 in which γαμέω and γαμίζω also appear. Jesus' response to the Sadducees in v. 25 states: 'When they are raised from the dead they neither marry nor are given in marriage, for they are like angels in heaven'. The evidence seems to support the conclusion that the anti-structure group knew of sayings valuing asceticism and was using them in its conflict with the pro-structure faction.

Mary Douglas's Model of Grid and Group

In 1 Corinthians 7 the clash centres on the relations of male and female Christians to one another and the social structures and organization within the church: should there be an absolute non-crossing of the sexual boundary (celibacy/singleness) or a selective crossing (sexual intercourse/marriage)? Two factions are in conflict and each is using the language of pollution and purity in its arguments: sin, immorality, holiness.[111] Mary Douglas's model of grid and group, through which she situates conflicting groups on a social map, will further focus the confrontation.

Mary Douglas sets pollution within the context of dirt:

> the idea of dirt implies system. Dirt avoidance is a process of tidying up, ensuring that the order in the external physical events conforms to the structure of ideas. Pollution rules can thus be seen as an extension of the perceptual process: insofar as they can impose order on experience, they support clarification of forms and thus reduce dissonance.[112]

Since the ordered relation of social units and the total structure of social life depend on a clear definition of roles and allegiances, beliefs about pollution are found guarding against disturbances of the social order.[113] These beliefs not only reinforce the cultural and social structure but also reduce ambiguity in the moral sphere.

Douglas speaks of three kinds of sex pollution. First, there is the desire to keep the body (physical and social) intact. Its rules are designed to control exits and entrances. Secondly, there is the desire to keep straight the internal lines of the social system. Rules control individual contacts that destroy these lines: acts of adultery, incest and so on. Douglas's description of the third type of sexual pollution has implications for 1 Corinthians 7:

111. Neyrey ('Body Language', pp. 138-42) interprets most of 1 Cor. as an application of purity concerns. Countryman (*Dirt*, p. 198) does not believe that all control over the sexual orifices necessarily springs from purity concerns. He interprets ch. 5 as an offense against family hierarchy rather than purity. Similarly, the issue in ch. 7 concerns the prevailing kinship system over a new model; however, some of the arguments of the factions are presented in terms of purity and holiness.

112. Douglas, *Implicit Meanings*, p. 53.

113. Douglas, *Implicit Meanings*, p. 55.

> On the one hand when the principle of male dominance is applied to the
> ordering of social life but is contradicted by other principles such as that
> of female independence. . . then sex pollution is likely to flourish.[114]

According to Douglas's theory, one group in Corinth, in its extreme
concern for purity of the sexual orifice, expressed through arguments
that speak of holiness and sin, wants to establish singleness and celibacy as the pattern for relationships between Christian men and wom-
en. Opposing it is another group that wants to confirm marriage and
sexual intercourse as the proper pattern. Neither group wants freedom
in sexual matters to order relationships within the church. At odds are
two different social systems: normative *communitas* and structure.[115]

The two key elements of social and cultural classification in
Douglas's model are 'group' and 'grid'. Societies vary according to
the strength of their group ties, which include any form of structuring
that is dependent upon group organization. The durability of group
life, the degree of the sense of 'them' versus 'us', the number of activities taken in common rather than individually all combine here. In
Douglas's words, 'group'

> expresses the possible range from the lowest possible of associations (on
> the left) to tightly knit, closed groups (on the right). . . The further we
> travel along the line from left to right, the more permanent, inescapable
> and clearly bounded (are) the social groups.[116]

The second dimension, grid, is made up of individually oriented
aspects of social structure, specifically the phenomenon described by
anthropologists as 'networks'. Networks are connections between particular individuals that do not carry with them group-centred consequences. As an example, Douglas speaks of classifications according to
ego-centred social categories such as sex or age and ego-focused categories such as kinship ties.[117]

114. Douglas, *Purity and Danger*, pp. 140-42.
115. See pp. 182-83, for an understanding of the relationship between normative
communitas and structure as social systems.
116. Mary Douglas, *Natural Symbols* (1970), p. 57.
117. In the latter category Douglas (*Natural Symbols*, p. 58) uses as an example
Anglo-Saxon vengeance groups and inheritance laws which defined a set of responsible kin radiating from each particular individual. She states: 'Just as a wedding
brings together a set of kin and friends relative to the married couple, who would
never otherwise meet or co-operate, so these ego-focussed kindreds fuse into groups

Grid measures individual ties; group measures group loyalties. A group-centred social structure and an ego-centred social structure may vary independently providing a two-dimensional field on which societies may be differentiated. 'Grid' and 'group' can be expressed diagrammatically in the following way:

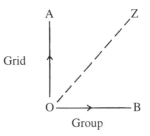

Z is the direction of maximal involvement of the individual in formalized social interaction. OB is the direction of maximum group organization. Moving along the line to B, group becomes a more and more effective principle of organization and so it imposes group-focused roles upon its members: stratification, leadership and sub-groupings will develop. OA goes toward the maximum for ego-centred categories of behaviour and the minimum of restraints of groups. Somewhere near zero is the minimum for either kinds of social variable.[118]

Using the criteria of stability, internal organization and external relations, Douglas specifies the stages of development of group organization along the line from O to B. A median point along this line is identified by fissions within the group and internal factions related to a struggle for a defined office of leader. This point on the line is a society in which roles are not yet clearly defined, and where the rules of succession are ambiguous.[119]

In social structures with little differentiation of roles, techniques for regulating and reconciling are little developed. In communities where authority has weak resources, survival demands that the structure of roles be defined more sharply.[120] Douglas describes a case of strong group and weak grid:

to prosecute a blood-revenge and are always potentially there so long as their focussing point is alive'.

118. Douglas, *Natural Symbols*, p. 60.
119. Douglas, *Natural Symbols*, p. 112.
120. Douglas, *Natural Symbols*, p. 114.

a man recognizes very strong allegiance to a social group, and at the same time does not know how he relates to others or what his expectations should be. He tends to use the image of the human body to express both the exclusive nature of the allegiance and the confused social experience. The group is likened to a human body; the orifices are to be carefully guarded to prevent unlawful intrusions; dangers from poisoning and loss of physical strength express the lack of articulated roles within it.[121]

The Christian community at Corinth reflected in ch. 7 fits a mid-strong group/low grid emplotment on Douglas's scale. Factionalism exists, and there is no clear definition of how the members should relate to each other. The individual is under considerable pressure to conform to community norms, but these norms are confused and in conflict. In the absence of a coherent system of internal classifications, deviance becomes difficult both to define and to contain within the group. Definition is problematic because one cannot be certain which behavioural patterns are acceptable. Pressure to conform is strong, but it is not clear what form conformity should take.[122]

A situation of diminishing grid reveals a pattern for increasingly ascetic behaviour.[123] Where grid is strong, the external manifestations of life such as marriage are positively valued. Where grid is weak two forms of asceticism appear: one arises out of a combination of weak group/weak grid while, in the other, although grid is weak, group is strong.

In Corinth ascetics and libertines are identified as one group opposing Paul.[124] Although Turner relates both asceticism and libertinism to the desire to liquidate the exclusive character of certain structural bonds such as marriage,[125] he admits that 'the organizational outcomes

121. Douglas, *Natural Symbols*, p. viii.

122. Dennis E. Owen, 'Spectral Evidence: The Witchcraft Cosmology of Salem Village in 1692', in Mary Douglas (ed.), *Essays in the Sociology of Perception* (London: Routledge & Kegan Paul, 1982), p. 280.

123. Douglas, *Natural Symbols*, p. 143.

124. Yarborough (*Not Like*, pp. 117-19) states the *communis opinio*: (1) that there were some in the Corinthian community who claimed that they had already experienced resurrection and (2) that the individual problems with which Paul deals in 1 Cor. were somehow related to this belief. Asceticism is fitted into this analysis as a special case: some Corinthians claimed that abstinence from sexual relationships was a sign of participation in the resurrection.

125. Turner (*Dramas*, p. 246) states that the institution of marriage, the basis of the family and of social structure in many cultures, comes under attack in many

of celibacy versus orgy must be very different as must the attitude of
the guardians of orthodox structure to movements of these rival
types'.[126]

At the level of organization, a group concerned for complete
freedom in sexual matters has a view of internal relationships which is
very different from that of a group espousing singleness/celibacy, and
it develops a different structure. Although both would be united ini-
tially in their opposition to the dominant structures and would represent a broad unified *communitas*, they would eventually organize into
separate factions.

Conclusion

In this chapter a first step analyzed the conflict in 1 Corinthians 7
according to Turner's description of a social drama. Questions based
on his analysis of how a situation of conflict is structured were addressed to the text, revealing evidence for the identity and the rhetoric
of the opposing factions.

In matters of sexual ethics at Corinth, as reflected in ch. 7, there are
two factions: one is demanding that Christians should remain single
and celibate, while the other is advocating marriage and sexual intercourse. The evidence from the text reveals the role that married
women played within the former group. It is probable that a married
woman provided the trigger that led to the breach within the community (vv. 10-11), and the breaks in the structure of Paul's argument
often relate to women (vv. 10-11, 12-16, 32-35). It is plausible to
suggest that the most volatile aspect of the controversy over marriage
concerns the right of married women to live a single/celibate existence. In vv. 25-40, where Paul argues that it is better if the marriage
does not take place, he addresses his arguments to the *male* believers
(vv. 27, 29b).

Previous research into 1 Corinthians has defined the factions within

religious movements. Some replace it with sexual promiscuity, while in others celibacy becomes the rule. Both attitudes towards sexuality are aimed at homogenizing
the group by 'liquidating' its structural divisions. Often an interdiction is laid on sexual relations during the liminal period in major rites of passage, and sexual licence
may follow periods of sexual abstinence in such ceremonies.

126. Turner, *Dramas*, p. 248 n. 3.

the community in terms of Greeks *versus* Jews or rich *versus* poor.[127] A detailed exegesis of ch. 7 reveals that, in the conflict over singleness and celibacy, marriage and sexual intercourse, there is a male-female polarity.[128] In addition, because the pattern of male-female relationships was in transition in the Graeco-Roman household structures, the women and men involved probably did not come from one particular cultural group.

To define the confrontation in ch. 7 in terms of a structural and an anti-structural presentation of a root metaphor forces the exegete throughout the explication of the text to keep the hypothesis of two groups at the forefront of the exegesis, and to look for evidence related to the arguments of both factions. Previous exegesis, even when it recognized that not all within the community agreed with the stance of anti-structure, has concentrated on Paul's response to that group and acknowledged only secondarily that he must respond to both factions in order to restore peace. This failure to include the pro-structure party as a factor in the conflict probably reflects a modern bias. Because marriage is the primary relationship within the Christian community today, and because the evidence from later texts[129] speaks against anti-structure and in favour of marriage, the exegete has difficulty acknowledging the influence of both factions.

When the model of social drama, with its emphasis on structure and anti-structure, and the exegetical data are held in tension, it is possible, by noting Paul's concessions and certain breaks in the pattern of his arguments, to identify the rhetoric of both factions. The arguments of the pro-marriage/sexual intercourse faction were heard in vv. 1-6 and 29-31, where the vocabulary referred to marital rights and obligations. This group also introduced a saying of Jesus (v. 10) into its arguments. The pro-singleness/celibacy faction appealed to Paul's own marital status (v. 7) and regarded marriage as a sin (vv. 28, 37) and polluting (vv. 14, 34). They also appealed to sayings of Jesus supporting celibacy (v. 38). The exegesis of ch. 7 revealed two sets of kinship terminology. These appear side by side in vv. 12-16,

127. See Richardson, 'Absence', pp. 59-74 and Theissen, *Social Setting* pp. 69-174.

128. This is not to suggest that the struggle aligned all women against all men. It is more likely that married women provided the catalyst for the anti-structure group, and that the group included both men and women.

129. For example, the Pastoral Epistles and *1 Clem.*; see discussion in Chapter 5.

and, once they are identified, the reason for the intensity of the confrontation becomes clear.

Although Christians at Corinth were being called upon to live out a brother and sister role in the church, many also related to each other as husband and wife. Each of these relationships represented a distinct kinship pattern, reflecting a different set of roles, obligations and structures for organizing the community. In other words, from an anthropological viewpoint, Christian husbands and wives in Corinth played two antithetical roles. The social drama arises when certain married women resolve the ambiguity of their situation by beginning to live as sisters to all men, including their husbands. By this step they initiated an egalitarian structure of relationships and organization within the church.

After the exegetical analysis was completed, the opposing factions were situated on a social map according to Mary Douglas's model of grid and group. From this emplotment it became clear that in the community at Corinth the members lacked a clear definition of how to relate to one another. In an attempt to reduce this ambiguity, each faction set out its system of roles and obligations as the proper way to order church relationships. This emplotment will form the basis for examining the function of Paul's arguments, which will be analyzed in the next chapter.

The use of the models of Douglas and Turner suggested that the ascetics in Corinth are to be separated from the libertines. Although similar in their origin, each group reflects a different understanding of social structure and organization within the community.

If the conflict in ch. 7 is defined in Douglas's terms, at the heart of the conflict lies an understanding of grid. A community, classified as a mid-strong group, has within it at least two factions which attempt in different ways to clarify the confused social experience of living as 'no male and female'.[130] One supports a selective crossing of the sexual orifice and a system of roles and responsibilities based on marriage and thus a movement to higher grid. The other faction, at odds with the dominant model, is demanding that an absolute non-crossing of the sexual orifice be made the identifying mark of the Corinthian community. This marks a move to lower grid.

130. In ch. 7 there is evidence of two factions, a pro-singleness/celibacy and a pro-marriage/sexual intercourse group. A third faction, identified in other sections of 1 Cor. and distinct from these two, is a libertine faction.

Both factions produce arguments to justify their positions, and Paul must de-escalate the crisis and bring the disputants to 'one mind' (1.10). According to Douglas's theory, the crisis developed 'in a specifiable social niche: important factions, externally distinct, internally competitive. Resolving it [crisis] demands an adjustment of the conditions in which power is sought and wielded.'[131] Paul's attempted resolution is the subject of the next chapter.

131. Douglas, *Natural Symbols*, p. xv.

Chapter 4

REDRESSIVE ACTION:
PAUL'S ATTEMPT TO RESTORE PEACE

> What do you wish? Shall I come to you with a rod, or with love in a spirit
> of gentleness? (1 Cor. 4.21).

The purpose of this chapter is to investigate how Paul acts to bring the
social drama to an end. We must not only understand what Paul is saying but also probe the function and effectiveness of his argumentation
with the two opposing factions. Mary Douglas's theory elaborated in
Cultural Bias will provide us with a tool to focus the analysis.
Expanding on her theory of grid and group, she seeks to identify and
understand the arguments that people use to bring others to their way
of thinking. But first it is necessary to ask about Paul's authority within the Corinthian community.

In Turner's model of social drama, the third stage is the phase of
redressive action: in order to limit the spread of the crisis,

> certain adjustive and redressive 'mechanisms'. . . informal or formal,
> institutionalized or ad hoc, are swiftly brought into operation by leading or
> structurally representative members of the disturbed social system.[1]

In ch. 7, Paul is acting as the structurally representative member of
the disturbed social system. In order to limit the crisis, he presents
arguments which seek to convince the Corinthians to act in a certain
manner. An important question in any social drama concerns the ade-
quacy of the redressive machinery in handling a crisis.[2] Is Paul's

---

1. Turner, *Dramas*, p. 39.
2. Turner (*Dramas*, pp. 40-41) states: 'I would give one piece of advice: study
carefully what happens in phase three, the would-be redressive phase of social
dramas, and ask whether the redressive machinery is capable of handling crises, so
as to restore, more or less, the status quo among the contending groups. Then ask, if
so, how precisely? And if not, why not?'

authority firmly enough established within the community that the Corinthians will listen to him?

Paul's Authority as a Redressive Agent

At the beginning of 1 Corinthians (1.10-17), Paul addresses the problem of rivalry within the community, and in v. 17 relates it specifically to two issues—baptism and wisdom:

> The connection between the parties and baptism (1.12-17) presents a social context of initiands in their relationship to a ritual elder. According to Turner, what is central to this kind of allegiance is the obedience of the initiands to their mentor and the value they place on the *gnosis* imparted by that person.[3] Since others baptized as well as Paul (vv. 13-17), allegiances within the community would be divided, and there would be no strong central authority.

The words Paul uses are σχίσματα (1.10) and ἔριδες (1.11), which imply a power struggle.[4] They are related to four names: Paul, Apollos, Cephas, Christ. Wellborn has investigated the relationship of the slogan, ἐγω μέν εἰμι, to the world of politics, where political parties are named after the individuals whose interests they serve and consist of clients and personal adherents of particular leaders.[5] In 3.4 and 4.6 Paul reduces the list to two, himself and Apollos; in 3.22 Cephas is included.

Some scholars suggest that in the phrase 'you are of Christ' (3.22) Paul is rebuking those who rally around the other three slogans.[6] In addition, they argue that he sees the party spirit expressed in

3.   Turner, 'Betwixt', p. 9.
4.   See Chapter 3 n. 6.
5.   Wellborn, 'On the Discord', pp. 90-93. For a history of interpretation surrounding these four names, see Hurd, *Origin*, pp. 96-107.
6.   For example, Ernst von Dobschütz, *Christian Life in the Primitive Church* (trans. G. Bremner; London: Williams & Norgate, 1904), p. 72 and Lake, *The Earlier Epistles*, p. 127 contra those who infer the presence of gnosticism in the Corinthian church from the existence of a Christ party. See Walter Schmithals, *Gnosticism in Corinth: An Investigation of the Letters to the Corinthians* (trans. J.E. Steely; Nashville: Abingdon Press, 1971). Wellborn ('On the Discord', p. 87) states that translations of 1.1, 3 fail to capture the political connotation that the verb μεμέρισται had for the first readers. Since μέρις is the customary term for 'party', Paul's inquiry may be stated, 'Has the body of Christ been split into parties?'

competing claims of authority[7] particularly those of himself and
Apollos.[8] Paul's authority is clearly not the only one recognized within the community,[9] and, therefore, according to Turner's social drama
model, he must first establish his right to act as a redressive agent if
he hopes to restore peace within the community.

In 1.10–4.21, in order to demonstrate his right to the Corinthians'
allegiance and his authority to act as a redressive agent, Paul presents

7.   In *Paul and Power: The Structure of Authority in the Primitive Church as
Reflected in the Pauline Epistles* (Philadelphia: Fortress Press, 1978), p. 135, Bengt
Holmberg defines authority in the following way: '"Authority" signifies a type of
social relation between at least two persons where one is the ruler. . . An authority
relationship is distinguished from a power relation by the fact that the subordinate is
caused to assent to the ruler's order, not by external constraint or out of sheer
calculative interest, but out of conviction. The conviction is part of a socially valid
and thus objective body of reason (ratio), which says, both to the ruler and to the
subordinate, that the ruler is entitled to give orders and that it is the moral duty of the
subordinate to obey and recognize the legitimacy of the ruler's position and orders.
The ruler's communications, within the sphere where he is ruler, are credited with
being capable of reasoned elaboration. This is upheld not by a permanent and explicit
rational demonstration of this capacity, but mostly by indirect means that inspire the
subordinate's trust in the ruler's legitimacy.'
8.   Several scholars have argued convincingly that Paul and Apollos were
antagonists. See Helmut Koester, 'Gnomai Diaphorai: The Origin and Nature of
Diversification in the History of Early Christianity', in James M. Robinson and
Helmut Koester (eds.), *Trajectories through Early Christianity* (Philadelphia: Fortress Press, 1971); Birger A. Pearson, *The Pneumatikos-Psychikos Terminology in
1 Corinthians: A Study in the Theology of the Corinthian Opponents of Paul and its
Relation to Gnosticism* (SBLDS 12; Missoula, MT: Scholars Press, 1973), p. 18.
Birger Pearson ('Hellenistic Jewish Wisdom Speculation and Paul', in Robert L.
Wilken [ed.], *Aspects of Wisdom in Judaism and Early Christianity* [Notre Dame:
University of Notre Dame, 1975, p. 59]) states that 'Paul's arguments provide hints
that Apollos was the one who was introducing the Corinthians to their "wisdom"
speculations, including the Hellenistic-Jewish traditions of "school of Apollos"
in Corinth'. Barrett (Charles Kingsley Barrett, 'Cephas and Corinth', in O. Betz,
H. Hengel and P. Schmidt [eds.], *Abraham unser Vater: Festschrift für O. Michel*
[Leiden: Brill, 1963], pp. 1-12) suggests that 'the evidence of 1 Corinthians shows
the certain influence and probable presence of Peter in Corinth'. He continues, 'he
(Peter) was an embarrassment to Paul, and his characteristically Jewish-Christian
opinions take some hard knocks; but Paul, who could not forget that Peter was the
primary witness of the resurrection, and did preach Christ, crucified and risen according to the Scriptures, did not attack him' (p. 11).
9.   Holmberg, *Paul and Power*, p. 187 speaks of other preachers and teachers
within Paul's church as a limitation on his authority.

an elaborate exposition of apostolic authority.[10] He begins, not by asserting his authority over someone else's, but with an explanation of the basis for his authority. He makes the cross the focus of the gospel in Corinth (1.23; 2.2). This moves the discussion away from baptism, with its emphasis on secret wisdom, and circumvents a direct confrontation with leadership allegiances based on ritual elder and initiands. δύναμις θεοῦ and the σοφία θεοῦ are one and the same (2.4) and are actually χριστὸς ἐσταυρωμένος (2.2).

In 2.1-5 Paul recalls what he did when he came to Corinth and how he did it. He presents his weakness as the corollary of his knowing only Christ crucified: both are the expression of δύναμις θεοῦ. God's power is demonstrated in the calling of the Corinthians and Paul's preaching.[11] This is the paradigm of apostolic authority and the model for the church. According to Schütz,

> if we ask about Paul's authority there emerges a picture. . . not unlike de Jouvenal's description of the *auctor*: the father and adviser whose primarily function is to augment the power at his disposal by seeing that it is diffused through those over whom he exercises authority, all the while guaranteeing the ultimate rightness and fitness of their actions so long as these are grounded in the power which he exhibits. It is a restricted view of authority which calls upon the *auctor* to assert not himself and his authority, but the primary source of power. When others perceive this power correctly and act accordingly, they share the same power with Paul and are themselves authoritative. When they misperceive, he exercises power over them.[12]

Paul describes his power among the Corinthians as χριστὸς ἐσταυρωμένος, who is δύναμις θεοῦ and the source of their κλῆσις Any other claim to power is secondary. After a study of Pauline parenesis in the context of conflict in 1 Corinthians, Wayne Meeks concludes that

> Paul uses the mediating symbol of Jesus crucified, not to achieve a theoretical synthesis of these opposing positions, but to signify a way in

10. παρακαλῶ occurs at 1.10 and again at 4.16. Both are connected to the problems of community strife and the Corinthians' 'declaration of independence' from Paul. Pearson ('Hellenistic-Jewish', p. 45) states 'The entire passage, 1.10-4.21, constitutes, therefore, an *apologia* in which Paul defends his apostolic authority. . .'

11. Schütz, *Apostolic Authority*, p. 202.

12. Schütz, *Apostolic Authority*, p. 204.

which persons who occupied the positions could understand their engagement with one another.[13]

In other words, Paul, through the symbol of the cross, tries to build
group consciousness and cohesiveness based on his leadership. A resolution of the issues which divide is secondary to this primary objective.

Paul also seeks to establish his authority over the community by his
use of metaphors of status. In 3.5-17 he employs a number of images
related to work, which lay out the roles of Apollos and himself, and
perhaps Peter,[14] in relation to God and to the community. These metaphors picture an economic system involving a boss who employs workers to tend a field and build a building. This boss will determine the
workers' wages according to their labour and the quality of their
work. Petersen understands this metaphor in the following way:

> Decoded, the system described above represents God as the boss, Apollos
> and Paul as his hired workers, the Corinthian community as the product
> of their labour, and the day of (eschatological) judgment as payday. With-
> in this system, Paul makes a number of distinctions, the most important of
> which sociologically are related to the equality of and differences between
> the principal workers.[15]

By these metaphors Paul points out to the Corinthians that their claim
to belong to Paul or Apollos is false. He also makes it clear, in metaphors of agricultural and building construction, that his job is tempo-
rally prior to and more fundamental than Apollos's (and Peter's). This
may be only implied in the agricultural metaphor. However, when
Paul refers to himself as a master builder who lays the foundation, he
clearly indicates that the foundation he lays is the only one that *can* be
laid. Anything built upon it must fit that foundation. Paul's lack of
confidence in what Apollos or others within the Corinthian community are doing to God's building is clear (3.12-15).[16]

Paul calls himself the 'father in Jesus Christ' (4.15) of the Corinthians. Although this relationship depends upon the fact that Paul has

13.   Meeks, *Moral World*, p. 136.
14.   Peter Richardson ('Absence', p. 65) has pointed out the possible reference
to the name Peter (rock, stone) in the building metaphor. Paul is developing a lengthy
pun on his own role as the 'foundation' despite the claim that Cephas is the rock on
which Jesus builds. (Mt. 16.18)
15.   Petersen, *Narrative*, p. 110.
16.   Petersen, *Narrative*, p. 111.

preached in Corinth, it represents an authority which extends beyond the preaching of the gospel. The extent of this authority is found in his use of παιδαγωγούς (4.15) to designate his competitors. This term refers to the household slave employed to teach manners and poise. Paul's obligation, by contrast, is to bring the Corinthians into life and to assume responsibility for them, as a father does for a child.[17] His patriarchal role is most clearly represented both in the 'rod' which he holds over the Corinthians (4.21) and in his appeal to them to imitate him. Paul can shame his children (4.14) or he can appeal, admonish and cajole (14.14, 16).

In a kinship system which speaks of all Christians as brothers and sisters and as children of God this patriarchal claim is paradoxical. Paul's alignment of himself with God, rather than with other Christians, is a strong authority move, one which implies definite obligations to Paul[18] and imitation and obedience to his ways.[19]

Bruce Malina's identification of three types of authority helps to clarify what Paul hopes to accomplish by his *apologia*:

> Legitimate authority is an ascribed right to obligate others, which is acknowledged by other members of a collectivity and sanctioned by some higher order norm. . . This form of authority ranges from personal or traditional authority to impersonal or rational authority. Personal legitimate authority inheres in the person, that is, flows from circumstances that befall a person and are not under the individual's control; such circumstances include birth, age, sex, physical size, and the status of one's family. These features are culturally interpreted as directly related to one's capacity to exercise authority. . . Impersonal legitimate authority is acquired by a person by means of some skill or competence deemed pertinent and useful to the realization of the ends of the institution in which authority is embedded. Such authority is occupational, being bound up with some job, task or office. . . [20]

In the light of this description, it is through Paul's metaphors of work and status, as well as through his 'preaching the cross', that he

---

17.   Petersen, *Narrative*, p. 130.

18.   Contra Holmberg (*Paul and Power*, p. 188), who concludes that Paul's choice of the 'father' image limits his authority. Holmberg underestimates the role of *paterfamilias* in the Graeco-Roman world and the obligations demanded in this kinship structure.

19.   Schütz (*Apostolic Authority*, pp. 228-31) affirms that whatever Paul means by 'imitate' he is demanding allegiance to himself, and this is an authority move.

20.   Malina, *Christian Origins*, p. 118.

exercises both personal and impersonal legitimate authority within the community.

Malina also helps us to understand how Paul presents his credentials to act as a redressive agent. Malina identifies four 'general symbolic media' (GSM) that people employ to have each other do what they want and value,[21] commitment, power, influence and inducement. Commitment is the capacity to command loyalty by means of internalized sanctions, such as guilt feelings, feelings of shame and disloyalty or fear of disapproval. Power is the capacity to produce conformity, the right to require others to perform some obligation because it is deemed necessary for the group. Influence presents another person with reasons for acting in a given way, and why acting or not acting makes sense or is to that person's own benefit. Inducement means the ability to lay claim on the goods and services of others because of one's special usefulness, resulting from one's social standing.[22] Paul's arguments in chs. 1–4 include appeals to three of these media.

Paul argues that he has a right to the Corinthians' loyalty because he is their father. He uses the sanctions of guilt and shame in 4.8-14.[23] His right to oblige them to do as he says is made clear in a number of ways: the right of physical force (4.21), Paul's closeness to God who is the source of power (2.7)[24] and his preaching the cross of Christ, which is the power of God (1.18). Paul accounts for his seeming lack of power by a series of inversions: weakness is strength, foolishness is

21.   '(F)rom the perspective of communication, a person (Source) embodying a given symbolic medium (Channel) applies the medium (Message) with a view to altering attitudes and/or behaviour (Effect) of another person or group (Receiver) in a given situation (Situation) in a direction which the source believes to be desirable'. See Malina, *Christian Origins*, pp. 76-77.

22.   Malina, *Christian Origins*, pp. 78-83.

23.   Malina (*Christian Origins*, p. 79) states that 'when people explain their activity "because my mother, father, sister, brother, friend, neighbour in great need" asked them to act, the trigger for their behaviour is the GSM (general symbolic media) of commitment'. The ironic statements in 4.8-14 express the sanctions that come from not responding to the activation of commitment. Malina (p. 79) explains that 'exclamations such as "Is that any way for a son to treat his mother, for a Christian to behave toward one in need, for a mother to help her children?"' are evidence of how such sanctions are used.

24.   In Hellenistic conceptions, God or the high god was the ultimate wielder of power; thus the closer one was to God in the hierarchy of power ranking, the more power one had. See Malina, *Christian Origins*, p. 83.

wisdom, and the cross of Christ is the power of God.

In chs. 1–4 Paul seeks to establish his right to act as a redressive agent in the social drama. He claims higher status than any other leader and thus a right to command the Corinthians' allegiance and obedience. However, the fact that Paul has to argue for this right in such detail indicates that, in reality, his authority is a weakened one.[25] The extent to which he has to justify his right to their obedience and loyalty suggests that his influence is inflated.[26]

According to Mary Douglas, a society in which authority is weak and factionalism prominent needs an adjustment in the conditions under which power is sought and wielded.[27] Baptism and the subsequent allegiance to those who did the baptizing was an important aspect of this power. Paul's attempt to redirect the dispute from baptism and secret wisdom to a focus on the cross sought to minimize the use of this power. His emphasis on himself as the ultimate authority would, if accepted, promote a stronger group, a move towards B from a midway point on the OB line,[28] and would result in Paul's redressive measures being approved within the community.

Structure and Anti-structure in Paul

Having completed those appeals by which he argues his right to mediate the crisis, Paul proceeds to address the disturbed social situation. Before analyzing his proposed solution in ch. 7, it is important to

---

25. In 4.21 Paul says he could come with the rod (power) or with persuasion (influence). Whether he has the luxury of choice is an important question.
26. A person whose word is taken immediately and directly has deflated influence. Conversely, one who has to explain in detail or needs to supply repeated verification for what (s)he states has inflated influence. See Malina, *Christian Origins*, p.18.
27. Douglas, *Natural Symbols*, p. xv.
28. Douglas, *Natural Symbols*, p. 60.

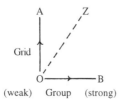

understand something of Paul's approach to structure and anti-structure.

In the last chapter a structural and an anti-structural presentation of the root metaphor, 'in Christ all are children of God, no male and female', was identified as the cause of the conflict in ch. 7. Then these two positions were plotted on Mary Douglas's grid/group map. Paul represents one more dynamic in the social drama in ch. 7; therefore an understanding of how he relates to structure and anti-structure at other points in 1 Corinthians will help the exegete understand the presuppositions that Paul brings to the dispute.

Other issues of a sexual nature provide insight into Paul's views on structure and anti-structure. In the case of the incestuous marriage (5.1-8), he demands that the offender be ejected from the assembly. His justification is given in 5.6-8, where he speaks of leaven as a polluting agent which threatens the social body. The man *must* be excommunicated because the incestuous marriage is a pollution of such magnitude that even outsiders would not tolerate such immorality. In these verses Paul limits sexual freedom, and bases his argument on a concern for the outsider as well as on an abhorrence of immorality.[29] According to William Countryman, this issue involves a violation of family hierarchy and the rights owed to the pater.[30] This being the case, Paul's resolution reaffirms the duties and obligations within the dominant kinship system; it is an affirmation of structure.[31]

In 6.12-20, also related to sexual orifices, Paul demands that the organism's boundary should be vigorously guarded and not illicitly crossed. His position affirms that the use of prostitutes is out of keeping with the Corinthians' understanding of themselves as members of

29. 'Yet one of the most obvious facts about the movement associated with Paul and his fellows was the vigor of its missionary drive, which saw in the outsider a potential insider and did not want to cut off communication with him or her. . . There is a tension in the literature of the Pauline groups between measures needed to promote a strong internal cohesion, including rather clear boundaries separating it from the larger society, and the intention to continue normal and generally acceptable interactions with outsiders'. See Meeks, *First Urban*, p. 107. Contra Atkins (*Integrating Function*, p. 67 n. 33), who separates missionary drive and acceptable interactions, and thus views the social context as sufficient to explain tensions without reference to missionary activity.

30. Countryman, *Dirt*, p. 198.

31. Richardson ('Judgment', pp. 44-46) suggests that the lawsuit referred to in vv. 1-11 also concerns the matter of proper kinship relationships.

the body of Christ and as belonging to God.[32] This kind of sexual freedom, as an anti-structural behaviour, is disallowed within the body of Christ, and the sexual orifice is regulated (bounded, structured).

In the controversy over idol meat (8.1–11.1) Paul regulates the mouth in two ways: if eating meat causes a brother or sister to stumble, it should not be eaten, nor should it be eaten if an unbeliever reveals that it has been sacrificed to an idol. Apart from these considerations, Paul is not opposed to those who eat idol meat and resists setting strict boundaries. According to John Hurd:

> . . . we reach the somewhat strange conclusion that Paul appears to have permitted the Corinthians to continue their current practices concerning idol meat virtually unchanged, that he had himself eaten such meat when he was in Corinth, and thus that he accepted to some extent the principles concerning Christian freedom which they expressed in their letter. Yet instead of immediately stating his large measure of agreement with the Corinthians, adding only a word or two of warning as to possible dangers in the matter, Paul devoted the major part of his reply to vigorous disagreement with them, and only at the close did he give them permission to behave as in fact they had been behaving.[33]

In a conflict situation, this lack of strong support for one's own position preserves group cohesiveness; however, it does so at the expense of the issue and, in this case it leaves the individual Christian somewhat confused about expectations concerning the eating of idol meat.

Paul's approach to formal structures is ambiguous. In 12.12-28 he begins by asserting an anti-structural view, based on baptism, and he rejects certain social and ethnic distinctions as a way to order the community (12.13).[34] Yet, he also speaks of structures within the church. He declares that 'God has arranged the organs in the body, each one as he chose' (12.18), and he clearly articulates roles within the body (12.28).

Paul's preference is not for a completely unstructured church. In

---

32. B. Malina (*The New Testament World: Insights from Cultural Anthropology* [Atlanta: John Knox, 1981], pp. 150-51, states that Christians began to establish new purity rules for the sacred 'based upon their group as analogous to a temple or holy space/people with immediate access to God in Christ'.

33. Hurd, *Origin*, p. 148.

34. In 12.13 the male/female pair does not appear. It is more probable that Paul eliminated it here, because of the controversies in 1 Cor., rather than that he added it in Gal. See Scroggs, 'Eschatological', p. 292.

his metaphor of the body in ch. 12, he distinguishes between the
superordinate and subordinate parts. Although the lowliest member of
the church has one or more gifts, like the apostle, this does not affect
the precedence of the apostle in a hierarchical ranking, and all the
parts are subordinated to the unity of the whole. After a discussion of
structure and anti-structure within the church as a whole, Petersen
concludes:

> Facing outward, anti-structure has an ideological purity deriving from a
> simple inversion of wordly distinctions, and its power derives from this
> radical contrast between opposites. . . [F]acing inward anti-structure
> loses this ideological simplicity and must therefore find its power else-
> where than in the mere polarization of opposites. It is, on the one hand,
> confronted with structures that it does not reject, and it is, on the other
> hand, confronted with concrete issues that defy simplistic antithetical solu-
> tions.[35]

Paul's Emplotment on the Grid/Group Map

According to Douglas's classification, Paul, who is committed to the
unity of the group even at the expense of the issue (8.1-11), would be
situated at strong group.[36] His ambiguity concerning structure and
anti-structure would place him in a medium position on the grid scale.
In other words, Paul subordinates individual concerns to a concern
for the group. Although he rejects some of the distinctions of the culture (Jew/Greek, slave/free), he emphasizes that order and structuring
are to be maintained. The fact that the male/female pair does not
appear in ch. 12 raises a question about whether Paul rejects this particular distinction. The omission, in light of 8.1–11.1 where a decisive
resolution of the issue became secondary to the unity of the group,
raises questions about how Paul will respond when conflict over the
male/female structural pattern threatens the unity of the community.

Development in Douglas's Grid/Group Theory in Cultural Bias

Mary Douglas's two dimensional social map, which we have used to
plot the actors in ch. 7, is but one of three distinct expressions of

35. Petersen, *Narrative*, p. 159.
36. See Douglas, *Cultural Bias,* pp. 19-21 for a description of each of the quadrants on her grid/group map.

grid/group theory. The two editions of *Natural Symbols* (1970, 1973) contain quite different versions, and *Cultural Bias* presents a third variant. In the third version,[37] as in the first, she maps the social universe by means of two intersecting social dimensions.

In this version, Douglas seeks to capture the individual's experience of social control. She is no longer concerned with the entirety of people's beliefs but wants to explain the ultimate justifications that people use to bring one another to account: '(Grid/group analysis) selects out of the total cultural field those beliefs and values which are derivable as justifications for action'.[38] Cosmologies are 'the sticks people use to coerce one another, and Douglas argues that different sticks will work in different social contexts'.[39] In other words, the explanations and justifications that work in each context generate an implicit cosmological bias; each social context develops arguments that 'naturally' sustain it. The drive to achieve consonance is no longer, as in the first version, directly between social experience and cosmology but it is now mediated by the arguments people use to sustain their social relations.[40]

> The argument throughout takes a particular kind of social environment as
> a starting point, and demonstrates how, given the premises involved in
> defining that social environment, certain distinctive values and belief sys-
> tems will follow as necessary for the legitimation of actions taken within
> it.[41]

37.   The second version, the 1973 edition of *Natural Symbols*, makes a false step which Douglas corrects in her later writings. James Spickard ('Mary Douglas's Three Versions of Grid/Group Theory: A Tool for New Testament Scholarship', unpublished paper presented at the Annual SBL Meeting, Boston, MA, 4–6 December 1987, pp. 12-13) describes this false step: 'This is her shift from graphing social experience along two *social* dimensions to charting it by the contrast of a *social* dimension with a *cosmological* one. . . If grid/group is intended to be "a diagram of possible social environments, across which an individual may move", then both of its dimensions must be social'.

38.   Douglas, *Cultural Bias*, p. 6.

39.   Spickard, 'Three Versions', p. 16. Douglas defines cosmologies as 'the ultimate justifying ideas which tend to be invoked as part of the natural order and yet which. . . are evidently not at all natural but strictly the product of social interaction'. See Douglas, *Essays*, p. 5.

40.   Spickard, 'Three Versions', p. 17.

41.   Douglas, *Cultural Bias*, p. 53.

Douglas sets forth the various grid/group quadrants and then proceeds

> to elucidate elements of cosmology which are not circularly implied in the
> definition of social context and to show that a distinctive cosmological
> bias is generated by the character of explanations and justifications that are
> plausible in each social context.[42]

She plots four variations on her grid/group map:

	−	Group	+
+ **Grid**	Insulated B		Strong Group C
−	Individualist A		Strong Group D

> As in the first version, societies with strong group loyalties appear on the
> right side of the diagram, while those with weak group loyalties appear on
> the left. Societies with elaborate role structures appear at the top, while
> those with little internal heterogeneity appear at the bottom. Hierarchists
> are in C, sectarians in D, competitive individualists in A. B is less
> coherent, being a repository for social fallout from C and A.[43]

At Corinth, as represented in ch. 7, there are two factions, both mid-strong in group but differing in grid. The rhetoric of one, situated in quadrant C, is pressuring all in the church to agree with its understanding of church relationships and structure. The other, in D, is equally forceful in demanding that its views be affirmed by the whole community.

In *Cultural Bias*, Douglas presents the kinds of arguments that would move each of these social biases to action. For example, the anti-structure group (D) would be moved by arguments which warn of sexual pollution or infiltration from the outside. Action to solve disputes takes 'the form of unmasking wolves in sheep's clothing and expelling spies from the ranks of the faithful'.[44] Quadrant C is concerned to justify its hierarchical structures. In order to do this it seeks

---

42. Douglas, *Cultural Bias*, p. 22.
43. Douglas, *Cultural Bias*, p. 7.
44. Douglas, *Cultural Bias,* p. 23.

'to make an explicit match between civilization and the purposes of God and nature'.[45] Going against nature means threat of failure.

Paul's Redressive Activity in Chapter 7

In 1 Corinthians 7 Paul is faced with a conflict which has reached crisis proportions. The anti-structural group has taken up its menacing stance in the open. When the woman divorced her husband (vv. 10-11) one crucial norm of social action was breached; if the man does not marry his virgin, another will be left unfulfilled (vv. 36-40). The extreme positions have hardened, and all in the church are being pressured to take sides in terms of deeply entrenched moral impera-tives and constraints.[46] Paul must de-escalate the crisis. Redressive action can consist in personal advice and informal mediation or for-mal judicial and legal machinery.[47] In 4.21 Paul affirms his right to use the rod (power), but asks if the Corinthians would not prefer a less harsh approach.[48]

General Comments

As the redressive agent, Paul is faced with two factions as well as those who are in the middle.[49] The justifications used by both groups to convince the uncommitted were made known to him in the Corin-thians' letter and through oral reports. In his appeal he needs to take these justifications into account, and then, in light of a weakened authority within the community, he must proceed to formulate argu-ments which would convince the conflicting social units to lessen the

45. Douglas, *Cultural Bias*, p.23. This reference and that in the previous foot-note are only two examples of the kind of analysis she makes. A complete discussion is found in *Cultural Bias*, pp. 22-36.

46. Turner, *Dramas*, p. 35.

47. Turner, *Dramas*, p. 39.

48. A less harsh approach is the general symbolic medium of influence, which aims to provide justifications why one ought to act in a given way. According to Malina (*Christian Origins*, p. 87), influence is basically consensual. It employs posi-tive sanctions and affects a person's opinions, attitudes and judgment. Malina views it as bearing qualities which befit the weak group.

49. Paul in 16.15 appeals to the Corinthians to submit to Stephanas. He would not risk the unity of the body by requesting allegiance to someone linked to either extreme position. The household of Stephanas was baptized by Paul (1.16), and, in all likelihood, remained committed to Paul; it therefore provides evidence that not all had decided for one of the two extreme positions reflected in ch. 7.

absoluteness of their positions. In addition, because of the priority he gives to a strong community at other points in 1 Corinthians (8.1–11.1; 12), his first priority is to prevent a schism.

According to Douglas's two-dimensional map, Paul's arguments must move on two fronts if they are to accomplish this. First, he must persuade both factions that their relationship to the community is of primary concern. In addition, he must bring the two quadrants closer together on the grid scale by persuading both to lessen the absoluteness of their demands about marriage/sexual intercourse and singleness/celibacy. According to Douglas, an over-emphasis on grid leads to a devaluing of group.[50]

Instead of emphasizing the theology of the factions, Paul organizes his arguments around marital status. This includes everyone at Corinth, not just the extreme positions, and every marital group would probably include those belonging to each extreme, as well as those in the middle. Therefore, before making his appeal, Paul cites arguments from each extreme position.

In vv. 1-7 and 8-9 he begins by siding with the anti-structure group. Then comes a directive which would appeal to the structure group. In vv. 10-11 he begins with the position of the latter. In vv. 12-16 Paul gives his judgment first and only secondarily refers to the arguments of the contending parties. Paul avoids a confrontation with the two extremes; nowhere does he address them directly.

The verbs he uses are in keeping with his goal. They are mainly verbs of persuasion and appeal (θέλω, δοκέω, λέγω, νομίζω, παραγγέλλω)[51] not command. This kind of argumentation serves to diffuse conflict rather than to intensify it. Paul considers his own instructions to possess authority, and he uses not only third person imperatives but also several verbs in the first person: λέγω (vv. 6, 8, 12, 35), θέλω (vv. 7, 32), παραγγέλλω (v. 10), διατάσσομαι (v. 17), γνώμην δίδωμι (v. 25), νομίζω (v. 26), φημί (v. 29), δοκῶ (v. 40). However, in the two places where he pointedly asserts his authority (vv. 25, 40),[52] the verbs that follow (νομίζω, δοκῶ) are those of weakened authority.

---

50. Douglas, *Cultural Bias*, p. 13.

51. παραγγέλλω (v. 10) is the exception that proves the rule. Although it is a strong verb, in the end it is the Lord that commands, not Paul.

52. Gooch, 'Authority and Justification in Theological Ethics', p. 66.

Verses 1-7

In vv. 1-7 the anti-structure statement (v. 1b) is followed by the arguments and rhetoric of the structure group (vv. 2-5a). In structuring the argument, Paul carefully affirms that men and women owe the same debts to each other and are obligated in the same way within marriage.[53] Although this solves little if the husband and wife disagree over sexual activity within marriage, Paul's intention is clear. It is a variation of the argument in ch. 8 concerning 'the weak', and it serves the same function: to strengthen group consciousness. In emphasizing mutuality Paul discourages a move to either lower grid (a valuing of autonomy which is measured in terms of the freedom of the individual to make his or her own choices[54]) or to higher grid (a valuing of a system of hierarchical roles over a concern for the other).

Paul does not give either side his full support. In v. 5 he tells married people not to defraud one another, yet immediately he proceeds to qualify the prohibition. In this same structure which emphasizes maintaining sexual relationships, certain exceptions are made, and the force of the prohibition is undermined. Temporary abstinence is permissible,[55] but to reject sexual intercourse absolutely in marriage constitutes fraud. Each side is demanding that its expression of the root metaphor becomes *the* way of clarifying the ambiguous social experience within the group. Paul's statements function to undercut the absoluteness of either position.

---

53. Scroggs, ('Eschatological', p. 294) states that an 'analysis of the structure shows that Paul in almost every instance addresses himself explicitly to *both* men and women in order to show that each sex has the same freedom and the same responsibility. The double address is, in fact, the determining moment in the structure and Paul carries out this pattern to the point of tautologousness and awkwardness.'

54. Douglas, *Cultural Bias*, p. 16.

55. Temporary abstinence is attested to in Roman, Greek and Jewish writings. In Roman and Greek society temporary abstinence would likely occur around the menstrual cycle. Lefkowitz (*Women's Life*, pp. 219-20) cites evidence to show that it was believed that conception was more likely to occur at the end of menstruation, 'for the time before menstruation is not suitable, the uterus already being overburdened and in an unresponsive state because of the ingress of material and incapable of carrying on two motions contrary to each other, one for the excretion of material, the other for receiving'. Soranus, *Gynecology* 1.34.1, 1.36.1-2, also quoted in Shelton, *As the Romans Did*, p. 24. Old Testament law prohibits intercourse with a menstruating woman (Lev. 18.19). A parallel for Paul's recommendation in v. 5 may occur in the *T. Naph.* 8.8.

In a chiastic arrangement, his compromise is bounded by a concern for immorality and lack of self-control, which would appeal to both groups.

a. διὰ δὲ τὰς πορνείας
  b. ἕκαστος τὴν ἑαυτοῦ γυναῖκα ἐχέτω, καὶ ἑκάστη. . . ἐχέτω
    c. τῇ γυναικὶ ὁ ἀνὴρ τὴν ὀφειλὴν ἀποδιδότω, ὁμοίως δὲ. . .
    c΄. ἡ γυνὴ τοῦ ἰδίου σώματος οὐκ ἐξουσιάζει ἀλλὰ ὁ ἀνήρ ὁμοίως δὲ
       καὶ. . .
  b΄. μὴ ἀποστερεῖτε ἀλλήλους, εἰ μήτι ἂν. . . ὑμᾶς ὁ Σατανᾶς
a΄. διὰ τὴν ἀκρασίαν ὑμῶν

Both quadrant C (pro-marriage/sexual intercourse) and quadrant D (pro-singleness/celibacy) are concerned with pollution; the latter group in particular, would have abominated unregulated sex.[56]

According to Douglas, those in a low-grid quadrant view the cosmos as irrational 'since in it evil is taken to be a foreign danger, introduced by perverted or defective humans'.[57] In v. 5 Paul directly links Satan's activity to a denial of normal sexual relations within marriage. Those Corinthians who favoured a move to lower grid, and many who were in the middle,[58] would be influenced by the argument that absolute celibacy would lead to evil infiltrating the group. David Ostrander states that in quadrant D,

> . . . we find people's views of society and of nature linked in disequilibrium. They are both fragmented into mutually antagonistic groups and both suffer constant danger from predators, human, natural and supernatural. Existence depends upon membership in a group, and therefore the goal of symbolic action is the protection of the group from outside threats.[59]

A concern for immorality is found at other points in the chapter. Absolute singleness/celibacy is presented as improper if there is danger of immorality or loss of control (vv. 8-9); the action recommended to the man in the situation described depends on whether or not there is danger of immorality (vv. 36-38). An argument which

56. Douglas, *Natural Symbols*, p. ix.
57. Douglas, *Natural Symbols*, pp. 103-104.
58. The community's experience of 'no male and female' is confused, producing an ambiguous situation in terms of social structure and organization which are grid concerns.
59. David Ostrander, 'One-and Two-Dimensional Models of the Distribution of Beliefs', in Douglas, *Essays*, p. 29.

warned of immorality or loss of control would serve to moderate the demands of both factions. In particular it would move those in the anti-structure faction to reconsider their stance.

The relation of vv. 6-7 to the argument in vv. 3-5 has been debated.[60] A pro-structure interpretation rests on three unlikely assumptions: that v. 6 refers to v. 2, not to vv. 3-5; that v. 2 is simply an exhortation to marriage; and that ἅπτεσθαι in v. 1 refers to marriage. John Hurd thinks that the ambiguity of v. 6 (τοῦτο δὲ λέγω) is the result of the unity of purpose in vv. 2-5: 'it matters little whether Paul's "concession" be referred to v. 5, to vv. 3-5 or to vv. 2-5. In any case Paul's meaning is the same: marital intercourse is his concession but not his command.'[61]

In his discussion of pilgrimages, Turner speaks of this same tension:

> Enough room is left to the individual to distance himself briefly from inherited social constraint and duty, but only enough room so as to constitute as it were, a public platform in which he must make by word or deed a public acknowledgement of allegiance to the overarching religious, political and economic orders. Yet even here appears the thin edge of the contractual wedge that will eventually lead to a major loosening up of the structure of society. Pilgrimages represent, so to speak, an amplified symbol in the dilemma of choice versus obligation in the midst of a social order where status prevails.[62]

In vv. 1-7, Paul's argument affirms both marriage and sexual

---

60. The words συγγνώμην, ἐπιταγήν (v. 6) are at the heart of this debate. The adversative particle δέ (v. 7) is replaced by γάρ in many manuscripts, and most English translations simply disregard it. Robertson and Plummer *(First Corinthians,* p. 136) state that δέ marks a slight opposition to the concession just mentioned and translate it 'rather'. While Orr ('Paul's Treatment', p. 12) concedes that δέ is primarily adversative, he points to its use in a string of sentences in chs. 6–7 to indicate a shift in subject. He translates δέ 'now'.

61. Hurd, *Origin,* p. 163. ἐπιταγήν is also found in v. 25. Gooch, ('Ethical Authorities', p. 94) maintains that the basic distinction between these two words (συγγνώμην and ἐπιταγήν) is between permission and obligation: sexual intercourse is permissible but not obligatory. David Daube ('Concessions to Sinfulness in Jewish Law', *JJS* 10 [1959], pp. 1-13 [1]) speaks of such concessions in terms of the disparity between what is ideal and what is found in practice but is in conflict with the ideal. He cites Roman authors who considered slavery unnatural, yet still retained it as a part of their positive system because it was found among all people. He also notes a number of rulings given by the Rabbis 'for the sake of the functioning of the social order' (p. 10).

62. Turner, *Dramas,* p. 177.

intercourse, singleness and celibacy to be proper to living as 'no male and female'. Neither lifestyle *absolutely* excludes the other. His compromise seeks to diminish the polarization which would be created if the whole community were forced to decide for one faction over the other. For Paul the issue, that is, an absolute non-crossing versus a selective crossing of the sexual orifice, is secondary to the unity of the group. The individual Christian has choice in the midst of a social order in which status prevails, but is left in doubt as to what the group's expectations are.

Verses 8-9
Widows and widowers are to remain single and celibate except in cases where self-control is impossible. These verses express the same position as vv. 1-7: neither side in the dispute is absolutely right; marriage and sexual intercourse are a concession aimed at preventing immorality and loss of self-control. From the perspective of Douglas's theory, Paul's seemingly negative view on marriage in v. 9 functions to convince the anti-structure group to lessen its absolute stance. According to Douglas, it would be a powerful argument for those in quadrant D.

Paul's appeal is presented in terms of the good and the better. In a social drama where positions harden and choice becomes a matter of either-or, a redefinition of the choice as being between two goods mitigates its intensity and serves to diffuse tensions. However, it does not clarify whether or not husbands and wives within the Christian community are to relate to each other as brothers and sisters.

Verses 10-11
In the next two sections, Paul's discussion follows a somewhat different form. The breach resulting in the social drama occurs because a woman has divorced or is about to divorce her husband. Paul will allow the divorce to stand; he only stipulates that the woman remain 'demarried' or else be reconciled with her husband. In this particular case the woman was not restricted in any way since a desire for the single/celibate state, not remarriage, was the reason why she sought to divorce her husband.[63]

63. Dungan's (*The Sayings*, pp. 91-92) investigation of the phrase, μενέτω ἄγαμος ἢ τῷ ἀνδρὶ καταλλαγήτω, has led him to the conclusion that the wife was wanting exactly what Paul denied her, another marriage. However, he views Paul's

Since those in the pro-structure group are the ones who need to be convinced of the appropriateness of this decision, Paul begins by citing their argument: Jesus did say that a woman should not divorce her husband. The limitation he places on the divorce is not primarily directed at the divorced woman; rather it aims to reassure the pro-structure group about his understanding of the wider ramifications of this changing pattern of male and female relationships.

Paul's position is a cautious anti-structure. In the situation that he is addressing, affirming a brother and sister kinship pattern, is an appropriate way of structuring relationships within the church. Divorce for this purpose is allowable but it must not be allowed to lead to a total lack of structure, because, where all social norms are swept away, a low sense of group results.[64] Paul's goal is to maintain a strong group, and, in a choice between the kinship pattern of marriage and a more general rejection of social norms, marriage is preferable.

Verses 12-16
Up to this point, Paul has dealt with various types of marital situations in which a believer is married to a believer. In vv. 12-16 he addresses Christians who are married to unbelievers. His mode of argumentation changes. He does not begin with a general statement which marks the argument of one or other faction. Instead, his advice, which throughout vv. 12-16 addresses two particular situations, has one common denominator: Paul takes the decision to divorce out of the hands of the believer and places it with the unbeliever.

According to the first εἰ clause, the believer is to remain in the marriage if the unbeliever agrees. While it has been shown that the holiness arguments used to justify this position reflect the rhetoric of the factions,[65] how they functioned in Paul's argument needs comment.

According to Douglas's description, these arguments would have special appeal for those in the anti-structure party. This faction places special emphasis on purging out evil that intrudes from the outside. To this group an unbeliever is an outside evil, yet Paul argues that marriage makes the unbeliever and the children pure and, therefore,

---

words in this section as addressed to the woman, and not as an appeal to the pro-marriage group.

64. Douglas, *Natural Symbols*, p. xvi.
65. See Chapter 3, pp. 123-24.

insiders. Through this argument he hopes to lead the anti-structure faction and all in the middle to reconsider their position that divorce is absolutely necessary in such a situation.

According to the second εἰ clause, Paul allows divorce if the unbeliever wants to separate. The theological rationale is that God has called community members to peace. In 14.33 εἰρήνη is placed in opposition to ἀκαταστασία, a word meaning disturbance, unruliness or even insurrection,[66] which is closely tied to the language of political intrigue and factionalism.[67] In Douglas's analysis, a high grid community values order and design; therefore in these verses, the connection which Paul makes between peace and divorce is an attempt to persuade the pro-structure faction to lessen the absoluteness of its opposition to divorce.[68]

In presenting arguments which should lessen the absoluteness of each position, Paul leaves the issue in the hands of the outsider. In a mixed marriage, the unbeliever is to decide between the alternatives of a husband and wife, or a brother and sister relationship. The believer is bound by this decision.

For Paul to place such a decision in the hands of the unbeliever is unusual,[69] and this strengthens the conclusion that he is less concerned about the outcome of the controversy than about the unity of the community. If the believers have no power over whether or not divorce occurs, there should be no reason for further conflict within the community.

Although Paul's question in v. 16 expects neither a positive nor a negative reply,[70] the fact that he uses the terminology of the dominant kinship pattern (γυνή-ἀνήρ) is revealing and indicates some form of allegiance to the structure of roles which is at the heart of the married relationship. This becomes especially important in light of the fact that the married woman in v. 13 is not called ἀδελφή. Paul seems willing to compromise her position in the interests of his primary goal, group cohesion and unity.

66.   Liddell and Scott, *Greek-English Lexicon*, p. 48.
67.   Wellborn, 'On the Discord', pp. 86-87.
68.   Douglas, *Cultural Bias*, pp. 26-27.
69.   The other instance of this phenomenon occurs in 1 Cor. 10.28.
70.   See Chapter 3 n. 91.

Verses 36-40

In these verses the right to decide the issue is again taken away from either faction. It is left to the man himself. He is to decide whether or not he has the gift of celibacy. In the grid/group model, individual choice marks a downward shift toward an individualist environment, or low grid. However, as will he seen from Paul's arguments in vv. 17-24, 25-35, this understanding of singleness/celibacy as a 'gift' is closely aligned with 'remaining as one is' (vv. 20, 24). If the man accepts Paul's arguments, both he and all who read Paul's advice will be pushed in a very specific direction.

In these verses Paul uses a 'good-better' argument, as in vv. 8-9. This strategy attempts to build consensus because, where no-one sins, neither option can be called deviant and no-one needs to be expelled from the group.

The status that Paul advocates in vv. 36-40 is not without structure.[71] The betrothed (vv. 39-40) remains bound (δέω) as if married. Only at the death of her 'husband' is she free to marry.[72] Paul's solution to a betrothal where the man has self-control is a bonding (permanent betrothal or 'marriage') which affirms structure and eliminates any move to disregard all social norms. However, the result is that the betrothed couple do not completely belong to either pattern of relationships. Although they are not in a sexual marriage, they are bound as if they were. Yet they are not to live according to the usual roles and obligations of the married state.

Paul seeks to end the social drama by strengthening group loyalties around his leadership, while maintaining a somewhat confused situation in the area of grid: his arguments advocate both marriage and singleness within the community. Through good/better arguments, appeals to mutuality, and the removal of the right to decide from either faction, he de-emphasizes the issue and attempts to build group unity.

---

71. See Chapter 3 n. 106 for the argument relating vv. 39-40 to 25-38.

72. Paul's use of γυνή and ἀνήρ in vv. 39-40 does not mean that these verses are out of place. Rather, a question must be asked about the function of Paul's use of marital language. Since his appeal in vv. 29-35 aims to convince the pro-structure party to allow the betrothal to remain as it is, Paul's use of wife and husband for that relationship functions to assuage the fears of this group for any lessening of the rules and obligations of a kinship pattern based on marriage. The betrothal is to continue and is to be binding in the same way as marriage.

For his redressive measures to be successful, Paul must persuade the pro-structure group to move to a point higher on the group scale and lower on the grid scale, thus strengthening their commitment to the community and lessening the value they place on ascribed status and definition in terms of social roles. The anti-structure group must be moved to stronger group, as well as to higher grid, so that their commitment to the group is strengthened. An absolute noncrossing of the sexual orifice is not to be a symbol of group identity. The fullest expression of Paul's pragmatic approach is found in vv. 17-24[73] and 29-35.[74]

Paul's Detailed Defense

Verses 17-24
Previous interpretation of these verses has been concerned primarily with what Paul says about slavery in v. 21: is Paul a social conservative or a social realist? Did his determination to maintain the status quo lead him to urge slaves to remain in slavery, even if this meant rejecting the opportunity to go free, or did he want Christian slaves to accept freedom, if it became available to them?[75]

μᾶλλον χρῆσαι (v. 21) needs to be completed and the question is whether τῇ δουλείᾳ or τῇ ἐλευθερίᾳ should be supplied. These are the two alternatives suggested by translators and found in the history of interpretation. A third possibility is that Paul's abrupt style left even the Corinthians unsure about its meaning. If Paul had completed 7.21d, the grammatical relationships and peculiarities in the rest of the verse would have called for only brief comment. As it is, the meanings of a number of words and phrases have been vigorously debated.[76]

---

73.   Murphy-O'Connor (*1 Corinthians*, p. 58) believes that vv. 17-24 shed light on the changes in the social status demanded in vv. 1-16. He sees these verses as part of an A-B-A pattern: A = vv. 1-16, B = vv. 17-24, A = vv. 25-40.

74.   Hurd (*Origin*, p. 178) views vv. 29-35 as another explanatory digression (like vv. 17-24), whose purpose is to defend Paul's preference for celibacy.

75.   Bartchy, *Slavery*, pp. 1-24, sets out the history of interpretation of this passage.

76.   These include: (1) χρῆσαι : is this verb to be translated 'make use of' (its usual meaning) or is the aorist imperative form sufficient ground for translating it with 'take' or 'grasp' (implying a new situation)? (2) μᾶλλον : is this adverb an elative comparison, to be translated 'by all means', or a contrasting comparative

Paul begins this section with an assertion of his authority: he commands (7.17)[77] everyone to live his or her life as the Lord has 'assigned' and as God has 'called'. Then he discusses two pairs of opposites in the same order in which they appear in Gal. 3.28: circumcision or uncircumcision (vv. 18-19), equivalent to Jew or Greek; slave or free (vv. 21-23). There is little difficulty understanding the first pair. Just as Paul carefully balanced his statements concerning men and women in vv. 1-16, so he balances his reference to

(expressing exclusion), to be translated 'rather'? If 'rather' is the correct translation, is the contrast with 'able to become free' (7.21c), with 'not being concerned about being a slave' (7.21ab), with following the general principle which Paul repeats in 7.17, 20, 24 or with 'being concerned about becoming a freedman' (in antithetical parallelism to 7.21b, with the 'concern' in this case, expressed perhaps in 'boasting' that one was not free)? (3) εἰ καί: should these two words be construed together as introducing a concessive clause: 'although' or 'even though' (of a condition represented as immaterial even if fulfilled)? Or should they be read separately, in which case εἰ would be construed with the 'indicative of reality' and translated 'if indeed', and καί would be an emphatic particle which could either stress the entire phrase 'if indeed you are able to become free' (contrasting it with 'were you a slave when you were called' in 7.21a) or emphasize only 'being able' (in which case the offer of freedom would be contrasted with seeking freedom by one's own effort, which could be implied in 'don't worry about being a slave' in 7.21b). (4) ἀλλά: does this adversative particle introduce a contrast to 'don't worry about it' in 7.21b? Is it to be translated 'but' or 'yet', or does it express an extension of μή in 7.21b? Is it to he translated 'rather (than being concerned about your slavery). . . ' or does this particle introduce a restriction of the general principle expressed in 7.20 (and in 7.17 and 7.24)? Finally, how is the unusual combination, ἀλλ᾽ εἰ καί, to be construed in view of the variety of possibilities for each word? (5) δύνασαι ἐλεύθερος: does this phrase refer to an action initiated by the Christian slave (such an action perhaps being already discouraged in 7.21b), or to an action initiated by the owner of the slave over which the slave would have no control (a case similar to that of the spouse in 7.15 whose believing partner breaks up the marriage)? (6) γάρ (7.22): does this conjunction, which expresses cause, inference or continuation, introduce a reason supporting 7.21ab (don't worry about being a slave), or 7.21cd (which would read 'even though you can become free, stay a slave')? See Bartchy (*Slavery*, p. 8), for this presentation of the debate.

77. The verb is διατάσσομαι which means 'order' or 'command'. Paul also uses it in 1 Cor. 9.14 where he reminds the Corinthians that the Lord has 'ordained' that those who preach the gospel have a right to support; in 11.34, where he promises to 'settle' other questions about conduct at eucharistic meals when he comes; and in 16.1, where he directs the Corinthians to follow his 'order' to the Galatian churches about the collection for the saints. This word contrasts with the verbs of persuasion that are used throughout the ch. 7.

circumcision and uncircumcision.[78] The inference is that neither circumcision nor uncircumcision is anything; what is important is τήρησις ἐντολῶν θεοῦ.[79] It is difficult to determine the meaning of this phrase in isolation; however its position in a chiastic structure sheds light on Paul's intent.

a. εἰ μὴ ἑκάστῳ ὡς ἐμέρισεν ὁ κύριος. . . οὕτως περιπατείτω
　　b. καὶ οὕτως ἐν ταῖς ἐκκλησίαις πάσαις διατάσσομαι
　　　　c. περιτετμημένος τις ἐκλήθη...μὴ περιτεμνέσθω
　　　　c´. ἡ περιτομὴ οὐδέν ἐστιν, καὶ ἡ ἀκροβυστία οὐδέν ἐστιν
　　b´. ἀλλὰ τήρησις ἐντολῶν θεοῦ
a´. ἕκαστος ἐν τῇ κλήσει ᾗ ἐκλήθη ἐν ταύτῃ μενέτω

Paul links 'keeping the commands of God', with no specific content, to what he commands in all the churches.

The second and more difficult pair is 'slave or free'. Verse 21ab (δοῦλος ἐκλήθης; μή σοι μελέτω) balances v. 18 (περιτετμημένος τις ἐκλήθη; μὴ ἐπισπάσθω), but then in vv. 21c-22 Paul adds a concession and the rationale for that concession (ἀλλ᾽ εἰ καὶ δύνασαι ἐλεύθερος γενέσθαι, μᾶλλον χρῆσαι ὁ γὰρ ἐν κυρίῳ κληθεὶς δοῦλος ἀπελεύθερος κυρίου ἐστίν.) As in vv. 10-11a, a statement is made (v. 21a) followed by an exception (vv. 21b-22a): 'Slaves, since you have been called by God, your legal status no longer determines your existence. Stop being concerned about it, but if. . . '

Since there is no evidence of a dispute between Jews and Gentiles over circumcision at Corinth, this part of the baptismal formula of Gal. 3.28 provided an excellent example for Paul's general principle. The second pair is more difficult to handle.[80] While it is unlikely that distinctions between slaves and free persons were involved in the factionalism at Corinth, Christian slaves and masters would have belonged to the Corinthian church, and manumission was a frequent occurrence

78.   It is preferable to consider both parts of this verse to be questions. See Kurt Aland, *et al.*, *The Greek New Testament* (London: United Bible Societies, 1966), p. 593. However there is little difference in sense if one takes both clauses as declarative statements.

79.   Paul uses τηρέω rarely (four times, of which two occurrences are in 1 Cor. 7). Similarly, ἐντολή is used infrequently (six times in Rom. 7, elsewhere only in Rom. 13.9; 1 Cor. 7.19; 1 Cor. 14.37). Only in 1 Cor. is it used in connection with θεός or κύριος.

80.   Bartchy, *Slavery*, pp. 129-32.

in Graeco-Roman society.[81] Paul wrote 7.21-22 not at the prompting of the slaves in the Corinthian congregation, but to provide a supporting argument to his understanding of how men and women were to view 'no male and female' within the congregation.[82]

The opposed pairs in 7.18-22, the gen words and nature words, assist Paul in making his point about the relationship of male and female (the kin words).[83] According to Bartchy v. 21b is best translated, 'but if, indeed,[84] you become manumitted',[85] and should be seen as an exhortation to the Christian slave to do something about the opportunity, namely, 'to live (as a freedman) according to God's call'.[86]

Paul uses καλέω/κλῆσις nine times in vv. 15-24.[87] It is unclear whether κλῆσει in 7.20 means the 'call from God in Christ', that is,

---

81.   Bartchy, *Slavery*, pp. 88-91.

82.   Bartchy, (*Slavery*, pp. 114-20) and James Crouch (*The Origin and Intention of the Colossian Haustafeln* [Göttingen: Vandenhoeck & Ruprecht, 1972], p. 126) disagree over whether the example of slave and free is illustrative or reflects a social reality in the Corinthian congregation.

83.   They serve an illustrative function for vv. 1-16 and vv. 25-40. See Chapter 3, pp. 102-105 for a discussion of root metaphor and its structural characteristics, that is, the gen words, the kin words and the nature words.

84.   Paul has used εἰ καὶ with the sense of 'even if' or 'although' in 2 Cor. 4.16; 7.8a, c and 12.11. In 1 Cor. 4 7; 7.11-12; 7.27-28 as well as in 2 Cor. 4.2-3; 7.8b-9 and 11.5-6, καὶ is used emphatically in the protasis of a conditional sentence, and thus is grammatically separate from εἰ. Margaret Thrall (*Greek Particles in the New Testament: Linguistic and Exegetical Studies* [Grand Rapids: Eerdmans, 1962], p. 81) concludes: 'It is probable that this verse (7.21) contains a third example of the idiom. That would mean Paul is advising Christian slaves to take advantage of the opportunity of emancipation.' See also C.F.D. Moule, *An Idiom Book of New Testament Greek* (Cambridge: Cambridge University Press, 1960), p. 167; J.D. Denniston, *The Greek Particles* (Oxford: Oxford University Press, 1959), p. 303.

85.   Bartchy (*Slavery* pp. 176-77) explains that the slave had no choice in the matter of manumission. It was something done to him. He notes that the use of δύνασαι is reminiscent of Agrippa's words to Festus in Acts 26.32: 'This man could have been set free if he had not appealed to Caesar'. Although Paul is the subject of ἐδύνατο, it was not Paul but Festus who could have set Paul free. Manumission was a common occurrence in the first century CE. The owner who manumitted a slave did so to serve his own advantage, since manumission increased the efficiency and contentment of those still in slavery, who could also hope to be manumitted. Slaves who did their work well could reasonably hope to be set free as their reward. Bartchy, *Slavery*, p. 175.

86.   Bartchy, *Slavery* pp. 178-79.

87.   These words occur thirty times in Rom., 1 Cor., Gal., 1 Thess., and Phil.

an act of calling, or whether it means 'status in society' or 'earthly condition'.[88] For Paul's readers both meanings would probably be suggested, raising the question: how do the circumstances of one's life relate to being called into the reign of God? Since neither circumcision nor uncircumcision matters, one's calling as a Christian[89] does not demand a change in one's station. However, if a change is brought about by another, as in manumission, it is to be seen as God's call and the individual is to live accordingly. If such a connection between God's call and earthly status were accepted in Corinth, it would be extremely difficult for individual Christians to initiate any change in marital status. Moreover, according to the prevailing pattern of relationships between the sexes a woman could not easily initiate a brother and sister relationship with her husband but, she could accept it if offered to her by her husband. If vv. 17-24 illustrate Paul's way of arguing throughout ch. 7, his arguments about marriage/sexual intercourse and singleness/celibacy will be seen to contain assumptions which support structure. Paul, in the interests of strong community, is willing to limit the freedom of a married woman who wants to live in a brother/sister relationship with her husband.

In vv. 22b-23, Paul advises those in a dominant position: although they are masters, they are slaves of Christ. This inversion is an antistructural move which prepares the reader for Paul's appeals in vv. 28b-31.

In vv. 17-24 Paul appeals to what Malina has labelled 'the generalized symbolic media of goal attainment' or power in order to produce conformity within the church.[90] He does this by appealing to the commands (ἐντολῶν) of God; keeping these commands is the only thing that matters. The gift of God (vv. 7, 17) and the call of God (vv. 15, 17, 18, 20, 21, 22, 94) seem to function in the same way.

88. According to Bauer (*Lexicon*, p. 436), while κλῆσις is used almost exclusively in a religious sense of the divine call, of the invitation to enter the reign of God, a secondary meaning is 'station', 'position', 'vocation'. Barrett (*First Epistle*, pp. 169-70) reads both 7.20 and 1.26 in terms of the second meaning. Conzelmann (*1 Corinthians*, p. 127) finds the first meaning in 1.26 but favours the second connotation in 7.20.

89. Bartchy (*Slavery*, p. 165) believes that for Paul there was a close connection between God's call and baptism. This connection is expressed in Paul's choice of examples to illustrate his 'theology of calling'. Perhaps because baptism is at the heart of the divisions in Corinth, Paul prefers to use the word 'calling'.

90. Malina, *Christian Origins*, p. 82.

Therefore, living according to the gift apportioned to the individual, and remaining as one was when [God's call was received], is to obey God's commands.[91]

In v. 17 Paul seems to identify the authority of God and the authority of 'the Lord'. Gooch proposes that his actual treatment does suggest a difference, if indeed the commands of the Lord are the sayings of Jesus. For those commands are specific and of necessity leave gaps to be filled in, but what ultimately fills them in is the authority of the gift and call of God.[92]

Each faction probably appealed to the sayings of Jesus as justification for its position (vv. 10, 36-38). In response, Paul sets forth as the ultimate authority the commands (gift, call) of God,[93] and Paul's right to demand conformity is clearly implied when he relates these commands to what he commands in all the churches. To demand allegiance to himself as the ultimate authority is a move to strengthen group loyalties. Paul must also provide arguments which will move the high grid faction lower on the grid line, where they will give less value to the hierarchical relationships based on marriage. At the same time the low grid faction must be moved higher on the same line, so that singleness/celibacy is not arbitrarily demanded as a sign of belonging within the community.

The worst scandal of low grid is disparity of status; thus those in this quadrant emphasize the dismantling of classifications and the increasing liberation of the individual.[94] In the Corinthian situation, those preferring low grid would judge any move towards erasing status disparity as liberating. When Paul describes slavery as freedom in Christ (7.22), he is attempting to stop any further move downward on the grid line.

Paul must also move the pro-marriage group to a lower point on the grid scale. He does this by referring to their having been bought with a price (v. 23a).[95] According to Douglas's analysis, the strong

91.   Gooch, 'Authority', p. 67.
92.   Gooch, 'Authority', p. 67.
93.   Gooch ('Authority', p. 67) states 'his [God's] authority is invoked by Paul to settle possible disagreements'.
94.   Douglas, *Cultural Bias*, p. 47.
95.   According to Bartchy (*Slavery*, p. 169) the words 'you were bought with a price; do not become the slaves of men' refer to and explain the words 'likewise a freeman who has been called is a slave of Christ'.

group/high grid quadrant is 'the kind of social environment in which doctrines of atonement flourish and which can make sense of a full [once-and-for-all] historical incarnational theology'.[96] This quadrant also seeks to make an explicit match between civilization and the purposes of God and views God as sustaining both nature and culture.[97] A connection between staying in one's station in life and Christ's sacrifice would work towards moving this group downward on the grid line to where what one was when one was 'bought with a price' would become more important than marriage, with its ascribed statuses and roles.

Verses 28b-31
This section begins with the statement that all those who marry[98] have bodily[99] distress.[100] Therefore, those who are free from any obligation to a woman should stay as they are, as should those who are bound by an oath. Paul's arguments, although addressed to the male in the situation, are written more generally to the pro-structure faction ('those who have wives', v. 29b). 'What I mean is this, brothers' (v. 29) signals the beginning of Paul's attempt to justify his position.[101] The argument is based on the imminence of the end of the world: 'the time has been shortened' (v. 29); 'the form of this world is passing away' (v. 31).

Verses 29-31 may reflect Paul's eschatological orientation. However, by his arguments, Paul is primarily trying to move the

---

96.   Douglas, *Cultural Bias*, p. 23.

97.   Douglas, *Cultural Bias*, p. 23.

98.   Barrett, *First Epistle*, p. 176 translates as 'all such people (who act against Paul's advice)'; Robertson and Plummer *(First Corinthians*, p. 154) say simply, 'such people who marry'.

99.   The word flesh, which often has a special theological sense in Paul, would seem here to be referring to the physical sphere, within which marriage means obligations. See Barrett, *First Epistle,* p. 176. In this context, the two meanings of the word would be associated at least subconsciously in the minds of the Corinthians.

100.   The word θλῖψις is used frequently in the LXX and the New Testament literature with the sense of 'oppression, affliction, tribulation'. The LXX uses θλῖψις for several Hebrew words which are sometimes also translated by ἀνάγκη (Job 27.9; Prov. 17.17). This latter term denotes the oppression and affliction of the people of Israel or of the righteous who represent Israel.

101.   τοῦτο δέ φημι can mean 'what I mean is this' indicating that what is to follow will provide the explanation. See Bauer, *Greek–English Lexicon*, p. 856.

Corinthian pro-structure faction to accept his advice to the betrothed couple. We must therefore concentrate on the function of his use of end-time language.

Nowhere else in this chapter is the eschatological motif developed further. The position of v. 29a (ὁ καιρὸς συνεσταλμένος ἐστίν) and v. 31b (παράγει γὰρ τὸ σχῆμα τοῦ κόσμου τούτου), which frame vv. 29b-31a, indicates the importance of this motif in providing a justification for Paul's exhortations.[102] Because the end is near, because the time has been shortened, the relationship of the believer to the world must be provisional, tentative and impermanent. The believer must deal with the world as though having no dealings with it. In this sense the end-time perspective provides not only the *motivation* for behaviour, but the *justification* for its content as well.[103] Gager concludes that, from a statement of 'fact' (the time has been shortened, the form of this world is passing away), Paul thinks he can derive a statement of obligation (therefore you ought to prepare yourself by living as if you were not married and by not marrying, if you still have that option).[104]

Douglas remarks that in all cosmologies there is a close relation between the sense of time past, the expectation of the future and the response to millennial prophecies.[105] At D quadrant (strong group/low grid), the sudden arrival of the millennium is more credible than at C (strong group/high grid). Thus, Paul's arguments concerning the end of the world must relate eschatology more specifically to the cosmological bias of the pro-structure group (quadrant C), in order to convince those at high grid. He proceeds to do this in v. 31b.

The words, παράγει γὰρ τὸ σχῆμα τοῦ κόσμου τούτου, provide a transition to Paul's reinterpretation and application of vv. 29b-31a in vv. 32-35. They also provide a conclusion to the previous section.

---

102. Various grammatical points in these verses which need to be clarified include: (1) τὸ λοιπόν: Thrall (*Particles*, p. 155) concludes that its position before is not unusual but is there for emphasis. (2) ἔχοντες: With and without an article this word indicates a distinction not between the situation of the persons referred to but the way they are to treat their situation. See Orr and Walther, *1 Corinthians*, p. 219. (3) σχῆμα: Orr and Walther (*1 Corinthians*, p. 219) believe that the word means 'the shape the world is in'. Conzelmann (*1 Corinthians*, p. 134) defines σχῆμα as 'the essence, that is, the world itself'.

103. Gager, 'End-Time', p. 332.

104. Gager, 'End-Time', p. 332.

105. Douglas, *Cultural Bias*, p. 29.

Douglas states that 'the uses of nature in moral justification are all pervasive in C group. Going against nature means threat of failure, unnatural vice is condemned'.[106] For those in this quadrant, the σχῆμα is almost a part of nature, and they are tempted to equate it with the purposes of God. Therefore Paul's reference to the passing away of the σχῆμα will make the pro-structure party take seriously what he proposes in vv. 30-31a.

In these verses five examples of worldly involvement, including marriage, are related to five corresponding modes of ideal behaviour. Wimbush concludes that all except the first and fifth are rhetorical. The first involves the immediate situation in Corinth, while the fifth functions as the umbrella under which all the examples can be subsumed. Paul's exhortations call for an equality or similarity 'not between two groups of persons, but between the actual situation of the persons and the way they are to treat their situation'.[107] Wimbush diagrams this comparison as follows:

persons	*situation*[108]
'those having wives	should be (=) not having wives'.

Paul, in addressing those who have wives, calls upon them to '"remain"' where they are in the world, but to adopt different *attitudes*, attitudes *associated* with different situations'.[109] What is contrasted is not so much the degree of involvement as the quality (moral, ethical) of involvement. According to Wimbush,

> [w]e can be certain only of the *goal* of the response or model of 'asceticism' and of the rejecting of other 'models', namely, the options for either changing stations in life (renouncing relationships with others), or remaining in one's station in life with all of the features typically associated with that station.[110]

A comparison with a passage in 6 Esdras[111] leads Wimbush to con-

106. Douglas, *Cultural Bias*, p. 23.
107. Orr and Walther, *1 Corinthians*, p. 219.
108. Wimbush, *Worldly Ascetic*, p. 30.
109. Wimbush, *Worldly Ascetic*, p. 30.
110. Wimbush, *Worldly Ascetic*, pp. 53-54.
111. 'Let him that sells be like one who will flee; let him that buys be like one who will lose, let him that does business be like one who will not make a profit; and let him who builds a house be like one who does not live in it. . . them that marry, like those who will have no children and them that do not marry like those who are widowed' (6 Esd. 16.35-44). The problem of dating this book leaves open the

clude that Paul wants those who are married to avoid the entanglements and responsibilities of marriage.

After a discussion of the possible Jewish and Graeco-Roman parallels,[112] Wimbush concludes that Paul is demanding the attitude of ὡς μή, a spiritual withdrawal or detachment. While the world is not evil, it does bring its own obligations, and in order to deal with them, an attitude of inner detachment is required. As the physical body must achieve freedom within from conflicting demands, so too must the social body. This call for inner detachment seeks to release both the physical and the social body from ambiguity.

Another clue to Paul's meaning is found in the change in predicate in the fourth (οἱ ἀγοράζοντες... κατέχοντες) and the fifth (οἱ χρώμενοι... καταχρώμενοι) examples. The emphasis here is not on the act of buying but on its result, the possession of goods; in the final pair, the contrast is between using the world and not using it fully.[113] These examples are taken from the economic structures of which kinship and marriage are an integral part.[114] J. Duncan Derrett relates these verses to marriage, considering v. 30c to be of particular importance: 'those that buy (i.e. those that put up the cash) (should act) as if they had acquired no right'.[115]

'Those who have wives are to live as those who do not' (v. 29d): Paul allows the marriage relationship to remain but calls upon the husband not to use his rights to the full. He is to cease relating to his

---

possibility that its pattern of argument may have been derived from Paul or from a Christian redactor. See Robertson and Plummer, *First Epistle*, p. 155; Conzelmann, *1 Corinthians*, pp. 133-34, n. 26.

112. These include Jewish piety, non-Jewish cultic asceticism and the spiritual detachment of the philosophers. Wimbush, *Worldly Ascetic*, pp. 54-69.

113. Robertson and Plummer, *First Epistle*, p. 156 paraphrases v. 30c 'as not entering upon full ownership' and v. 31a 'as not using it to the utmost'.

114. British anthropologists stress the rights and duties transferred at marriage from the kin group of one spouse to that of the other and/or the rights and duties created by the marriage itself. A woman is viewed in terms of the rights her kin have to her domestic labour, to the property she might acquire, to her children and to her sexuality. In many societies the marriage ceremony and the payment of bride-wealth give these rights to the husband and residually to his kin. See Lamphere, 'Strategies', p. 98. *Coemptio* in Roman tradition was that ceremony by which a woman was transferred to a new family. It was an application of the old form of sale and purchase.

115. Derrett, 'Disposal', pp. 189-90.

wife as a structural superior, except in the residual legal sense which attaches to the identities of husband and wife in the world. In other words, to live as 'not married' means being uninvolved with those statuses and roles which are integral to the proper ordering of a patrilineal kinship system. Since a kinship system orders private relationships with a view to an orderly society, the corollary is that order within the church should also not be based on the hierarchical statuses and roles of the patrilineal kinship system.

Comparing Paul's use of apocalyptic language here and in Galatians, Meeks says that

> on the face of it, then, Paul's employment of apocalyptic categories here (in Corinthians) seems to be the reverse of that in Galatians. There he used the present experience of factors traditionally associated with the messianic age to warrant a radical innovation, abandoning the use of the Mosaic Law so as to set boundaries between Jew and gentile. Here he uses eschatological language in the future tense to restrain innovation and to counsel stability and order.[116]

Meeks is only partially correct. He fails to see that the group addressed in these verses is the one favouring a social structure of kinship and marriage ('those who have wives'). The eschatological justification seeks to prevent their move to higher grid: if they accept Paul's advice, this would pave the way for new forms of status and structure.

In another way Meeks is quite correct. Paul's arguments are addressed to the individual in the structurally dominant role: the husband. In these verses the married woman is not given a part in the decision making process. Further, in light of Paul's advice in vv. 17-24, the implication is that wives must wait until equality is offered to them by their structural superiors, namely, their husbands.[117]

Paul's willingness to argue from the structure of roles and obligations laid down by the kinship pattern based on marriage[118] confirms

116. Meeks, *First Urban*, p. 179.

117. Meeks is quite correct when he affirms that the consistent factor in Paul's use of eschatological language is his concern to build 'the solidarity and stability of the congregation'. See Meeks, *First Urban*, p. 179.

118. This was recognized by Countryman (*Dirt*, p. 198) in his discussion of 5.1-8. In 1 Cor. 7 there is no indication that Paul demands of husbands the 'even more than' that he expects of Philemon's relationship to Onesimus in v. 21. Petersen (*Narrative*, pp. 97-98) interprets the 'even more than' to mean that Paul is calling for

the suspicion that arose in connection with his use of the terminology in v. 16. In the interests of group cohesion and unity, Paul is willing to sacrifice the freedom of married women who are involved in the anti-structure group. The final proof comes when the breaks in the pattern of his argument in vv. 32-35 are noted.

Verses 32-35
Paul continues here to justify to the pro-marriage group his demand that they live as 'not married'. He wants them to be free from anxieties (ἀμέριμνοι) which, in v. 35, is taken to mean 'waiting on the Lord with good order and devotion, without distraction (ἀπερισπά- στως)'. Some of these words occur in Stoic literature,[119] and, in at least one description, the situation involves a concern for the entanglements which marriage brings, especially that of children.[120] The

the abolition of the legal vestiges of the relationship between master and slave. In 1 Cor. 7, except in vv. 10-11 where the divorce has already taken place, Paul reacts against the Christian moving to a legal dissolution of marriage.

119. There is a longstanding debate as to whether or not Paul used Stoic philosophy. Representative of one side are the conclusions of Johannes Weiss *Der Erste Korintherbrief* (Meyer Commentaries; Göttingen: Vandenhoeck & Ruprecht, 1970 [1910]), p. 205 n. 2 and Herbert Braun 'Die Indifferenz gegenuber der Welt bei Paulus und bei Epiktet', *idem, Gesammelte Studien zum neuen Testament und seiner Umwelt* (Tübingen: Mohr, 1962), pp. 159-67. The opposite position is argued by Wolfgang Schrage 'Die Stellung zur Welt bei Paulus, Epiktet und in der Apoka- lyptik. Ein Beitrag zu 1 Kor. 7.29-31', *ZTK* 61 (1964), pp. 125-54. Commenting on the adverb ἀπερισπάστως, Weiss asserts, 'Here we have an exact Stoic-Cynic parallel to the view of Paul.' Schrage wonders how one can use Cynic-Stoic parallels to clarify Paul's exhortations when they have a clear eschatological basis. David Balch's position ('Stoic Debate', pp. 429-30) is useful: 'Paul accepted and used certain Stoic values, which were indeed in logical tension with other values he held, but which were useful in his debate'.

120. Epictetus writes as follows: 'But in such an order of this as the present, which is like that of a battlefield, it is a question, perhaps, if the Cynic ought not to be free from distraction (ἀπερισπάστον), wholly devoted to the service of God, free to go about among men, not tied down by the private duties of men, nor involved in relationships which he cannot violate and still maintain his role as a good and excel- lent man, whereas on the other hand, if he observes them, he will destroy the mes- senger, the scout, the herald of gods, that he is. For see, he must show certain ser- vice to his father-in-law, to the rest of his wife's relatives, to his wife herself; finally he is driven from his profession, to act as a nurse in his own family and to provide for them. To make a long story short, he must get a kettle to heat water for the baby, for washing it in the bathtub; wool for his wife when she has a child, oil, a cot, a cup

unmarried man is free to give his loyalty to a fictive kinship system, and thus God receives the duties and obligations that would normally be due to a wife. The married man, however, being divided in his loyalties, cannot serve God in the same way.

This section (vv. 28b-35) seeks to convince those within the Corinthian community who are in favour of high grid to renounce voluntarily the roles and statuses that accompany it. Paul tries to make his point, however, without giving further support to those who are part of the anti-structure faction. Thus, he does not describe the married woman as divided in her loyalties. Neither does he equate being unmarried, in her case, with proper service to the Lord. Singleness in women is related to purity (v. 34).

Paul argues that if his advice is taken, certain things will follow: personal advantage (σύμφορον), good order (εὔσχημον) and an ability to serve God with an undistracted or undisturbed mind (ἀπερισπά- στως). According to Gooch,

> the first result is directed to the self: his readers will find their own good promoted by following Paul's advice. The second is a reason related to more general values: their lives will be fitting, honourable, attractive. The third does contain a religious element: by so ordering their lives, they will be free from the cares and concerns which intrude upon one's sitting down and staying with the Lord. . . Paul does not say do this because it is divinely commanded, but rather do this because it will produce certain valued experience. . . This form of argument is non-authoritarian in the sense that there are reasons for rules apart from any moral authority whatever, the reasons being linked to the consequences which result from those rules and actions.[121]

This manner of appeal uses the symbolic media (GSM) of influence, which is the ability to get another to change opinions and actions so that intended actions might follow. Whether or not one's advice is followed depends on the degree to which one's influence is deflated or inflated.[122]

Paul's appeal is to the high grid group. He wants them to live as

---

(the vessels get more and more numerous); not to speak of the rest of his business, and his distraction (περισπασμόν). Where, I beseech you, is left now our king, the man who has leisure for the public interest?' Quoted in Balch, 'Stoic Debate', pp. 430-31.

121. Gooch, 'Authority', p. 70.

122. Malina, *Christian Origins*, p. 81.

married, yet not to exercise the roles and obligations of the married state, and he argues that such ambiguity will produce order and integrated living. Paul's task is not an easy one, because this group is arguing that marriage, with its way of ordering relationships, will clarify the confused social situation which already exists. Paul appeals to them to live with the ambiguity, and the results which Paul asserts will come from living this way are those that would appeal to this quadrant: structure, order and things being in their place.[123]

The example of Philemon, a high-grid Christian, helps us understand vv. 29-35. In his letter to Philemon, Paul does not attack the institution of slavery as such or even the involvement of a believer in owning slaves. Rather, he creates a conflict between identities, since it is logically and socially impossible to relate to one and the same person as both inferior and equal. Petersen concludes,

> In Paul's view the ultimate issue is the identity of believers as sibling children-to-be of God, and therefore as equals. Because Onesimus is no longer a slave but a brother, both in the flesh and in the Lord, his *being* a brother to Philemon means that he cannot also *be* a slave to Philemon in any domain. In other words, *being* in Christ or *being* in the Lord is a state of social being that governs the relationships between believers even outside the spatial and temporal boundaries of the church. Being in Christ/the Lord, therefore, excludes all other forms of social being for those who are 'in' him.[124]

Paul does not explicitly state how he expected Philemon to deal with his worldly position as the owner of Onesimus. However, his line of argument suggests that Philemon ought to free him (v. 21).

The issue in 7.25-35 also concerns a conflict of identities: how to live as children of God when, in the domain of the world, brother and sister are husband and wife or bound by an oath that should lead to a husband and wife relationship. In the latter case to remain unmarried is Paul's preference. However, if the brother and sister are husband and wife, Paul allows the marriage to stand, but, at the same time, he urges the high-grid Christians to abstain from the rights and obligations of marriage, as the proper way of serving God.

---

123. Douglas (*Cultural Bias*, pp. 26-27) identifies how each quadrant responds to gardening. Strong group/high grid would 'use this medium (gardening) to justify and expand its view of society as hierarchised, trained and compartmentalized'. This produces ingenious arrangements dominated by design and order.

124. Petersen, *Narrative*, p. 289.

If his advice here were the same as in his letter to Philemon, Petersen could be rephrased: 'because a woman is no longer a wife but a sister, both in the flesh and in the Lord, her being a sister to her husband means that she cannot be a wife to her husband in any domain'. In both Philemon and 1 Corinthians the initiative is to come from the structurally superior individual; however, in 1 Corinthians, Paul argues that the legal vestiges of the relationship are to remain.[125]

Conclusion

In the anthropological model of social drama, stage three is the phase of redressive activity. Its structure directs the exegete to look closely at the degree of authority that the redressive agent has within the community. When chs. 1–4 are understood in the context of an apostolic *apologia* in which Paul attempts to establish his right to act as a redressive agent, the weakness of his authority within the community becomes clear. He does not have the power to command; instead, he must persuade the Corinthians that his advice represents the proper course of action for them to follow. What Paul recommends in this particular situation is not necessarily his own preference; it may reflect a compromise required because of his weakened authority. In other words, his advice might have been different had the balance of power been different.

Paul cannot just appeal for group loyalty; he must attempt to clarify grid concerns, if the factionalism is to end and the conflict is to be resolved. In the end, he leaves the structure of relationships within the community ambiguous.

The evidence suggests that the drive within the community for living anti-structure came from married women. In disallowing them the right to initiate any further move to celibacy, Paul is sacrificing their interests in order to strengthen group cohesion. At the same time, he attempts to ensure that group ties are strong enough to prevent either a split within the community or the expulsion of one faction as deviant or polluting. If, however, wives fail to acquiesce in his call to stay as they are unless their husbands agree to a change in the relationship, they risk being considered deviant and polluting.

For survival, a group needs to be precise about its definition of roles. According to Douglas, the resolution of the kind of crisis we

125. Petersen, *Narrative*, pp. 97-98.

find in 1 Corinthians 7 and the ultimate survival of the group demands that the structuring of roles becomes unambiguous.[126] Paul is unable to bring this about because of his own uncertain authority at Corinth and his ambivalence over structure and anti-structure, especially when the issue threatens to undermine the unity of the community. Paul's failure to address the issue decisively suggests that the social drama will remain unresolved.

Successful redressive action leads either to a reintegration of the disaffected group or to the social recognition and legitimization of an irreparable schism between the contending parties. When redress fails, the crisis usually recurs.[127] The next chapter will attempt to trace the success of Paul's redressive measures.

126. Douglas, *Natural Symbols*, pp. 111, 114.
127. Turner, *Dramas*, pp. 40-41.

Chapter 5

THE RESOLUTION OF THE SOCIAL DRAMA: THE JOURNEY OF A METAPHOR

> Men [and women] have to organize structurally in order to exist materially
> at all. . . One great temptation in this milieu is to subordinate *communitas*
> totally to structure so that the principle of order will never be subverted.
> The opposite temptation is to opt out of structure altogether. The basic and
> perennial social problem is to discover what is the right relation between
> these modalities at a specific time and place.[1]

In the social drama represented in 1 Corinthians 7, there are two
interpretations of the root metaphor, 'in Christ all are children of
God, no male and female'. These two interpretations are vying for the
right to order male and female relationships within the church. Paul
takes redressive measures, and the social drama moves to its final
stage. According to Turner's comparison of certain types of social
processes with dramas on the stage, with their acts and scenes, this
final stage is the climax, resolution or outcome. This point in the
social drama provides an opportunity to analyze the total course of
events in Corinth.

Characteristics of the Resolution Stage in the Social Drama

Turner states that in the final stage there will be changes both in the
nature and intensity of the relations between the parties and in the
bases of political support. Some factors in the drama will have less
support, others more. Still others will have fresh support, and some
will have none. Furthermore, what is viewed as legitimate and what is
not legitimate will have changed, as will the techniques used by the
leaders to gain compliance.[2]

1. Turner, *Dramas*, p. 266.
2. Turner, *Dramas*, pp. 42-43.

In this phase in the social drama a new order will be established, with a new balance of power, new relationships, new statuses and new bases of legitimation.[3] But if redressive action fails, this stage can signal a reversion to crisis.[4] If the central authority is not strong enough to address the conflict, force may be used: war, revolution, violence, repression and rebellion.[5]

The purpose of Paul's redressive action in ch. 7 was to strengthen group ties and to emphasize group loyalties around his leadership. To accomplish this, he de-emphasized the issue under dispute and allowed the structure of roles and the organization within the community to remain ambiguous. Although Paul stated a preference for singleness/ celibacy, he did not impose either a hierarchical system of marital rights and responsibilities or an egalitarian structure of sibling relationships. How individual Christians were to relate to one another remained unclear. A discussion of Paul's attempt to resolve the crisis must focus on two factors: group loyalties (group) and the patterning of individual relationships as they relate to 'no male and female' (grid).

Evidence for the success or failure of Paul's intervention in 1 Corinthians 7 must be traced through later correspondence to that community. Victor Turner argues that it is important to study the history of a single group or community over an extended period of time, for it is in this kind of extended study that the explanations of constancy and change are to he found.[6] When social dramas and social enterprises are analyzed over a period of decades, changes become evident even in a society thought to be 'stagnant'.[7]

1 and 2 Corinthians and 1 Clement provide rich data for such an extended case study. Between 2 Corinthians and 1 Clement, there is no primary description of the Corinthian community; however, there are *other* communities, namely those described in Colossians, Ephesians and the Pastorals, which looked to Paul as a leading authority and which continued to struggle with the root metaphor, 'in Christ all are

3.   Flanagan, *David's Social Drama*, p. 108.
4.   With the failure of redress, another escalation of the crisis, with an accompanying state of liminality, can occur. At each step the parties waver between resolution and further revolt.
5.   Turner, *Dramas*, p. 41.
6.   Turner, *Dramas*, p. 43.
7.   Turner, *Dramas*, p. 43.

children of God, no male and female'.[8] The letters addressed to these communities provide important commentary on social process within the communities founded by Paul.

2 Corinthians

An understanding of the final phase of the social drama depends on information about what happened in Corinth immediately after the writing of 1 Corinthians, and how Paul responded, what visits Paul made and what letters he wrote. In 2 Corinthians there are a number of difficult literary problems, particularly the unity of the letters[9] and the identity of Paul's opponents.[10] A discussion of these problems is limited to their bearing on the question: was Paul successful in redressing the social drama at Corinth?

In 1 Corinthians Paul claimed the authority to act as a redressive agent. This authority derived from the fact that he was the 'father in Christ' of the Corinthians, that is, the one who had laid the foundation of the community and an apostle. In 2 Corinthians Paul continues to fight for the recognition of his authority and apostolic legitimacy.[11]

8.   Margaret MacDonald in *The Pauline Churches: A Socio-Historical Study of Institutionalization in the Pauline and Deutero-Pauline Writings* (Cambridge: Cambridge University Press, 1988), p. 89, states that '(t)he important point is. . . that a system of symbols associated with the life of the Apostle remained relevant after his death, undergoing changes as it stood in a dialectical relationship to communitas in new times and circumstances'.

9.   For a detailed history of interpretation see, Hans Dieter Betz, *2 Corinthians 8 and 9: A Commentary on Two Administrative Letters by the Apostle Paul* (Philadelphia: Fortress Press, 1985), pp. 3-27. The three main questions are: (1) Do chs. 10–13 belong to the same letter as chs. 1–9? If they form part of a different letter, is this letter to be dated before or after chs. 1–9? (2) Do chs. 8 and 9 belong together, or are they two separate notes, dealing with different aspects of the collection? (3) Is 2.14–7.4 to be regarded as a misplaced insertion which interrupts Paul's account of his meeting with Titus (2.13; 7.5)? Within this section a special problem is raised by 6.14–7.1, which some think is part of the Previous Letter (1 Cor. 5.9), and others believe not to have been written by Paul.

10.   For a discussion of Paul's opponents see, Dieter Georgi, *The Opponents of Paul in Second Corinthians* (Philadelphia: Fortress Press, 1986).

11.   Francis Young and David F. Ford (*Meaning and Truth in 2 Corinthians* [Grand Rapids: Eerdmans, 1987], p. 12) state that 'the letter is about two closely related things. One of these is the glory of God, the other is the reputation of Paul'. Contra C.K. Barrett (*Essays on Paul* [London: SPCK, 1982], pp. 14-15) who states

Other Christian missionaries who had arrived at Corinth were challenging Paul's authority. Malina's understanding of three kinds of authority: reputational authority, impersonal legitimate authority and personal legitimate authority is illuminating.[12] Reputational authority derives from 'the successful criticism and dislocation of the higher order norms which legitimate the authority prevailing in a given society', and emerges 'from a person's effective ability to convince members of a given society no longer to recognize some higher order norm as binding'.[13] Whatever the rationale upon which legitimate authority, personal or impersonal, is based, reputational authority will attempt to demonstrate that it depends on force, trickery, conspiracy or inconsistency.

In 2 Corinthians the outsiders challenge Paul's authority by laying charges against him. They accuse him of being inconsistent in his dealings (10.1), acting in a worldly fashion (10.2),[14] not being of Christ (10.7b), and boasting too much of his authority (10.8). The charge that causes Paul the greatest difficulty is that he 'robbed the other churches' (11.8). This relates to the collection and to Paul's refusal of remuneration for his services. Paul is forced to defend himself against such accusations.[15]

---

that 'in reading through the epistle one might have supposed that Paul was defending himself, his integrity and also his position and authority. This is not so; what he is doing he does as a responsible Christian and apostle... His language is in the strictest sense theological language and his objectives are theological'. Mary Douglas (*Cultural Bias*, p. 6) calls attention to the fact that theology and social environment are interrelated and that a social context develops arguments that naturally sustain it. Traditionally, biblical studies have focused on conflict in terms of conflicting theologies; a social sciences model points out the need to consider rivalry, competition and even jealousy as integral to any conflict.

12.   Impersonal legitimate authority is that which inheres in the person, and impersonal legitimate authority is that which inheres in the office or task. See Malina, *Christian Origins*, p. 117-19.

13.   Malina, *Christian Origins*, pp. 118-19.

14.   'Acting in wordly fashion' (2 Cor. 10.2) can be understood two ways: Paul is acting out of worldly egocentric motives, or he is without spiritual power. See Talbert, *Reading Corinthians*, p. 113.

15.   Accepting money demonstrates the superiority of the missionary over the congregation as well as the importance of the congregation for the missionary's task. In 12.16b Paul compares himself ironically with his opponents. The comparison suggests that they viewed Paul as staging a clever deception: what he did not dare to

The outsiders also challenge the basis of Paul's authority: his claim to have laid the foundation of the community and his apostolic credentials. They seek for themselves the Corinthians' loyalty and obedience. In this controversy, the following elements must be considered: (1) the titles claimed by Paul's adversaries; (2) their concern for measuring competence; and (3) the importance of letters of recommendation.

The titles associated with the outsiders include διάκονοι χριστοῦ (2 Cor. 11.13), ἀπόστολοι (2 Cor. 11.13),[16] ἐργάται δόλιοι (2 Cor. 11.13). Like Paul, the outsiders see themselves as Christ's representatives; they claim to be apostles and missionaries, like the other apostles and missionaries of the early church. These terms reveal different convictions about the proper manner and legitimate basis of representation. At stake is the meaning of 'apostle'.[17] From the beginning of ch. 10, the polemic focuses on how an apostle is to appear in public.

The outsiders, presenting themselves as apostles in their own right, lay before the Corinthians their claims to impersonal legitimate authority, namely, their status as apostles; and their credentials are impressive.[18] They also claim an authority based on personal qualifications.[19] In 11.22–12.10 Paul boasts of his merits, asserting that he has been forced to do so because of the boasts of others. Their standards of competence include: background (11.22), accomplishments (11.23-33), visions and revelations (12.1-10), and miracles (12.11-13). Using these standards, the outsiders are able to prove their

request directly by remuneration, he tried to get indirectly, through the collection. See Georgi, *Opponents*, pp. 241-42.

See J. Paul Sampley, 'Paul, His Opponents in 2 Corinthians 10–13, and the Rhetorical Handbooks', in J. Neusner, P. Borgen, E.S. Frerichs and R. Horsley (eds.), *The Social World of Formative Christianity and Judaism: Essays in Tribute to Howard Clark Kee* (Philadelphia: Fortress Press, 1988), pp. 162-77 (165-67).

16.   Paul refers to the outsiders as ψευδαπόστολοι. He would not have done this unless his opponents had seen themselves as ἀπόστολοι.

17.   For a discussion of 'apostolate' see Georgi, *Opponents*, pp. 32-39.

18.   Malina, *Christian Origins*, p. 118. According to Georgi *(Opponents*, p. 39) the outsiders came to Corinth as 'missionaries of the early church who thought they were good at what they were doing, apparently with good reason. In so doing they had not acted contrary to the general practice of their contemporaries and the applicable criteria; on the contrary one may ask whether the zeal of professional missionaries of the early church is not manifested here before a congregation with missionary interest'.

19.   Malina, *Christian Origins*, pp. 117-18 defines both personal and impersonal legitimate authority.

worth in the missionary competition and to impress the Corinthians.

In his boastings Paul cites three titles used by the outsiders: Ἐβραῖοι, Ἰσραηλῖται, σπέρμα Ἀβραάμ. These titles claim superior and primary status[20] and are set over against Paul's claims to be the 'father', that is, the founder of the Corinthian community.

συστατικῶν ἐπιστολῶν are an important factor in the debate,[21] and another element in the adversaries' propaganda. Letters of recommendation contained the achievements of the persons recommended and served to introduce their carriers to a community and to attest to what they were able to do. Georgi sees a reference to this kind of recommendation in 2 Cor. 12.11,[22] where Paul reproaches the congregation for not recommending him. In Paul's view, it is the community's responsibility to recommend its preachers.

Therefore, letters of recommendation as well as official titles and personal qualifications provided proof of the outsiders' right to the Corinthians' loyalty and obedience. Some in the Corinthian community were holding up the outsiders as the model for true apostleship;[23] by comparison, Paul comes off second best. His attempt in 1 Corinthians to build group loyalties around his leadership seems to have failed.

Although Titus, whom Paul sent to Corinth shortly after the writing of 1 Corinthians, was well received and succeeded in organizing the collection for Jerusalem (2 Cor. 12.18; 8.5, 10; 9.2), Paul's primary objective was not realized: after Titus's departure there were renewed tensions.[24] The Corinthians give their loyalty to outsiders, who presented themselves as apostles. Paul sends a letter (including 2.14–7.4)[25] to redress the situation and to persuade those wavering in their loyalty to him. He briefly visits Corinth, and the conflict reaches a climax (2 Cor. 2.1-11 and 7.5-16). Paul then writes another letter (2 Cor. 10–13) in which he risks making a fool of himself (2 Cor. 12.11).

---

20. See Georgi, *Opponents*, pp. 41-60 for a full discussion of these terms.

21. The phrase occurs sixteen times in the New Testament; thirteen of these are in Paul's authentic letters, eight are in 2 Cor. 2.14–7.4 and 10–13.

22. Georgi, *Opponents*, p. 244.

23. Talbert, *Reading Corinthians*, p. 118.

24. If the conflicts causing the social drama are not effectively resolved, there will be disturbances within the social unit. See Turner, *Dramas*, p. 41.

25. The tone of this letter is still conciliatory. It is hard to imagine that ἀδικία (2 Cor. 7.12) had already taken place. See Georgi, *Opponents*, p. 24 n. 65.

The letter regains the Corinthians' loyalty.

This is the sequence of events reconstructed by Dieter Georgi;[26] 1.1–2.13 and 7.5-10 form a final letter of reconciliation. Barrett considers chs. 10–13 the final fragment of the letters; chs. 2–7 are Paul's overly optimistic reaction to Titus's overly optimistic report. Barrett believes that the conflict to which chs. 10–13 respond erupted after this communication.[27] For our purposes, it is not crucial whether chs. 10–13 followed or preceded 1.1–2.13 and 7.5-10. Both Georgi and Barrett believe that this section represents Paul's most impassioned plea and the means by which he regains the loyalty and obedience of the Corinthians.[28]

In 2 Corinthians 10–13 Paul is obliged once again to address the situation in Corinth. This time his relationship to the Corinthians is in jeopardy; he is 'fighting in a corner for his life',[29] and he uses numerous arguments to convince the community. The paramount question is: who will command the group's loyalties?

One important argument is found in 11.2-3 and in 11.13-14. Here Paul accuses his opponents of being agents of Satan. He compares the community to a spotless bride whose purity is under attack (11.2). As Eve was deceived by the devil, represented by a snake, so now the Corinthians are in danger of pollution at the hands of Satan's envoys.[30] These verses are linked to 11.14, where Satan is said to be capable of disguising himself as an angel of light, as in the deception

26.   Georgi, *Opponents*, pp. 16-18.

27.   Barrett, *2 Corinthians*, pp. 10-21.

28.   See Barrett, *2 Corinthians*, p. 21 and Georgi, *Opponents*, p. 17. If ch. 10–13 preceded 1.1–2.13 and 7.5-10, their place at the end of 2 Cor. is evidence of Paul's success. If chs. 10–13 followed 1.1–2.13 and 7.5-10, their survival is evidence of Paul's success in winning over the Corinthians. Clement's letter to Corinth refers to 1 Cor. and to Paul as an example whom the Corinthians could respect (1 Clem. 5.5-7). Ernest Best in *Second Corinthians* (Atlanta: John Knox, 1987), p. 139 concludes that the author of 1 Clem. would not have argued in this way had not Paul and his writings been held in honour in Corinth, nor would the Corinthians have preserved so trenchant a criticism of themselves had they permanently rejected Paul.

29.   Turner, *Dramas*, p. 41.

30.   Talbert (*Reading Corinthians*, p. 120) relates 11.3 to a historical evil as described in Gen. 3 and a metaphysical evil originating with the watchers of Gen. 6 or with Satan. In the context of 2 Cor. 11.3, it is not certain whether Eve's deception is simply that of being led astray or is to be understood in terms of sexual seduction by the snake, through which she lost her virginity. Talbert believes the latter alternative fits Paul's image better.

of Eve.[31] The Corinthians must guard their bodily orifices against Satan's agents who will corrupt their innocence with false teaching. There is the threat of 'another Jesus' and 'a different gospel' (11.4) being preached.

In anthropological analysis this is called 'witchcraft accusation'.[32] It is not about black cats and broomsticks; it is a social phenomenon: one's enemy or rival is accused of being either the devil or someone acting under the devil's power.[33] Mary Douglas describes the witch as

> someone whose inside is corrupt; he works harm on his victims by attacking their pure, innocent insides. Sometimes he sucks out their soul and leaves them with empty husks, sometimes he poisons their food, sometimes he throws darts which pierce their bodies. And then again he needs access to their inner bodily juices, faeces, semen, spittle before he can hurt them. Often such bodily excretions are the weapons of his craft. If we were to make an analysis of the symbols of attack, I predict we would find a close correspondence between the experience of the social system and the kind of attack most feared. Soul sucking and poisoning we would expect to be practised by the witch within the local community.[34]

Consequently, a community must discern and expel the devil's envoy.

One of Satan's most dangerous advantages is the ability to appear other than he is. Accordingly, his human agents do not show their true colours; instead Satan uses an apparently good person to lead others

31. In *Apoc. Mos.* 17 Eve recalls the event: 'When the angels ascended to worship God, then Satan appeared in the form of an angel and sang hymns like the angels. And I bent over the wall and saw him, like an angel.' In the related *Vita Adae et Evae* 9.1, Satan transformed himself into the brightness of angels and went to Eve. The Slavonic text, 38.1 reads: 'The devil came to me, wearing the form and brightness of an angel'. See Barrett, *Essays on Paul*, p. 67.

32. Douglas, *Natural Symbols*, p. 111.

33. Douglas, *Natural Symbols*, p. 113: 'Somehow we must bring the association with cats and broomsticks under control by eliciting some general characteristics of these beliefs. First to accuse of witchcraft is to accuse of evil practice on a cosmic scale. The witch is no ordinary thief or adulterer, or even a common traitor. He is accused of a perverted nature, or of alliance with the enemies of human kind, in Europe with the devil, in other continents with carnivorous predators. He is associated symbolically with the reverse of the way that a normal human lives, with night instead of day. His powers are abnormal, he can fly, be in two places at once, change his shape. Above all, he is a deceiver, someone whose external appearance does not automatically betray his interior nature.'

34. Douglas, *Natural Symbols*, pp. 113-14.

astray. 'The more impressive the person, the more godly the appearance, the greater became the chance that Satan's ally would be effective.'[35]

In 2 Cor. 10.3-6 Paul describes the battle he is waging with these
agents of Satan. The metaphor is extensive: Paul has weapons which
will demolish fortifications (πρὸς καθαίρεσιν ὀχυρωμάτων); he is
waging a campaign (στρατευόμεθα, στρατεία); he has spiritual
weapons (ὅπλα); he is prepared to punish every disobedience (πᾶσαν
παρακοήν).[36] At Corinth a state of war exists, and the whole
community is in peril.[37]

Paul's attempts to persuade the Corinthians to give him their loyalty
presents a dualistic view in which the cosmos is divided into opposing
forces of good and evil: Paul the Apostle against the Super Apostles or
False Apostles; the Gospel of Christ against Another Jesus or a Different Gospel; the Authorized Preacher from God against Unauthorized
Agents from Satan. According to Neyrey, Paul argues that

> he is legitimate, they are not; his doctrine is authentic, theirs is not; his
> spirit is pure, theirs is demonic and polluted. He is spiritual, they are
> worldly; he is God's representative, they are Satan's henchmen.[38]

In the context of a competitive society, marked by rival claims of
leadership, this accusation serves to defame Paul's rivals and to undermine their leadership claims. In essence, witchcraft accusations are the
language of social control.[39] If the witches, that is, Paul's opponents,
are expelled, schism is prevented and Paul regains his position of
authority within the community.

Besides witchcraft accusations Paul also uses the symbolic media
(GSM) of belonging or commitment and goal attainment or power.[40]
Paul refers to his 'acts and services' on behalf of the Corinthians. He
preached the gospel (10.14b) without any cost to them (11.7) and
without burdening anyone (11.9; 12.13-14, 16). The Corinthians are
the beneficiaries of 'signs and wonders and mighty works' which Paul
did among them (12.12). Since they are in his debt, he has a right to

35. See Dennis Owen, 'Spectral Evidence', p. 238.
36. Abraham Malherbe, 'Antisthenes and Odysseus, and Paul at War', *HTR* 76
(1983), pp. 143-73 (144).
37. Neyrey, 'Witchcraft Accusations', p. 165.
38. Neyrey, 'Witchcraft Accusations', p. 167.
39. Neyrey, 'Bewitched', p. 97.
40. See Malina, *Christian Origins*, pp. 76-83.

their loyalty. They are his children, and, like a parent, he will gladly spend everything to help them, without demanding financial compensation (12.14-15). In speaking this way Paul evokes feelings of shame from the Corinthians for their disloyalty.[41]

In responding to the charges laid against him by his opponents (10.1-8; 11.8), Paul appeals to the emotions[42] of the Corinthians by cataloguing his hardships and sufferings (11.21b-27). He also mentions the daily pressure of his anxiety for all the churches (11.28). Paul's language in 11.21b ('whatever anyone dares to boast of... I also dare to boast of') suggests that the Corinthians owe *him* greater loyalty than they owe to anyone else.

Commitment can be either weak or strong. It is weak when persons feel emotional ties to many people or groups of people; it is strong when a person has only a few loyalties. Commitments are ranked in terms of priorities: here Paul is asking the Corinthians to give priority to their commitment to him.[43]

Power implies the threat of physical coercion (1 Cor. 4.21), and inflated power has too little coercion to make it effective.[44] In 1 Corinthians there were indications that Paul knew his ability to command obedience might be weak.[45] According to 2 Cor. 7.12, there has been an attack upon him within the congregation. When he departed suddenly after this episode, he was accused of being a person with weak bodily presence (10.10-11), that is, with inflated power.

To counter this accusation, Paul threatens not to 'spare' his opponents in the community (13.2). His recitation of his visions and revelations (12.1-4) implies a divine right to require the Corinthians to do

---

41. Malina, *Christian Origins*, pp. 78-80.

42. Paul uses the GSM of influence when he justifies his refusal to take remuneration. However this appeal is minimal, when compared with the other two GSM. Sampley ('Rhetorical Handbooks', p. 167) states, '... the rhetoricians realized that such proofs and disputations of charges were merely a part of the total effort to cause the judge, jury or audience to decide in favour of the defendants. Proofs, it is true, may induce the judges to regard our case as superior to that of our opponents, but the appeal to the emotions will do more, for it will make them wish our case to be better. And what they wish they will also believe (Quint. 6.2.5).'

43. Malina, *Christian Origins*, p. 79.

44. Malina, *Christian Origins*, pp. 82-83.

45. He uses the GSM of influence, which is a secondary type of appeal in a strong group setting. It is consensual rather than obligatory and suggests that the ability to demand compliance is weak. See Malina *Christian Origins*, p. 88.

what he says. In the Hellenistic world, God or the high god was the
ultimate wielder of power. Hence, the closer one was to God in the
hierarchy of power ranking, the more power one had.[46] Paul's presence in highest heaven, where he heard 'things which cannot be told'
(v. 4), confirms his place in the hierarchy of power.

When Paul calls himself a 'fool'[47] and boasts of his weakness and
suffering (12.7-10), he is appealing to inter-dependency and commu-
nion.[48] Turner gives us an example of this kind of appeal: after
forcing a political opponent into exile, the main political faction of
Muhanza village began to have second thoughts about their actions.
Their consciences began to trouble them, and they began to think:

> Was he not blood of their blood, born from the same womb. . . as they?
> Had he not been part of their corporate life? Had he not contributed to
> their welfare, paying for the education of their children, finding jobs for
> their young men when he was a foreman on a government road gang for
> the PWD?[49]

The end result was that the man's plea to return was allowed; a new
divination found him not guilty of the charges and made an outsider
responsible for the use of sorcery.[50] Paul hoped that the use of images
of inversion[51] would enable him to return to power and would lead to
the expulsion of the outsiders.

The battle in 2 Corinthians is over power and loyalty: who is in
control? Outsiders[52] have come to Corinth and challenged the legiti-

46. Malina, *Christian Origins*, p. 83.
47. Paul calls himself a fool or foolish many times in these chapters: 11.1,
ἀφροσύνης ; 11.16, ἄφρονα (twice); 11.17, ἀφροσύνη; 11.19, ἀφρόνων; 11.21,
ἀφροσύνη; 12.6, 11 ἄφρων.
48. Turner, *Dramas*, pp. 49-50.
49. Turner, *Dramas*, p. 49.
50. Turner, *Dramas*, p. 49.
51. Carolyn Walker Bynum, 'Women's Stories, Women's Symbols: A Critique
of Victor Turner's Theory of Liminality', in Robert L. Moore and Frank E. Reynolds
(eds.), *Anthropology and the Study of Religion* (Chicago: Centre for the Scientific
Study of Religion, 1984), p. 106. Images of inversion occur when Paul calls himself
a fool and boasts of weakness.
52. Paul's opponents have been taken to be: (1) Judaizers who wished to force
the Jewish law on new converts; (2) enthusiasts who desired a wholly spiritual and
charismatic faith; (3) 'divine men' who claimed to have supernatural powers;
(4) gnostics. Barrett (*Essays on Paul*, p. 4) argues that Paul is opposed by two
groups. See Georgi, *Opponents*, pp. 1-9 for a history of interpretation.

macy of Paul's leadership. Factionalism had already pervaded the community, and the arrival of outsiders created an escalation of the crisis. Whether the outsiders were able to bring the disparate groups at Corinth into some sort of unity or whether they somehow rendered powerless the other factions which were identified in 1 Corinthians is difficult to determine, since Paul's overriding concern is to counter their claims to authority and priority within the community.[53]

Since the issue in 2 Corinthians is group loyalty around Paul's leadership, the contest of grid, so prominent in 1 Corinthians 7, seems no longer important.[54] Although there is no mention of marriage or celibacy, David Balch finds the theme of asceticism in ch. 3. He believes that ascetic ideas were still a part of the Corinthians' practice, since the interpretation of Exodus 34 in ch. 3 is consonant with that found in 1 Corinthians 7:

> If the opponents of Paul in II Cor. iii took their theology seriously, then some members of this Corinthian Christian party would have become ascetics. More concretely, I think that the theology of Paul's opponents in II Cor. iii was one source of the asceticism which appears in I Cor. vii.[55]

Balch's arguments would link the opposition to Paul in 2 Corinthians with the anti-structure faction in 1 Corinthians 7. 2 Corinthians cannot be used as proof that the issues of grid which predominated in 1 Corinthians 7, no longer exist; rather, concern about grid has become secondary in a competition for leadership.

In *Cultural Bias* Douglas speaks of the relationship between grid and group. When one pulls against the other, the tension promotes dialogue within society. However, when one wins out against the other, there is a slide towards strong group or low grid.[56] If there was no movement in the conflict reflected in 1 Corinthians 7 after Paul's redressive measures and each faction maintained the absoluteness of its stance, the Corinthians' loyalty would be to their particular faction, rather than to the church. As a result, not only would the community

---

53.   Although Paul speaks to the Corinthians as a whole in chs. 10–13, it is doubtful whether all the Corinthians supported the person who attacked Paul. Perhaps they were confused by what was taking place and therefore did not act.

54.   Some interpreters believe that issues of grid were no longer a problem within the community. See Barrett, *Essays on Paul*, p. 6.

55.   Balch, 'Backgrounds', p. 361.

56.   See Douglas, *Cultural Bias*, p. 13.

be threatened but Paul's relationship to that community would be undermined.

Accordingly, Paul's need to build group strength and to reassert his authority over the community would override all other concerns. However, the persistent question of authority and leadership within the community also indicates that Paul was unsuccessful in 1 Corinthians in convincing the Corinthians' that their commitment to one another and to him was more important than the issue raised in 1 Corinthians 7. Probably each side continued to maintain the absoluteness of its stance in the dispute over marriage.

There is evidence that Paul's appeals for the Corinthians' loyalty in 2 Corinthians 10–13 were successful,[57] How that would specifically affect the conflict over marriage is difficult to determine except that, according to Douglas, 'every time a member appeals successfully to the paramount need to ensure the survival of the group, its being in existence can be used as a more powerful justification for controlling individuals.'[58]

As long as a community is small, it can remain viable even with an ambiguous role structure; however, when the community reaches a certain size, only certain limited targets can be achieved without defining this structure more sharply.[59] The need for this kind of clarification is seen in the struggle over the root metaphor which took place in those communities that recognized Paul's authority, but sought to reinterpret him for their own time and situation. It is also visible in 1 Clement

Colossians and Ephesians

The debate over the authenticity of Colossians focuses on style, language and thought. Even though this letter was probably not written by Paul, the similarities between it and the authentic epistles favour a close connection between the author and the apostle.[60] The linguistic,

---

57. See n. 29.

58. Douglas, *Cultural Bias*, p. 13.

59. Douglas, *Natural Symbols*, p. 114.

60. In favour of Deutero-Pauline authorship, see E. Lohse, *Colossians and Philemon* (Philadelphia: Fortress Press, 1971), pp. 177-83; E. Schweitzer, *The Letter to the Colossians* (London: SPCK, 1982), pp. 13-16; E.P. Sanders, 'Literary Dependence in Colossians', *JBL* 85 (1966), pp. 25-45 (28-45). In favour of Pauline

stylistic and theological features of Ephesians make its pseudonymity even more probable.[61] The parallels between Ephesians and the other letters in the Pauline corpus suggest that the purpose of the author was to use Pauline traditions to exhort the community.[62]

Paul's understanding of the Christian faith was embedded in the minds and actions of the members of these communities, and therefore the traditional materials in Colossians and Ephesians were used to interpret new situations.[63] As in Gal. 3.28, 1 Cor. 12.13 and 7.18-23, the pairs 'Jew and Greek', 'slave and free' appear in Col. 3.11. Again the context refers to baptism.[64] Galatians and Colossians refer respectively to 'putting on Christ' (Gal. 3.27) and 'putting on the new person' (Col. 3.11).

However, there are also striking differences. In Colossians, Barbarian or non-Greek and Scythian are not juxtaposed antithetically but listed side by side. 'Male and female' (Gal. 3.28) is not included in the Colossians passage.

Furthermore, the two pairs are used for different purposes in the three passages. In Gal. 3.28 Paul explains how the entry of Jews and Gentiles and slaves and free persons into one community is to be understood. In 1 Cor. 7.17-24 he urges those in all four groups to 'remain as you were when called'. This advice served to unify the group, while at the same time, it left the structure of roles and

authorship, see R. Martin, *Colossians and Philemon* (London: Oliphants, 1974), pp. 32-40; F.F. Bruce, *Epistles*, pp. 28-33; W.G. Kümmel, *Introduction to the New Testament* (Nashville: Abingdon Press, 1975), pp. 340-46.

61. See E.J. Goodspeed, *The Meaning of Ephesians* (Chicago: University of Chicago Press, 1933); C.L. Mitton, *The Epistle to the Ephesians* (London: Marshall, Morgan & Scott, 1973), pp. 2-18. In favour of Pauline authorship, see Bruce, *Epistles*, pp. 229-46.

62. On the connection between Eph. and authentic Pauline writings, see Mitton, *Ephesians*, pp. 13-17. Mitton understands Eph. to be a presentation of Pauline theology made relevant for the author's own day. As an example, he points to Eph. 2.8-9, which includes a description of Paul's teaching but also shows how interpretative modifications are introduced to make Pauline affirmations more intelligible to the later situation addressed in Eph.

63. See MacDonald, *Pauline Churches*, p. 88. A process of constancy and change sees traditional materials being expanded to include new understandings while at the same time providing categories against which to interpret new understandings.

64. In 1 Cor. 7.17-24 Paul speaks not of baptism but of 'calling'. However, Bartchy, (*Slavery*, p. 165, n. 568) relates 'calling' to baptism.

relationships within the community unclear.

In Colossians the author's intention is to generate unity among group members:

> The unity generating function of Col. 3.11 is especially visible when one considers its location within a series of ethical exhortations. Numerous virtues are associated with putting on the new man (Col. 3.15-17).[65]

After the baptismal formula comes a pattern for living based on a sharper definition of roles than we find in 1 Corinthians 7. The unity described by the author is specifically related to structure, and roles and relationships within the community are defined in hierarchical terms. Although there are opposing viewpoints about the origin and function of the New Testament *Haustafeln*, the patriarchal kinship structure, with roles and relationships based on marriage is clearly the model for relations among church members.[66]

But although the structure of church relationships is clarified, some ambiguity concerning grid remains: a woman named Nympha has a church in her house (Col. 4.15). At this stage, leadership within the church community is not restricted to a household structure dominated by a male who is husband, master and father.

In Colossians the relationships between church members affirm the patrilineal kinship system. Believers are encouraged as part of their Christian duty to obey their superiors (5.18, 22). Their 'being in Christ' demands a respect for societal distinctions; it does not bring equality.

It is within the slave and master relationship (Col. 3.22–4.1) that justifications encouraging societal distinctions appear at greatest length. The slave will receive a heavenly reward for showing proper respect and obedience. However, both master and slave are under the same master, Jesus Christ, and the master of the household is

65. MacDonald, *Pauline Churches*, p. 104.
66. An interpretation of the origin and function of the New Testament *Haustafeln* has a lengthy history; see, L. Hartman, 'Some Unorthodox Thoughts on the "Household-Code Form"', in Neusner, Borgen, Frerichs, Horsley (eds.), *Social World*, pp. 220-22 and Verner, *Household*, pp. 16-23. Verner concludes his history: 'these opposing viewpoints underline the fact that there is still little clarity on the way in which the *Haustafeln* were composed and/or transmitted and on how they functioned'. Crouch's (*Origin*) contention that the *Haustafeln* reveal social tension and a move toward social liberation among women and slaves is rejected by other scholars. See Balch, *Wives*.

reminded of the equality of all Christians in the heavenly order.[67]

The author seeks to clarify the ambiguity in Paul's symbolic universe in favour of a hierarchical pattern of relationships. Unlike the letter to Philemon, in which Paul uses 'master', 'slave' and 'brothers' to order the relationship between Philemon and Onesimus, in Colossians there is only the language of hierarchy and structure. Here also some ambiguity concerning grid remains: although the preference is for structure which emphasizes differences among Christians, qualifying statements about how the obligations of hierarchy should be lived out by the individual in the dominant role lessen the absoluteness of the reinterpretation.

In the Ephesians code (5.21–6.9) it is the husband and wife relationship that is most developed. Thirteen verses concern this pair of opposites, while only nine are directed to the remaining groups. The exhortation to married persons contains ideas related to the structural understanding of the root metaphor found in 1 Corinthians.

The author refers to Christ's 'sanctification' of the church (Eph. 5.26-27; 1 Cor. 7.14); the husband is called as the head of the wife (Eph. 5.23; 1 Cor. 11.3). However, certain other statements in the authentic Pauline text are strikingly absent: man is not independent of woman (1 Cor. 11.11); man is born of woman (1 Cor. 11.12); 'how do you know, wife or husband, whether or not you will save your spouse?' (1 Cor. 7.16); each spouse should give the other his or her conjugal rights (1 Cor. 7.3); each spouse is master of the other's body (1 Cor. 7.4).

In 1 Corinthians 7 Paul says that marriage and sexual intercourse is 'good' but singleness and celibacy is 'better' (v. 38); he urges those who are married to live as though the roles and statuses associated with marriage no longer existed (vv. 29-31); he associates purity in women with the single state (v. 34). In Ephesians, however, purity is related to the obligations of the marriage relationship (submission/ nurture and love), and these obligations include sexual intercourse (Eph. 5.32-33). The author compares the relationship between husband and wife to that between Christ and the church, and, in this way, provides a powerful theological justification for an ordering of

---

67. Theissen (*Social Setting*, p. 108) calls this conception love-patriarchalism, a system in which the social differences continue, although all relationships are to be marked with a spirit of concern and respect.

husband and wife relationships within the church according to a hierarchical pattern.

The author cites Gen. 2.24 (Eph. 5.31) and interprets the union between Adam and Eve as prefiguring the great mystery of Christ's union with his church (Eph. 5.32). This great mystery, in turn, offers a paradigm for Christian marriage.[68] Macdonald states:

> In light of the elaborate argumentation made to support the subjection of wife to husband and to elevate the married state, it seems likely that the development visible in Ephesians represents an important step in the patriarchalization of Pauline communities. The wives in the Ephesian community or communities who heard the household code, were being given clearly defined roles in the household which undoubtedly had ramifications for their roles in the church.[69]

A move to higher grid is visible, but at the same time, although the justification for hierarchy and structure is more elaborate than in Colossians, leadership within the Christian church is still not specifically tied to the patriarchal household structure.

The Pastoral Epistles and the Apocryphal Acts of the Apostles

The struggle between structure and normative *communitas* or permanent anti-structure can be seen most clearly when the Pastoral Epistles and the Apocryphal Acts of the Apostles are set side by side. Although scholarship has been unable to agree on the relationship between the stories in the *Acts* and the Pastoral epistles,[70] Dennis MacDonald concludes that the author of the Pastorals sought to show the socially

---

68.   Pagels, 'Adam and Eve', pp. 149-50.
69.   MacDonald, *Pauline Churches*, p. 120.
70.   Dennis R. MacDonald, *The Legend and the Apostle: The Battle for Paul in Story and Canon* (Philadelphia: Westminster Press, 1983), pp. 17-53 and Dennis R. MacDonald, 'Virgins, Widows and Paul in Second Century Asia Minor', in P.J. Achtemeier (ed.), *SBLSP* (Missoula, MT: Scholars Press, 1979), pp. 169-84. The author of these Acts alludes to the Pastorals only to set the scene. He censures Demas who, 'in love with this present world' (2 Tim. 4.10), deserted Paul; Alexander the coppersmith, who did the apostle 'great harm' (2 Tim. 4.14); and Hermogenes, whom the Paul of the Pastorals includes among 'all those in Asia' who 'turned away from me' (2 Tim. 1.15), apparently offended by the 'bitter' severity of his preaching (Act. Pl. and Thekl.l).

radical Paul of the legends to be a distortion and thus to silence the storytellers.[71]

Since folk-stories and legends[72] adapt themselves to the cultural, social, economic and physical characteristics of the community in which they are told, they may reveal historical information, particularly the points of conflict within that community.[73] Burrus finds three historical realities reflected in the chastity stories: (1) The woman's proper place is in the inner world of her husband's home. By remaining in the home she accepts her place in society, marriage and sexual relationship. Every time she leaves the house she is crossing boundaries and provoking disapproval, hostility and suspicion; (2) the role that the Roman government plays in backing the social order of the communities also reflects the world of the storytellers. The social order is that of marriage and the household, and marriage becomes a political as well as a social concern; (3) the narrators and audiences of these folk-stories are women who experienced tension within the institution of marriage and felt themselves in conflict with

---

71.   The *Acts* are difficult to date. In their written form they date from the late second and early third century; however, if they are literary adaptations of folk-stories, rather than *ad hoc* creations, their origins can be much earlier. See MacDonald, *Legend*, pp. 62-66. Martin Dibelius and Hans Conzelmann (*The Pastoral Epistles* [Philadelphia: Fortress Press, 1972], p. 36 n. 89) conclude: 'it seems likely that they (the *Apocryphal Acts*) point to movements similar to those which must be presupposed for the context of our author, and especially of his opponents'.

72.   See Burrus, *Women*, p. 107. Scholars disagree over whether the chastity stories are literary works or based on folk-stories. See Virginia Burrus 'Chastity as Autonomy: Women in the Stories of the Apocryphal Acts', *Semeia*, 38 (1986), pp. 101-17 (103-104) for arguments supporting the folk-story theory. Although many have favoured the theory that the chastity stories are literary creations modelled on the genre of the Hellenistic romantic novel, a striking difference is found in how each genre views society. The romantic novel affirms the values of marriage and family, both of which are aspects of the traditional social order. The Christian chastity story is opposed to the traditional social order and, above all, to marriage and family. 'Whereas the novel begins with mutual love and ends with marriage and reunion with family, the chastity story begins with the woman's attraction to the apostle and his message and ends with the woman's triumphant attainment of singleness. The heroine and the hero of the novel leave home and discover persecution; the woman of the chastity story does not journey but experiences alienation in her own family and community.' Burrus, 'Chastity as Autonomy', p. 106.

73.   Burrus, *Women*, p. 108.

the social and political powers that backed the institution.[74]

Although she admits that 'unassailable historical "facts"' are not available to support her reconstruction, Burrus considers other features of these stories to be also historically accurate.[75] The heroines in the *Acts* reflect historical characters who, inspired by Christianity, defied their husbands, families, societal and political rulers, and renounced marriages.[76] After leaving their husbands, these women belonged to groups of so-called 'widows' who were supported by the church.[77] Whatever their financial status, 'it is likely that the women who separated from their families would have found new "families" in communities of single women'.[78] The role of the apostle is to legitimize the unmarried life-style of the women who told these stories.[79]

The women in the *Acts* resist family pressure, ostracism, threats of rape, torture and sentences of death in order to follow the virgin life. In some of these stories the celibate's bridal purity is explicitly contrasted with the pollutions of sexuality incurred through the fall. The virgin disciple of the *Acts of John*, promising darkly to 'reveal more fully the mystery of the marital union', declares that 'it is a device of the serpent... an ambush of Satan, a device of the jealous one... a shedding of blood... a falling from reason, a token of punishment... a comedy of the devil, hatred of life...'[80] The *Acts of Thomas*, which shows traces of the baptismal symbolism associated with the root metaphor,[81] juxtaposes the images of an earthly and heavenly marriage. Those who repudiate their obligation to procreate receive the incorruptible and true marriage. In the *Acts of Thomas*

---

74.   Burrus, *Women*, pp. 87-96.

75.   Burrus, *Women*, pp. 96-103.

76.   Burrus, *Women*, p. 97 sees a contemporary parallel in Justin Martyr's *Second Apology*.

77.   S. Davies, *The Revolt of the Widows: The Social World of the Apocryphal Acts* (Carbondale: Southern Illinois University Press, 1980), pp. 70-94.

78.   Burrus, *Women*, p. 102.

79.   Burrus, *Women*, pp. 103-106. She disagrees with Davies (*Revolt*, p. 35-36), who views the apostles as the last of the charismatic preachers prior to the triumph of institutionalized leadership. Burrus sees a psychological function at work as well as one of social legitimation.

80.   Pagels, 'Adam and Eve', p. 157 citing Act. Jn Fr. 3 in the Ps.-Titus Epistle, Henn.-Wilson II, pp. 160, 209-10.

81.   MacDonald, *Male and Female*, p. 129. In the *Acts of Thomas* asceticism is set forth as a requirement for baptism.

the bride, converted to chastity declares that, in rejecting temporal marriage, she is 'bound to another marriage' with Christ himself.[82] In the worldly bridal chamber the pair are separated and unyoked, but in the true bridal chamber, baptism, they are yoked together. Because the two have become one, they can no longer respond to each other as male and female but must remain sexually ascetic.[83]

By contrast, the Pastoral Epistles are permeated with a concern for the opinion of contemporary society. The advice to bishops (1 Tim. 3.7), young widows (1 Tim. 5.14), young wives (Tit. 2.5), young men (Tit. 2.8), and slaves (1 Tim. 6.1; Tit. 2.10) betrays an anxiety about the effect of the behaviour of these groups of Christians on the reputation of the church.[84]

When these writings are examined from the perspective of the root metaphor which, in 1 Corinthians, encompassed two ways of understanding 'no male and female', we see how the Pastorals attempt to suppress the activity of teachers who appear to threaten the conventional male and female roles in the household of God.[85] Behind the stereotypical accusations of immorality in these letters, Robert Karris finds evidence of an ascetic, gnosticizing group which challenged this church and enjoyed particular success among women. He argues that the author has employed a schema which is traditional to the polemic of philosophers against sophists. Applying form and redaction

82. Pagels, 'Adam and Eve', p. 157.

83. MacDonald, *Male and Female*, pp. 57-60.

84. For example, obedient servanthood is portrayed as Christian witness. MacDonald (*Pauline Churches*, p. 178) states: 'Severe departures from traditional slave-master relationships would be a visible violation of the household relationships fundamental to the society embracing the Christian community and would most certainly provide a stumbling block for the evangelization of the society. There may have been a tendency among the slaves of Christian masters to overstep the traditional boundaries of slave-master relationships on the grounds that Christians were "brothers and sisters". In fact, slaves could find justification for their actions if they read Paul's letter to Philemon. The author of the Pastorals, however, views the slaves among the congregation from the perspective of the slave-owner. The concern is that Christian slaves in general not damage the church's public image by insubordination.'

85. MacDonald (*Pauline Churches*, p. 178) states that the origin of these teachers is unknown, while C.K. Barrett (*The Pastoral Epistles* [Oxford: Clarendon Press, 1963], p. 12) points out that the author of the Pastorals was more concerned to combat the evil effects of their teaching and to note their moral deficiencies than to analyze their beliefs.

criticism to the Pastorals, he concludes that

> [t]he opponents are Jewish Christians who are teachers of the law (1 Tim.
> 1.7; Tit. 3.9; cf. Tit. 1.14). They teach Jewish myths (Tit. 1.14; cf.
> 1 Tim. 1.4; 4.7; 2 Tim. 4.4) and genealogies (1 Tim. 1.4; Tit. 3.9). They
> forbid marriage and enjoin abstinence from food (1 Tim. 4.3-5). They
> teach that the resurrection has already occurred (2 Tim. 2.18). They may
> have had significant success among the womenfolk, especially because of
> their teaching about emancipation (2 Tim. 3.6-7; cf. 1 Tim. 2.11-15; 5.13;
> Tit. 2.5).[86]

2 Timothy 3.6 associates women with false teaching. No other social group in the church is mentioned in this connection. The false teachers are described as making secret attacks on households and capturing gullible women.

The activity of widows is of great concern to the author, and in 1 Tim. 5.3-16 the relationship of widows to the church structure is addressed. These verses contain many difficulties. In spite of the evidence supporting the unity of the text,[87]

> the criteria put forward in it are so numerous and occasionally so
> contradictory that it seems difficult to maintain that vv. 3-8, 16 and vv. 9-
> 15 refer to the same group, that is, that the true widows, (v. 3) are
> identical to the enrolled (καταλέγειν) widows (v. 9). Verses 3-8 and 16,
> for example, emphasize the need and piety of the real widow who is to
> receive assistance (honour) from the church. Verses 9-15, however,
> present standards of age (not less than sixty years) and past behaviour
> (wife of one husband, well attested for good deeds, having brought up
> children, shown hospitality, washed the feet of the saints, relieved the
> afflicted) for the widows who are to be enrolled.[88]

If the passage is viewed as a unity, the implication is that the church would give no financial assistance if a widow did not meet the age requirement. A further anomaly excludes a young widow who follows the injunction to marriage from the circle of widows and from any future assistance from the church, if she were to be widowed a second time. Real widows are poor widows who must depend on the church

---

86.   Robert Karris, 'The Background and Significance of the Polemic of the Pastoral Epistles', *JBL* 92 (1973), pp. 549-64 (562-63).

87.   These verses refer to widows throughout, and there is an inclusio frame (vv. 4, 16).

88.   J.M. Bassler, 'The Widow's Tale: A Fresh Look at 1 Tim. 5.3-16', *JBL* (1984), pp. 23-41 (33-34).

for support and are not necessarily identical with enrolled widows.[89]

Both sections of this passage (vv. 3-8, 16, 9-15) seek to reduce the circle of widows to a minimum. The most stringent restrictions are applied to the younger widows. They are encouraged to marry and cannot be enrolled as widows. The author of the Pastorals wants them to serve the household of God as wives and mothers, and the 'Paul' of the Pastorals stands ready to challenge any ascetic interpretation of Paul's teaching. Enrolled widows are encouraged to teach the younger women to love their husbands and children and to be sensible, pure, domestic, kind and submissive.

The author of the Pastorals seeks to reduce the size of the circle of widows and gives three reasons to support his position: some of the widows are going from house to house saying things with which the author disagrees (5.13); some of the younger widows have broken their pledges to celibacy (5.15); the church is financially burdened (5.16). The primary objection would seem to be their activity as itinerant teachers.[90]

Jouette Bassler raises questions about the increase in the number of widows in the community. If χήρα is understood to include the 'demarried', many recently converted Christian women may have divorced their pagan husbands and other women may have espoused singleness and chastity. She states that the sociological advantages to the latter category of women are numerous:

> The widows of the Pastoral epistles were like the vestal virgins, under special restrictions, but, again like the vestals, these restrictions were not those binding ordinary women. Indeed, widows were remarkably free of these ordinary restraints. Freed from the hierarchical dominance of either father or husband, freed from the demands of childbearing and rearing,

89.   While the mention of enrollment does not necessarily mean that there was an office of widows, the fact that the church keeps such a list and that membership is limited makes the existence of an office seem likely. See MacDonald, *Pauline Churches*, p. 185. The requirement for the enrollment of widows resembles the requirements for the office of bishop, elder and deacon (1 Tim. 3.1-13; Tit. 1.6-9). The expectation that a male office holder should be the husband of one wife is paralleled in the statement that an enrolled widow should have been ἑνὸς ἀνδρὸς γυνή (1 Tim. 5.9). Moreover, the virtues of hospitality (1 Tim. 5.10; 1 Tim. 3.2; Tit. 1.6) are demanded of the widows, as well as of male leaders in the church. See Verner, *Household*, pp. 163-64. Another argument favouring the existence of this office is the rejection of younger widows from enrollment.

90.   MacDonald, *Legend*, p. 74.

freed even from pressing economic concerns, the 'widows' were granted
a degree of freedom usually reserved for the *hetairai*, yet now enhanced
by ecclesiastical respectability and esteem.[91]

If the Pastorals are understood as a reaction to the attitude towards
marriage put forth in the *Acts*, the struggle between structure or
marriage/sexual intercourse and normative *communitas* or singleness/
celibacy in the early second century becomes apparent.[92] The ambiguity of the 'real' Paul provides the material to support the positions
of both sides in the struggle.

In Colossians and Ephesians the struggle between structure and
normative *communitas* led to increasing controls on the role of married women within the household of God. In responding to the popularity of the theology of the *Acts* among women, the Pastorals try to
regulate the circle of widows, which was likely the practical arm of
this movement. Although older widows retain somewhat more power
than married women, their function is to promote the stability of the
household structure within the church:

> The church defined proper widowhood, established for it a code of
> behaviour, and offered social legitimacy to those widows who fulfilled the
> requirements. The clergy, who were men, acted as representatives of the
> community of believers and assumed a spiritual tutelage over widows
> parallel to the legal and social responsibilities exercised by fathers over
> daughters and husbands over wives.[93]

In the Pastorals the patriarchal household structure is affirmed as a
paradigm not only for ordering relationships within the Christian
community but also for defining leadership roles within the church,
and any anti-structural response to this ordering is discouraged.
Household and church are not conceived as separate settings, but constitute a unified sphere within the Christian community. The pattern of
church order is derived from the regulations for family life; the
structure of the house of God is built upon the hierarchical structure

91. Bassler, 'Widow's Tale', p. 36.
92. Scholars who accept the pseudonymity of the Pastorals date them anywhere
between the 80s and the mid-second century. J.L. Moulden (*The Pastoral Epistles:
1 and 2 Timothy, Titus* [Harmondsworth: Penguin Books, 1976], p. 401) and
MacDonald *(Pauline Churches*, p. 159) favour the first quarter of the second century.
93. Marjorie Lightman and William Zeisel, 'Univira: An Example of Continuity
and Change in Roman Society', *CH* 46 (1977), pp. 19-32 (29).

within the family, with its various roles and obligations.[94] However, these structural affirmations are a reaction against the popularity and success of the forces of *communitas*.

Paul intended his redressive measures in 1 Corinthians 7 to build group loyalties. As a result, he left the structure of roles and relationships within the community unclear. Disputes continued, and certain leaders within those communities that claimed allegiance to Paul wrote letters to clarify Paul's ambiguity concerning roles and structure. In the canonical works, his cautious preference for an egalitarian order based on anti-structure is rejected, and ascetic interpretations of his words are excluded.

Other evidence from the second century confirms that the tension between the exponents of singleness/celibacy and those of marriage/ sexual intercourse was not restricted to the *Apocryphal Acts* and the Pastoral Epistles. Disputes existed which involved not only complex doctrinal issues but also controversies over sexual practice. Sayings of Jesus (Mk 10.2-10 and parallels; Mk 12.18-27 and parallels; Lk. 20.30) and Paul's Corinthian correspondence are used by both sides.

Above all, the story of Adam and Eve, which both Jesus and Paul had introduced into the discussions of marriage and sexual relationships, formed the storm centre of the controversy. The anti-structure exponents assumed that Eve was originally meant to remain a 'pure bride' in spiritual union with Adam; marital intercourse with Adam was the sin of *porneia*. For one who is related to Christ as a bride to a bridegroom, marital and extra-marital intercourse become equally adulterous.[95]

As a result of this image, however, singleness/celibacy for women is patterned on the patrilineal kinship model. The duties and obligations of 'wife', which included submission and obedience, are owed to Christ, the 'husband'. Instead of male and female Christians being in an egalitarian relationship of brother and sister, all women, including

94.   The *Haustafeln* in the Pastoral epistles are so different in content and form from that of Col. and Eph. that there is no general agreement as to what verses properly belong to them. The material in 1 Tim. 2.1–6.1 can be considered either as *Haustafeln* that have been expanded by material dealing with church order or as a church order that has incorporated *Haustafeln*. See Dibelius and Conzelmann, *Pastoral Epistles*, pp. 5-6.
95.   Davies, *Revolt*, p. 84.

virgins and widows, were in a hierarchical structure as someone's wife or bride.[96] In spite of this development and the increasing support for marriage and hierarchical relationships within the church, the tension between structure and anti-structure continued to be played out within many Christian communities.[97]

1 Clement

The Christian community at Corinth reflects this tension. 1 Clement is a letter written at the end of the first century to the church in Corinth by the church in Rome.[98] It attests to continued factionalism within that congregation. The letter was occasioned by a revolt against the leaders in the community (1 Clem. 3.3; 44.6–45.1).

What kind of persons stood behind this rebellion? The rebels seem to have claimed to possess spiritual gifts which were not receiving adequate recognition. Bornkamm observes:

> We can recognize fairly clearly that the group of younger men who revolted against the office-bearers in the congregation consisted of pneumatics (23.1; 38.1-2; 48.5-6) and thus were not dissimilar to the opponents of Paul in 2 Corinthians.[99]

Cyril Richardson finds hints in 1 Clement that, besides being pneumatics, the 'younger men' are ascetics who observe continence (38.2)

---

96.   Kraemer (*Ecstatics*, pp. 180-82) describes this image as leading to the social control of women who have attempted to break away from their prescribed roles. Once virginity is related to the hierarchical kinship pattern, women are expected to fulfil certain obligations and roles which are integral to the system. In other words, the ideology of virginity failed to challenge the dominant pattern; rather it adopted the pattern, adding a theological dimension which produced an even more restrictive and coercive system. See Elizabeth Castelli, 'Virginity and its Meaning for Women's Sexuality in Early Christianity', *JFSR* 2 (1986), pp. 61-88 (75-77).

97.   Pagels, 'Adam and Eve', pp. 146-75.

98.   The *Letter of the Church at Rome to the Church of Corinth* was written about 96 CE, and was so highly esteemed in Christian antiquity that for a time it was even reckoned as part of the canon in Egypt and Syria. Ancient tradition ascribes it to a certain Clement, who according to early episcopal lists, was the third bishop of Rome. See C.C. Richardson, *Early Christian Fathers*, I (Philadelphia: Westminster Press, 1953), p. 33.

99.   G. Bornkamm, 'The History and Origin of the So-Called Second Letter to the Corinthians', in K. Aland, *et al.* (eds.), *The Authorship and Integrity of the New Testament* (London: SPCK, 1965), p. 81.

and boast of *gnosis* revealed only to the elite (48.5). They may have spoken in tongues, although the passages in question may also mean simply that they were persuasive speakers (21.5, 57.2).[100]

Women or wives are another group referred to frequently in the letter, often in conjunction with the young men. In 1.3 Clement addresses the congregation and praises them for their former obedience and respect for elders and rulers, for their discipline of younger members and their proper instruction of women or wives. Further, in 21.5-9 the author appeals for respect for rulers, honour for elders, young people who fear the Lord and women who do what is good and show purity of character, modesty and reticence, as well as loving all equally.

In 2.2 the present situation of 'rivalry and envy, strife and sedition, persecution and anarchy, war and captivity' is declared to be the result of an uprising: '"the dishonoured" rose up "against those who were held in honour", those of no reputation against the notable, the stupid against the wise, "the young against their elders"' The theme of rivalry is drawn out in numerous examples (chs. 4–6) which conclude with the statement that 'it was rivalry that estranged wives from their husbands and annulled the saying of our father Adam, 'This is now bone of my bone and flesh of my flesh' (6.3-4).

After pleas to repent, to give up rivalry and to receive God's mercy and kindness (chs. 7–8), the author gives examples of many who have followed God's way and received his benefits (chs. 9–10). In 11.1 Lot is cited as an example of someone who has shown hospitality and religious devotion and so was delivered and not punished like those who turned away. The author continues,

> Of this latter, to be sure, his wife became an example. After quitting the city with him, she changed her mind and fell out with him, with the result that she became a pillar of salt. . . (11.2) In this way it was made quite evident to all that the double-minded and those who question God's power are condemned and become a warning to all generations (11.2).[101]

By falling out with her husband, Lot's wife questioned God's power and so was punished.

Women figure prominently in chs. 54–55. In 54.1 the author speaks of those who caused the schism and suggests that they should say these

---

100. Richardson, *Early Christian Fathers*, p. 34.

101. Richardson, *Early Christian Fathers*, pp. 48-49. All quotations from 1 Clem. are from Richardson's translation.

words: 'If it is my fault that revolt, strife and schism have arisen, I will leave. I will go away wherever you wish, and do what the congregation orders', so that the congregation may live in peace with its appointed leaders. In 55.1 the author continues this theme by referring to kings and rulers who 'have quit their own cities to put an end to sedition'. Specific examples of this kind of sacrifice are women, Judith and Esther, who have gone out from their people and been used by God.

At the end of his letter, the author, on behalf of the rebels, prays to God for forgiveness. Part of his prayer states: 'do not take account of every sin of your slaves and slave girls but cleanse us with the cleansing of your truth, and "guide our steps so that we walk with holy hearts and do what is good and pleasing to you" and to our rulers' (60.2). Young men may be at the heart of the revolt in Corinth, but equally, the evidence points also to the centrality of women or wives in the rebellion.[102]

The author of 1 Clement appeals for order and stability, and relates the Corinthians' former good name to their honouring and respecting elders and rulers and to the hierarchical ordering of the household (1.2-3; 21.6-8). For him church membership implies a specific set of responsibilities toward the group and an acknowledgment of one's place in it.

> Just as Rome remains in peace because all obey the emperor, the Christian community will remain in peace when all obey God, the Master, and remain in subjection to the congregation's leaders. This peace and stability does not arise out of a belief shared by the rulers and the ruled in specific principles of authority, such as those found in Paul's writings. Rather it is posed from above.[103]

---

102. Evidence that the root metaphor of 1 Cor. 7 may have been involved in the rhetoric of the conflict comes from 2 Clem., which K. Donfried (*The Setting of Second Clement in Early Christianity* [Leiden: Brill, 1974]) argues was written by the leaders shortly after their reinstatement. 2 Clem. 12.2 interprets the saying, 'When the two shall become one, and the outside like the inside, and the male with the female, neither male nor female', to mean: 'Furthermore "the male with the female, neither male nor female" means this: that when a brother sees a sister he should not think of her sex, any more than she should think of his'. See C.C. Richardson, 'An Early Christian Sermon: An Anonymous Sermon, Commonly Called Clement's Second Letter' in *idem, Early Christian Fathers*, pp. 183-202. See *Early Christian Fathers*, p. 198.

103. James Jeffers, 'The Influence of the Roman Family and Social Structures on

The author of 1 Clement refers twice to the household: 1.2-3; 21.6-8. In both passages, the *paterfamilias* is the only one addressed directly unlike the *Haustafeln* in Colossians and Ephesians. Furthermore, the obligations of husbands and fathers toward the family are defined simply in terms of their responsibility to govern its conduct.[104] Each passage begins by demanding honour and respect for rulers and elders and then proceeds to describe the duties of the young and wives.[105]

The message is clear: order and harmony must be imposed on the community if dire consequences are to be avoided. This stability comes from treating the church leader as a *paterfamilias* with all other members of the community giving him the respect due to his office. As in the Pastorals, the pattern of church order is derived from the regulations for family life; the structure of the church is built upon the hierarchical structure of the family with its various roles and obligations.

The author of 1 Clement also uses the patron-client model in his arguments, thus demonstrating that he had come to accept social distinctions among Christians as a basis for ordering their interrelationships. Hierarchy based on social status is accepted as proper. He states that '[t]he strong must take care of the weak, and the weak must look up to the strong. The rich man must provide for the poor; the poor must thank God for giving him someone to meet his needs (38.2).'[106]

In Corinth at the end of the first century, factionalism has become

Early Christianity in Rome', in D.J. Lull (ed.) (SBLSP; Chico, CA: Scholars Press, 1988), pp. 373-74.

104. In Col. 3.18–4.1 and Eph. 5.23-69 wives, husbands, children, fathers, slaves and masters are addressed. Also in these codes the duties of those in the dominant position are more extensive. For example, the husband must love his wife like his own body (Eph. 5.33, Col. 3.19); fathers are not to embitter their children (Eph. 6.4, Col. 3.21). See Jeffers, 'Early Christianity', p. 378.

105. At 1.3 the author tells the Corinthian Christians: 'you instructed your women to do everything with a blameless and pure conscience, and to give their husbands the affection they should. You taught them, too, to abide by the rule of obedience and to run their homes with dignity and thorough discretion'; at 21.6-8 we read: 'Let us direct our women to do what is good. Let them reveal a genuine sense of modesty. By their reticence let them show that their tongues are considerate. Let them not play favourites in showing affection but let them love all equally, who fear God'. See Richardson, *Early Christian Fathers*, pp. 43, 54.

106. Richardson, *Early Christian Fathers*, p. 61.

rebellion, and the leaders within the congregation have been removed by young men and women or wives. Although the new leaders are supported by the majority of the congregation,[107] the author of 1 Clement demands that the original leadership be reinstated, and he justifies this move to high-grid by an appeal to Roman political ideology:

> In the same way that the Romans had imposed order on many different nations, order among Roman congregations and in their constituent families could not be expected to arise naturally but must be imposed from above. Like good citizens, the laity needed to recognize that peace would come through their orderly obedience to their office holders. Like obedient members of a *familia*, they needed to realize that peace would result from accepting the direction of their *paterfamilias*, whether the head of a household or an office holder. Finally like good clients they need to show proper deference to their social superiors, who were their leaders.[108]

In 1 Clement none of the ambiguity found in 1 Corinthians 7 remains. Hierarchical structure based on the husband and father is applied to family relationships, but more particularly to church structure. The 'rulers and elders' who are to be honoured and obeyed are like the *paterfamilias*. However, the context of these assertions is a rebellion led by the forces of *communitas*.

Conclusion

According to Turner, the fourth stage in the social drama provides an opportunity to analyze the total course of events and a chance to observe those things which have changed and those things which have stayed the same. In 1 Corinthians 7 both structure and normative *communitas* or permanent anti-structure were recognized within the community. Although Paul expresses a preference for *communitas*, he recognizes a hierarchical ordering in relations between husband and wife when he frames his redressive measures.

2 Corinthians provides no evidence of any development in the preference for structure or normative *communitas*. There the battle is over leadership, authority and group loyalty within the community. If Paul's position of authority was restored, as seems likely, then the Corinthians' loyalty to him and to the community would become more

---

107. Jeffers, 'Early Christianity', p. 374.
108. Jeffers, 'Early Christianity', pp. 383-84.

important than the issue, and an ambiguous relationship between structure and normative *communitas* would persist. However, Paul's authority within the community would create a period of stabilization.

In 1 Clement the author, as the redressive agent, affirms structure and a hierarchical ordering of social relationships as authoritative inside and outside the church. Structure is to prevail over normative *communitas*. Yet the context of this advice is a rebellion led by the forces of normative *communitas*, which are actively receiving community support.

In the period between 2 Corinthians and 1 Clement, those communities which appealed to Paul's authority have provided us with details of a distinct movement towards structure, as structure and normative *communitas* faced each other in new times and new circumstances.

An extended case study seeks to describe constancy and change over a period of time. Mary Douglas uses a grid/ group analysis to chart social change, and by way of illustration points to the continuous cycle of transformation between an egalitarian political order and a hierarchical system among the Kachin people of Burma:

High	2. Higher status obtained through community feasting and territorial expansion to produce absolute surplus. 1. Increasing productivity permits acquisition of wives and therefore children to increase the work force	3. Diminishing yields weaken structure. Inflation makes bride-wealth payments difficult. Loss of status by all except dominant lineage.
Grid		4. Village chiefs rebel against paramount chiefs and assert equality of lineage and status.
Low	5. Mechanisms for future development of surpluses remain intact. Redispersal of population permits forest regrowth for future high yields.	
	Low High	
	Group[109]	

This schema is useful in charting the trajectory of the root metaphor in 1 Corinthians 7.

The social drama at Corinth began at number 4, a mid group/low

109. In Gross and Rayner, *Measuring Culture*, p. 13.

grid position on the diagram. The root metaphor, 'all are children of God, no male and female', brought two kinship systems into conflict, the hierarchical structure of the dominant society and an egalitarian order expressed in anti-structural living. Paul's redressive measures, although showing a preference for the latter, maintained a tension within the social unit between these two structural possibilities. The likelihood is that as long as Paul is able to command the loyalty of the Corinthians, the community is stabilized.

In his redressive measures, Paul lays the basis for the future development of arguments (#5). Subsequent societal pressure gives ascendancy to hierarchical structures and a move to higher grid results (#1). This system seeks to maintain itself through elaborate justifications, using the patrilineal structure to order its religious life (#2). But a tension persists: the egalitarian impulse continues to plead for its worldview and, through folk-lore and anti-structural justifications, exerts pressure for a recognition of the continuing validity of normative *communitas* (#3). A rebellion occurs at Corinth, and the structural representatives are replaced, a move supported by a majority of the congregation (#4). However, the defenders of structure, typified by the author of 1 Clement, reassert their arguments and, the cycle begins all over again.

This cyclical portrayal of the relationship between a hierarchical and an egalitarian order within the Corinthian community reveals the importance of both structure and *communitas* to the process of constancy and change. According to Turner, both are indispensable for human continuity, especially in the area of social creativity where new societal and cultural forms are engendered.[110] If structure is rigorously imposed, it invites either violent revolution or uncreative apathy. In the same way, if *communitas* is maximized, it becomes totalitarian in suppressing all tendencies to develop structural independencies and interdependencies.[111] Both archmodalities need to be safeguarded, 'for in destroying one we destroy both and must then present a distorted account of man with man'.[112]

Using the words of Mario Bunge, Turner describes the proper relationship between structure and anti-structure:

110. Turner, *Dramas*, p. 268.
111. Turner, *Dramas*, p. 268
112. Turner, *Dramas*, p. 52.

Without imagination, without inventiveness, without the ability to conceive hypotheses and proposals, nothing but the 'mechanical' operations can be performed... The invention of hypotheses, the devising of techniques, and the designing of experiments are clear cases of imagination (purely 'liminal') operations, as opposed to 'mechanical' operations... Logic *alone* is incapable of leading a person to new ideas as grammar *alone* is incapable of inspiring poems and as a theory of harmony *alone* is incapable of inspiring sonatas. Logic, grammar and musical theory enable us to detect formal mistakes and good ideas, as well as to develop good ideas, but they do not, as it were, supply the 'substance', the happy idea, the new point of view.[113]

If creativity and growth are to take place within a social unit, neither structure nor *communitas* can exist without the other. When one modality is the form of relationships and order within the social unit, the other is to be looked for in 'the interstices, niches, intervals and on the peripheries'.[114] This means that the scientific observer, through all the changes that take place in a social unit, must watch for those norms and relationships which persist.

Paul's work at Corinth has been referred to as 'community-building institutionalization':

[at] this stage much ambiguity surrounds the question of how members of the community should act and how beliefs should be interpreted. Institutionalization is relatively free to proceed in different directions. We can expect that as the body of tradition grows larger, institutionalization will become set along a more definite course. As problems of management increase, more firmly established guidelines for living will be required.[115]

Because of the severity of the conflict within the community and his own lack of authority, Paul's redressive measures continued to recognize both structure and normative *communitas* or structured anti-structure. The result was a compromise which preserved both structure and *communitas*. The guidelines provided by the redressive agents in Pauline communities after Paul's death gradually resolved this ambiguity in favour of a hierarchical system of statuses and roles. When this system was officially accepted, a new balance of power and

113. Mario Bunge, *Intuition and Science* (Englewood Cliffs, NJ: Prentice–Hall, 1962, p. 80, as quoted in Turner, *Dramas*, pp. 51-52.
114. Turner, *Dramas*, p. 268.
115. MacDonald, *Pauline Churches*, p. 84.

a new basis of legitimation was set up within the church.[116]

Marriage and the household became the way of ordering not only Christian family relationships but ecclesiastical authority and office. Male and female relationships emphasized husband over wife, father over children, especially daughters, and male church leaders over widows and virgins.[117] Thus each female role (wife, widow, virgin) is brought under the authority of the representatives of structure and ordered according to their principles.

However, the anti-structural response, normative *communitas*, is not completely erased. The primary role of women in normative *communitas* which was seen in 1 Corinthians 7 is also evident in 1 Clement and in the folk-lore of the later period. In addition, at Corinth and in other Pauline churches the voice of anti-structure and *communitas* continued to be heard within the hierarchical structure. Christians continued to refer to themselves in terms of a fictive kinship system. They called themselves 'brothers' and acknowledged the fatherhood of God.[118] In addition, features of anti-structure continued in the church's life at baptism and in the celebration of the Lord's Supper.[119] Although a kinship system based on marriage became the ordering principle within the church, anti-structure and *communitas* continued to exist in baptismal symbols and other symbolic activities of the church's life, that is, sibling language and the Lord's Supper. Consequently, the possibility existed for transformations of social relationships.

Turner warns that any analysis of a social unit must take cognizance

116. Turner (*Dramas*, p. 42) identifies the various possibilities that can take place in the resolution phase.

117. The image of the virgin as the bride of Christ is important for subsequent structural affirmations: celibacy for women is patterned on the patrilineal kinship model, and the duties and obligations of submission and obedience are owed to Christ, the husband.

118. Although fewer in number than in the genuine Pauline epistles, references to 'brothers' include: Col. 1–2; 4.7, 15–16; Eph. 6.21, 23; 1 Tim. 4.6; 2 Tim. 4.19; also 1 Clem. 14.1; 33.1; 37.1; 50.1; 52.1. The one reference to 'sister' is specifically related to hierarchy, as are some of the references to 'brother'. In 1 Tim. 5.1 brothers and sisters become young men and women, while older men and women are referred to as mothers and fathers. 1 Clem. 41.1 speaks of 'each of us brothers in our own rank'.

119. L. William Countryman, 'Christian Equality and the Early Catholic Episcopate', *ATR* 63 (1981), pp. 115-38 (124-25).

of both structure and *communitas*; a failure to investigate both modalities results in a partial understanding of the process of constancy and change. Turner also recognizes that there has been an almost total identification in anthropological theory of the social with the social structural. This has led to the view that what is not social structural is 'psychological' and of secondary status. Moreover, when structure and *communitas* regard each other as antagonists, each 'becomes what it beholds'. Turner continues:

> What seems to be needed, to quote William Blake again, is 'to destroy the negation' and thus 'redeem the contraries', that is, to discover what is the right relationship between structure and communitas at a given time and place in history and geography, to give each its due.[120]

In the end, it was the structural viewpoint that became official in the church. In consequence, normative *communitas* became the pattern of deviance and heresy.[121] At the official level, the possibilities which *communitas* presented for structuring and organizing the Christian community were undermined, but the popularity of anti-structure remained in those areas of the church's life where the egalitarian impulse persisted.[122]

In the development of the Christian tradition, the move toward institutionalization has been identified with the development of the social structural. The canonical process gave legitimacy to this identification, and thus, the complex and subtle relationship between *communitas* and structure was neglected. *Communitas*, if recognized at all, was viewed as secondary or heretical.[123] Today, almost two thousand

120. Turner, *Dramas*, p. 269.

121. Georgi (*Opponents*, p. 345) reflects on his statements about Paul's opponents in 2 Corinthians: 'what I regret is a certain theological defensiveness which expresses itself in a doctrinaire attitude extolling orthodoxy and denouncing heresy'. Shirley Jackson Case in *Social Origins of Christianity* (repr.; Chicago: University of Chicago Press, 1973), p. 199 defines heresy as 'fundamentally a social phenomenon rather than an intellectual problem. Differences of opinion that were always present even in the most peaceful community never resulted in heresies until rival social attitudes crystallized around specific centres of interest and thus gave real vitality to the opinions in question.'

122. See MacDonald, *Legend*, pp. 90-96 for a discussion of the victory of the Apocryphal Acts, which represent the position of normative *communitas* at the time of the Pastorals.

123. Turner (*Dramas*, p. 268) states that from the standpoint of the structural individual, the one who is in *communitas* is someone who by his or her very

years after the formulation of the metaphor, 'in Christ all are children of God, no male and female', Christians continue to struggle to define the right relationship between structure and normative *communitas* in their own particular time and place. The greatest stumbling block to this task is the continuing assumption that structure is the norm and that *communitas* is abnormal.

existence calls into question the whole normative order.

Chapter 6

SUMMARY AND CONCLUDING REMARKS

Summary

The purpose of this study has been two-fold: (1) to investigate the conflict over marriage in 1 Corinthians 7, in order to uncover the social dynamics at work within the Christian community; (2) to probe the function of Paul's argumentation in light of those dynamics. In order to accomplish this goal, the method and models of cultural anthropology have been appropriated to guide the inquiry.

As a result of our analysis we have concluded that the conflict reflected in 1 Corinthians 7 arose as the result of two antithetical views of the root metaphor, 'in Christ all are children of God, no male and female'. One group in the Corinthian church supported a kinship system based on patrilineal marriage and hierarchical community structures. A second group demanded that normative *communitas* should order the community. This latter system was based on a sibling relationship that affirmed equality between men and women and valued achieved status over ascribed status, namely, preferment within the community based on gifts rather than on one's gender, race, or condition in life.

The two groups came into conflict when a female member of the community divorced her husband (v. 10). The ambiguities created by these conflicting patterns could no longer be ignored, and each faction increased its efforts to win over uncommitted church members to its point of view. An engaged couple was caught in the middle (v. 36).

Paul responds at this point in the crisis. His attempts at redress seek to persuade both factions that their commitment to each other and to him is more important than the issue of marriage. He tries to accomplish this in various ways: by emphasizing mutuality (vv. 2-4), by using arguments of 'good' and 'better' (vv. 8-9, 36-38, 39-40) and by removing the right to decide the issue from both factions (vv. 12-16, 36-38).

In addition, Paul presents arguments which seek to move each group to reconsider the *absoluteness* of its stance and to persuade all members of the community to live with ambiguity. The arguments Paul uses to convince the anti-structure group appeal to their fear of Satanic influence (v. 5), of unregulated sexual activity (vv. 2, 5; 9, 36-38), and of pollution (vv. 14, 32). His appeals to the group affirming structure include an emphasis on order and things being in their place (vv. 14, 35), eschatological considerations (vv. 29b, 31) and the importance of serving the Lord without distraction (vv. 32-35).

Paul uses the language and assumptions of structure as a basis for his arguments (vv. 2-5, 16, 20-22, 29-31). While he states a preference for anti-structure (vv. 7, 8-9, 10-11, 25-40), the assumptions of structure that are part of his redressive measures (vv. 2-5, 16, 29-31) indicate his unwillingness to negate the obligations owed within the marriage relationship (vv. 16, 29-31). His appeal to structure points out the strength of the pro-marriage group, and in all likelihood, Paul's own socialization.

The breaks in the pattern of his argument in vv. 12-16 and vv. 32-35 point to the prominence of married women in the anti-structure faction. In addition, these verses indicate Paul's reluctance to encourage married women within the community to take the initiative in moving to a brother and sister relationship with their husbands. In effect, Paul's redress denies them the right to initiate such a relationship.

Paul nowhere denies the rights and obligations that were at the heart of the patrilineal kinship structure; however, he does attempt to lessen the absoluteness of their hold on the Christian. But, by the end of ch. 7, the structural arguments used by later generations to resolve the conflict over marriage are firmly in place. After Paul's death, other redressive agents moved to discount relationships based on normative *communitas*, and so this way of ordering relationships no longer served as the pattern for authority and leadership within the church.

The continuing struggle over male and female relationships within the Corinthian community and in other Pauline communities permits an extended case study of the social drama. At the end of the trajectory we find a situation in which the structural leaders within the community unambiguously affirm both marriage and a system of hierarchical relationships within the church. However, the persistence of the egalitarian order can be seen in the anti-structural revolt that broke out within the Corinthian community and in the continuing, if muted, allegiance to a fictive kinship system.

This study in sociological exegesis[1] provides an interdisciplinary approach to the issues in 1 Corinthians 7. We have not only asked what the text 'said', but also how that text was designed to function, and what its impact upon the life and activity of its recipients and formulators was intended to be.[2] However, we have addressed the traditional concerns of New Testament exegesis. We offer not only a historical reconstruction of the situation but an improved understanding of the text.[3]

The methods and models of cultural anthropology, particularly the insights of Mary Douglas, have attracted the attention of a number of biblical scholars. The value of this approach is shown in the light it sheds on texts which have resisted analysis by more traditional methods.

We have used anthropological theory in two ways in our analysis of ch. 7. First, we have set our description of marriage in Graeco-Roman society within the anthropological category of kinship. Then, guided by Victor Turner's model of social drama and Mary Douglas's model of grid and group, we have undertaken an exegesis of 1 Corinthians 7. In order to uncover the social dynamics of the conflict, we have employed the four stages in Turner's description of a social drama. We have used Mary Douglas's model of grid and group to situate the information which we uncovered. In addition, the 'cosmological' justifications that individuals use to persuade others, according to Douglas, have provided us with a schema for analyzing Paul's argumentation.

Kinship and Chapter 7

The anthropological category of kinship has helped us to situate the struggle over marriage at Corinth. Rather than being limited to ethics and theology, the confrontation in ch. 7 emerged as a conflict over

1. This term is taken from Elliott, *Home for the Homeless*, p. 1.
2. Elliott, *Home for the Homeless*, p. 8.
3. S.B. Reid ('Enoch: The Rising Elite of the Apocalyptic Movement', *SBLSP* [Missoula, MT: Scholars Press, 1983], p. 147) states that the goal of sociological exegesis must not only be historical reconstruction but must also include a better understanding of the issues in the text.

organization, social structures and relationships within the church. When marriage/sexual intercourse and singleness/celibacy were identified with two opposite kinship patterns that reflected two patterns of organization, the one hierarchical, the other egalitarian, the importance of this conflict, not just at Corinth but for the history of the Christian church, became evident.

Anthropology studies not only kinship proper but also what it calls fictive kinship. An investigation of the use of kinship language in ch. 7 revealed the terminology of two relationships: husband and wife, and brother and sister. What happens when a Christian is called to live, at one and the same time, in accordance with *two* patterns of kinship. More particularly, how are believers who are husband and wife to relate to each other as brother and sister?

We identified kinship terminology at a number of points in ch. 7 (vv. 1-6, 12-16, 29-31). Of particular importance was Paul's use of kinship terminology in vv. 12-16. In these verses he failed to use the term 'sister' for the married woman, when addressing the anti-structure group, but he did use husband and wife terminology in v. 16. As our exegesis proceeded, the involvement of married women in the anti-structure party became increasingly clear, as did Paul's unwillingness to encourage any initiative on their part to live as sisters with their husbands.

In vv. 1-6 and 29-31, where kinship language occurs, the kinship pattern of marriage, with its debts and obligations, is used as a basis for Paul's arguments. In the former passage, both partners are called to live out these obligations, including sexual intercourse; and in the latter passage Paul appeals to husbands not to use the rights they have. In effect, he recognizes the structures and obligations of this kinship pattern to be binding, but tries to lessen the absoluteness of their hold on Christians by encouraging temporary abstinence and by calling for a voluntary relinquishing of such rights.

Social Drama and Chapter 7

Victor Turner's model of social drama has provided the investigative tool for analyzing the conflict situation in this chapter. From his analysis of conflict in African society and in historical and literary texts, he delineates the causes of conflict and identifies certain recognizable phases. The exegete must pay attention to certain details within the text, in order to trace the course of the conflict.

An understanding of the presence and function of a root metaphor in a conflict situation enables the exegete to relate the baptismal formula in Gal. 3.26-28 to the conflict in ch. 7. In addition, Turner's understanding of conflict in terms of structure and anti-structure helps the exegete to identify the two viewpoints in the text which are in tension. Often in exegesis the existence of two viewpoints within the Corinthian community has been lost.

To maintain the tension between two factions throughout the exegesis of ch. 7 points out the need for models in the analysis of biblical texts. As the social drama developed, singleness/celibacy became the way of deviance, while marriage/sexual intercourse with its hierarchical structure, became the primary pattern for Christian relationships and for church organization. In 1 Corinthians 7 neither of these patterns has yet prevailed. Turner's model provides a method for keeping distinct the two responses to the root metaphor.

Turner's model also pays particular attention to the stage of redressive activity in a social drama: is the redressive agent's authority secure enough to effect a resolution to the conflict? In the situation reflected in ch. 7, Paul appears to act as he does not by choice but because his authority within the community has been weakened. His manner of argumentation betrays an uncertainty as to whether he can command the community's loyalty and obedience. Because he is unable to demand obedience, Paul is forced to appeal and to compromise.

A complete description of a social drama needs to include the stage of resolution. Since 1 Corinthians 7 sheds no light on this phase, the exegete cannot stop there. Paul's relationship to the Corinthian community after writing 1 Corinthians must also be investigated.

It has often been assumed that Paul's word was enough to resolve the conflict; however, 2 Corinthians and 1 Clement show that a tension between structure and *communitas* at Corinth remained even after the establishment of roles and relationships based on structure. We have also been able to study the forces of constancy and change in other Pauline communities.

Turner's insistence on the importance of both structure and *communitas* for human creativity and continuity is a challenge to the biblical exegete to investigate both patterns in order that the description of the process of change may be complete. *Communitas* must not he relegated to a secondary or heretical role in the history of institutionalization within the church.

Grid and Group and Chapter 7

Mary Douglas's model of grid and group focuses on the individual and the community. By using her model, we have been able to identify those arguments by which Paul sought to strengthen community allegiances. In addition, we could delineate his appeals to each faction and the points at which he sacrifices the individual in the interests of the community. In particular, we have seen how he restricted the freedom of those married women who were at the heart of the anti-structure movement.

Concluding Remarks

Biblical studies have traditionally drawn on other disciplines in the task of interpretation. Scholars have used historical, philosophical and literary analyses to shed light on the text. An exegesis which uses the methods and models of cultural anthropology to investigate the social dynamics within an early Christian community is neither surprising nor out of place.

Our contribution to the exegetical task has concentrated on the human dimension of one early Christian community. We have sought to clarify the social dynamics in that community that produced tension and conflict, as leaders and people alike tried to grasp their new faith. The theological and ethical affirmations in the text reveal a process of reflection and compromise which not only gives us greater insight into early Christianity but also brings a new perspective to faith statements in our own time and place.

BIBLIOGRAPHY

Abbott, F.F., *Society and Politics in Ancient Rome* (New York: Scribner's Sons, 1909).

Allo, E.B., *Saint Paul: Première épître aux corinthiens* (Paris: Gabalda, 1935).

Ardener, E., 'Belief and the Problem of Women', in S. Ardener (ed.), *Perceiving Women* (London: Malaby House, 1975), pp. 1-18.

Arthur, M.B., ' "Liberated" Women: The Classical Era', in R. Bridenthal and C. Koonz (eds.), *Becoming Visible: Women in European History* (Boston: Houghton Mifflin, 1977), pp. 60-89.

Atkins, R., 'The Integrating Function of Adoption Terminology Used by the Apostle Paul: A Grid-Group Analysis' (PhD dissertation, Northwestern University, 1987).

Baird, W., *The Corinthian Church: A Biblical Approach to Urban Culture* (New York: Abingdon Press, 1964).

—*1 Corinthians, 2 Corinthians* (Atlanta: John Knox, 1980).

Balch, D.L., Background of 1 Cor. VII: Sayings of the Lord in Q; Moses as an Ascetic ΘΕΟΣ ANHP in II Cor. III', *NTS* 18 (1972), pp. 351-64.

—'1 Cor. 7.32-35 and Stoic Debate about Marriage, Anxiety and Distraction', *JBL* 102 (1983), pp. 429-39.'

—'Household Ethical Codes in Peripatetic, Neopythagorean and Early Christian Moralists', in P.J. Achtemeier (ed.), *SBLSP* (Missoula, MT: Scholars Press, 1977), pp. 397-404.

—*Let Wives Be Submissive: The Domestic Code in I Peter* (Chico, CA: Scholars Press, 1981).

Balsdon, J.P.V.D., *Life and Leisure in Ancient Rome* (New York: McGraw-Hill, 1969).

—*Romans and Aliens* (London: Gerald Duckworth, 1979).

—*Roman Women: Their History and Habits* (London: The Bodley Head, 1962).

—'Women in Imperial Rome', *History Today* 10 (1960), pp. 24-31.

Banks, R., *Paul's Idea of Community: The Early House Churches in their Historical Setting* (Grand Rapids: Eerdmans, 1980).

Banton, M., *Anthropological Approaches to the Study of Religion* (London: Tavistock Publications, 1966).

Barbour, I., *Myths, Models and Paradigms: A Comparative Study in Science and Religion* (New York: Harper & Row, 1974).

Barre, M.L., 'To Marry or to Burn: πυροῦσθαι in 1 Cor. 7.9', *CBQ* 36 (1974), pp. 193-202.

Barrett, C.K., 'Cephas and Corinth', in O. Betz, M. Hengel and P. Schmidt (eds.), *Abraham unser Vater: Festschrift für O. Michel* (Leiden: Brill, 1963), pp. 1-12.

—*Commentary on the First Epistle to the Corinthians* (BNTC; London: A. & C. Black, 1968).

—*Essays on Paul* (London: SPCK, 1982).

—*The Pastoral Epistles* (Oxford: Clarendon Press, 1963).

Bartchy, S., μαλλον χρησαι: *First Century Slavery and the Interpretation of 1 Corinthians 7.21* (SBLDS; Missoula, MT: Society of Biblical Literature, 1973).

—'Power, Submission and Sexual Identity among the Early Christians', in C.R. Wetzel (ed.), *Essays on New Testament Christianity: A Festschrift in Honor of Dean E. Walker* (Cincinnati: Standard Publishing, 1978), pp. 50-58.

Bartlett, D., 'Biblical Scholarship Today: A Diversity of New Approaches', *The Christian Century* 98 (1981), pp. 1090-94.

—'John G. Gager's "Kingdom and Community": A Summary and Response', *Zygon* 13 (1978), pp. 109-22.

Bartling, W.J., 'Sexuality, Marriage and Divorce in 1 Corinthians 6.12–7.16: A Practical Exercise in Hermeneutics', *CTM* 39 (1968), pp. 355-66.

Barton, S., 'Paul and the Cross: A Sociological Approach', *Theology* 85 (1982), pp. 13-19.

—'Paul and the Resurrection: A Sociological Approach', *Religion* 14 (1984), pp. 67-75.

Bassler, J.M., 'The Widow's Tale: A Fresh Look at 1 Tim. 5.3-16', *JBL* 103 (1984), pp. 23-41.

Bauer, W., *Orthodoxy and Heresy in Earliest Christianity* (ed. R.A. Kraft and G. Krodel; Philadelphia: Fortress Press, 1971).

Beare, F.W., *St. Paul and his Letters* (London: Adam and Charles Black, 1962).

Belkin, S., 'The Problem of Paul's Background: III Marrying One's Virgin', *JBL* 54 (1935), pp. 49-52.

Benko, S., and J.J. O'Rourke, *The Catacombs and the Colosseum: The Roman Empire as the Setting of Primitive Christianity* (Valley Forge, PA: Judson, 1971).

Benoit, P., 'Christian Marriage according to Saint Paul', *Clergy Review* 65 (1980), pp. 309-21.

Berger, P., *The Heretical Imperative: Contemporary Possibilities of Religious Affirmation* (Garden City, NY: Doubleday, 1979).

—*The Sacred Canopy: Elements of a Sociology of Religion* (Garden City, NY: Anchor, 1967).

—'A Sociological View of the Secularization of Theology', *JSSR* 6 (1967), pp. 3-16.

Berger, P., and T. Luckmann, *The Social Construction of Reality: A Treatise in the Sociology of Knowledge* (Garden City, NY: Doubleday, 1966).

Best, E., *Second Corinthians* (Atlanta: John Knox, 1987).

—*Paul and his Converts* (The Sprunt Lectures 1985; Edinburgh: T. & T. Clark, 1988).

Best, E.E., 'Cicero, Livy and Educated Roman Women', *Classical Journal* 65 (1970), pp. 199-204.

Best, T., 'The Sociological Study of the New Testament: Promise and Peril of a Discipline', *SJT* 36 (1983), pp. 181-94.

Betz, H.D., *2 Corinthians 8 and 9: A Commentary on Two Administrative Letters by the Apostle Paul* (Philadelphia: Fortress Press, 1985).

—'Orthodoxy and Heresy in Primitive Christianity', *Int* 19 (1965), pp. 299-311.

Black, M., *Models and Metaphors: Studies in Language and Philosophy* (Ithaca, NY: Cornell University Press, 1962).

Bornkamm, G., 'The History and Origin of the So-Called Second Letter to the Corinthians', in K. Aland *et al.* (eds.), *The Authorship and Integrity of the New Testament* (London: SPCK, 1965), pp. 73-81.

—'The Missionary Stance of Paul in, 1 Corinthians 9 and in Acts', in L.E. Keck and J.L. Martyn (eds.), *Studies in Luke–Acts* (Nashville: Abingdon Press, 1966), pp. 194-207.

Boucher, M., 'Some Unexplored Parallels to 1 Cor. 11, 11-12 and Gal. 3, 28: The NT on the Role of Women', *CBQ* 31 (1969), pp. 50-58.

Bowerstock, G.W., *Augustus and the Greek World* (Oxford: Clarendon Press, 1965).

Braun, H., 'Die Indifferenz gegenüber der Welt bei Paulus und bei Epiklet', in *Gesammelte Studien zum neuen Testament und seiner Umwelt* (Tübingen: Mohr, 1962).

Broneer, O., 'The Apostle Paul and the Isthmian Games', *BA* 25 (1962), pp. 1-31.

—'Corinth: Centre of Saint Paul's Missionary Work in Greece', *BA* 14 (1951), pp. 78-96.

—'Paul and the Pagan Cults at Isthmia', *HTR* 64 (1971), pp. 169-84.

Brooten, B., 'Inscriptional Evidence for Women as Leaders in the Ancient Synagogue', in K.H. Richards (ed.), *SBLSP* (Chico, CA: Scholars Press, 1981), pp. 1-12.

Brown, P., *The Body and Society: Men, Women and Sexual Renunciation in Early Christianity* (New York: Columbia University Press, 1988).

—'The Rise and Function of the Holy Man in Late Antiquity,' *JRS* 61 (1970), pp. 80-101.

Bruce, F.F., *The Epistles to the Colossians, to Philemon and the Ephesians* (Grand Rapids: Eerdmans, 1984).

—*1 and 2 Corinthians* (NCB; London: Oliphants, 1971).

—*Paul, Apostle of the Heart Set Free* (Grand Rapids: Eerdmans, 1977).

Brunt, P.A., *Italian Manpower 225 BC–AD 14* (Oxford: Clarendon Press, 1971).

Bultmann, R., *The Second Letter to the Corinthians* (trans. R.A. Harrisville; Minneapolis: Augsburg, 1985).

Burrus, V., *Chastity as Autonomy: Women in the Stories of the Apocryphal Acts* (Lewiston, NY: Edwin Mellen, 1987).

—'Chastity as Autonomy: Women in the Stories of the Apocryphal Acts', *Semeia* 38 (1986), pp. 101-17.

Bynum, C.W., 'Women's Stories, Women's Symbols: A Critique of Victor Turner's Theory of Liminality', in R.L. Moore and F.E. Reynolds (eds.), *Anthropology and the Study of Religion* (Chicago: Centre for the Scientific Study of Religion, 1984), pp. 105-25.

Cadbury, H.J., 'Erastus of Corinth', *JBL* 50 (1931), pp. 42-58.

Caird, G.B., 'Paul and Women's Liberty', *BJRL* 54 (1972), pp. 268-81.

Cameron, A., 'Neither Male nor Female', *Greece and Rome* 27 (1980), pp. 60-68.

Cameron, A., and A. Kuhrt, *Images of Women in Antiquity* (London: Croom Helm, 1983).

Cantarella, E., *Pandora's Daughters: The Role and Status of Women in Greek and Roman Antiquity* (trans. M.B. Fant; Baltimore: The Johns Hopkins University Press, 1981).

Carcopino, J., *Daily Life in Ancient Rome* (trans. E. Lorimer; New Haven: Yale University Press, 1940).

Carney, T.F., *The Shape of the Past: Models and Antiquity* (Lawrence, KS: Coronado Press, 1975).

Carp, T., 'Two Matrons of the Late Republic', in H.P. Foley (ed.), *Reflections of Women in Antiquity* (New York: Gordon and Breech Science Publishing, 1981), pp. 343-54.

Cartlidge, D., 'Competing Theologies of Asceticism in the Early Church' (PhD dissertation, Cambridge, MA: Harvard University, 1969).

—'1 Cor. 7 as a Foundation for a Christian Sex Ethic', *JR* 55 (1975), pp. 220-34.

Case, S.J., 'The Nature of Primitive Christianity', *AJT* 17 (1913), pp. 63-79.

—*Social Origins of Christianity* (repr.; Chicago: University of Chicago Press, 1973).

—'Whither Historicism in Theology?', in M.H. Krumbine (ed.), *The Process of Religion:*

Essays in Honor of Dean Shailer Mathews (New York: The Macmillan Company, 1933), pp. 53-71.

Castelli, E., 'Virginity and its Meaning for Women's Sexuality in Early Christianity', *JFSR* 2 (1986), pp. 61-88.

Catchpole, D.R., 'The Synoptic Divorce Material as a Tradition Historical Problem', *BJRL* 57 (1974), pp. 92-127.

Chadwick, H., 'All Things to All Men', *NTS* 1 (1954–55), pp. 261-75.

Clark, E.A., *Ascetic Piety and Women's Faith: Essays on Late Ancient Christianity* (Lewiston, NY: Edwin Mellen Press, 1986).

—'Ascetic Renunciation and Feminine Advancement: A Paradox of Late Ancient Christianity', *ATR* 63 (1981), pp. 240-57.

Clark, G., 'The Women at Corinth', *Theology* 85 (1982), pp. 256-62.

Colish, M.L., *The Stoic Tradition from Antiquity to the Early Middle Ages*. I. *Stoicism in Classical Latin Literature* (Leiden: Brill, 1985).

Collins, A.Y., 'The Function of "Excommunication" in Paul', *HTR* 73 (1980), pp. 151-63.

Collins, J.J., *Between Athens and Jerusalem: Jewish Identity in the Hellenistic Diaspora* (New York: Crossroad, 1983).

—'Chiasmus, the "ABA" Pattern and the Text of Paul', in *Studiorum Paulinorum Congressus Internationalis Catholicus*, 2 (Rome: Pontificio Instituto Biblico, 1963), pp. 575-83.

Collins, R.F., 'The Unity of Paul's Parenesis in 1 Thess. 4.3-8: 1 Cor. 7.1-7, a Significant Parallel', *NTS* 29 (1983), pp. 420-29.

Conzelmann, H., *1 Corinthians: A Commentary on the First Epistle to the Corinthians* (Hermeneia; Philadelphia: Fortress Press, 1975).

Corbett, P.E., *The Roman Law of Marriage* (Oxford: Oxford University Press, 1930).

Coser, L. (ed.), *The Idea of Social Structure* (New York: Harcourt, Brace, Jovanovich, 1975).

Countryman, L.W., 'Christian Equality and the Early Catholic Episcopate', *ATR* 63 (1981), pp. 115-38.

—*Dirt, Greed and Sex: Sexual Ethics in the New Testament and their Implications for Today* (Philadelphia: Fortress Press, 1988).

—'Welfare in the Churches of Asia Minor under the Early Roman Empire', in P.J. Achtemeier (ed.), *SBLSP* (Missoula, MT: Scholars Press, 1979), pp. 131-46.

Crook, J.A., *Law and Life of Rome 90 BC–AD 212* (Ithaca, NY: Cornell University Press, 1967).

Crouch, J.E., *The Origin and Intention of the Colossian Haustafel* (Göttingen: Vandenhoeck & Ruprecht, 1972).

Dahl, N., 'Paul and the Church at Corinth according to 1 Corinthians 1.10–4.21', in *Studies in Paul* (Minneapolis: Augsburg Press, 1977).

Darr, J.A, 'A Review, "Rediscovering Paul: Philemon and the Sociology of Paul's Narrative World"', *RelSRev* 14 (1988), p. 118.

Daube, D., 'Concession to Sinfulness in Jewish Law', *JJS* 10 (1959), pp. 1-13.

—*Roman Law: Linguistic, Social and Philosophical Aspects* (Edinburgh: Edinburgh University Press, 1969).

Davies, S.L., *The Revolt of the Widows: The Social World of the Apocryphal Acts* (Carbondale: Southern Illinois University Press, 1980).

Davilá, M., 'Compadrazgo: Fictive Kinship in Latin America', in N. Graburn (ed.), *Read-*

ings in Kinship and Social Structure (New York: Harper & Row, 1971), pp. 396-405.

Davis, J.J., 'Some Reflections on Galatians 3.28, Sexual Roles and Biblical Hermeneutics', *JETS* 19 (1976), pp. 201-208.

Deissmann, G.A., *Paul: A Study in Social and Religious History* (trans. W.E. Wilson; London: Hodder & Stoughton, 2nd rev. edn, 1926).

Delling, G., 'ἁγιασμο´', *TDNT*, V, pp. 826-37.

Deming, W., *Paul on Marriage and Celibacy: The Hellenistic Background of 1 Corinthians 7* (Cambridge: Cambridge University Press, 1995).

Den Boer, W., *Private Morality in Greece and Rome* (Leiden: Brill, 1979).

Denniston, T.D., *The Greek Particles* (Oxford: Clarendon Press, 1959).

Derrett, J.D., 'The Disposal of Virgins', in *idem, Studies in the New Testament.* I. *Glimpses of the Legal and Social Presuppositions of the Authors* (Leiden: Brill, 1977), pp. 184-92.

Dewey, A.J., 'A Matter of Honor: A Socio-Historical Analysis of 2 Corinthians 10', *HTR* 78 (1985), pp. 209-17.

Dibelius, M., and H. Conzelmann, *The Pastoral Epistles* (Philadelphia: Fortress Press, 1972).

Dill, S., *Roman Society from Nero to Marcus Aurelius* (New York: Meridian Books, 1956).

Dixon, S., 'Family Finances: Terentia and Tullia', in Rawson, B. (ed.), *The Family in Ancient Rome*, pp. 93-120.

Dobschütz, E., von, *Christian Life in the Primitive Church* (trans. G. Bremner; ed. W.D. Morrison; London: Williams & Norgate, 1904).

Donfried, K.P., *The Setting of Second Clement in Early Christianity* (Leiden: Brill, 1974).

Douglas, M., *Cultural Bias* (Occasional Paper No. 34, Royal Anthropological Institute of Great Britain and Ireland; London: Bakers Trade Finishers, 1978).

Douglas, M. (ed.), *Essays on the Sociology of Perception* (London: Routledge & Kegan Paul, 1982).

—*Implicit Meanings: Essays in Anthropology* (London: Routledge & Kegan Paul, 1975).

—*In the Active Voice* (London: Routledge & Kegan Paul, 1982).

—*Natural Symbols: Explorations in Cosmology* (New York: Random House, 1970).

—*Natural Symbols: Explorations in Cosmology* (London: Barrie and Jenkins, 1973).

—*Purity and Danger: An Analysis of Concepts of Pollution and Taboo* (Harmondsworth: Penguin Books, 1970).

—'Social Preconditions of Enthusiasm and Heterodoxy', in R.F. Spencer (ed.), *Forms of Symbolic Action: Proceedings of the 1969 Annual Spring Meeting of the American Ethnological Society* (Seattle: University of Washington Press, 1969), pp. 69-80.

Drane, J.W., 'Tradition, Law and Ethics in Pauline Theology', *NovT* 16 (1974), pp. 167-87.

Dulau, P., 'The Pauline Privilege', *CBQ* 13 (1951), pp. 146-52.

Dungan, D., *The Sayings of Jesus in the Churches of Paul* (Philadelphia: Fortress Press, 1971).

Edwards, A., 'Review of Bruce Malina, "The New Testament World" ', *New Blackfriars* 65 (1984) pp. 42-44.

Edwards, O.C., Jr, 'Historical-Critical Method's Failure of Nerve and a Prescription for a Tonic: A Review of Some Recent Literature', *ATR* 59 (1977), pp. 115-34.

—'Sociology as a Tool for Interpreting the New Testament', *ATR* 65 (1983), pp. 431-48.

Elliot, A., 'The Theory of Cognitive Dissonance in Current Perspective', in L. Berkowitz (ed.), *Cognitive Theory in Social Psychology* (New York: Academic Press, 1978), pp. 181-220.

Elliott, J.H., *A Home for the Homeless: A Sociological Exegesis of 1 Peter, its Situation and Strategy* (Philadelphia: Fortress Press, 1981).

—'Review Article of W.A. Meeks, The First Urban Christians', *RelSRev* 11 (1985), pp. 329-34.

—'Social Scientific Criticism of the New Testament: More on Method and Models', *Semeia* 35 (1986), pp. 1-33.

Elliott, J.K., 'Paul's Teaching on Marriage in I Corinthians: Some Problems Considered', *NTS* 19 (1973), pp. 219-25.

Ellis, E.E., 'Paul and his Opponents: Trends in Research', in J. Neusner (ed.), *Christianity, Judaism and Other Greco-Roman Cults: Studies for Morton Smith at Sixty*. I. *The New Testament* (Leiden: Brill, 1975), pp. 264-98.

Esler, P., *Community and Gospel in Luke–Acts* (Cambridge: Cambridge University Press, 1987).

Evans, E., *The Epistles of Paul the Apostle to the Corinthians in the Revised Version* (The Clarendon Bible; Oxford: Clarendon Press, 1930).

Farber, B., *Comparative Kinship Systems: A Method of Analysis* (New York: John Wiley & Sons, 1968).

Fee, G., '1 Corinthians 7.1 in the NIV', *JETS* 23 (1980), pp. 307-14.

Feeley-Harnik, G., 'Is Historical Anthropology Possible? The Case of the Runaway Slave', in G.M. Tucker and D.A. Knight (eds.), *Humanizing America's Iconic Book* (SBL Centennial Addresses; Chico, CA: Scholars Press, 1980), pp. 95-126.

—*The Lord's Table: Eucharist and Passover in Early Christianity* (Philadelphia: University of Pennsylvania Press, 1981).

Field, J., Jr, 'The Purpose of the *Lex Iulia et Papia Poppaea*', *Classical Journal* 40 (1944–45), pp. 398-416.

Filson, F.V., 'The Significance of the Early House Churches', *JBL* 58 (1939), pp. 105-12.

Finley, M.E., 'The Silent Women of Rome', *Horizon* 7 (1965), pp. 57-64.

Finley, M.I., *Aspects of Antiquity* (New York: Offset Paperback, 1917).

—*The Politics of the Ancient World* (Cambridge: Cambridge University Press, 1983).

Fiedlander, L., *Roman Life and Manners under the Early Empire* (trans. L.A. Magnus; New York: Dutton, 1913).

Fischer, J.A., '1 Cor. 7.8-24: Marriage and Divorce', *BR* 23 (1978), pp. 26-36.

—'Paul on Virginity', *TBT* 72 (1974), pp. 1633-38.

Fitton, J.W., 'That Was No Lady, That Was . . .', *Classical Quarterly* 64 NS 20 (1970), pp. 56-58.

Flacelière, R., 'D'un certain féminisme grec', *Revue des Etudes Anciennes* 64 (1962), pp. 109-16.

Flanagan, J.W., *David's Social Drama: A Hologram of Israel's Early Iron Age* (JSOTSup, 73; Sheffield: Almond Press, 1988).

Ford, J. Massingberd, 'Levirate Marriage in St. Paul (1 Cor vii)', *NTS* 10 (1963–64), pp. 361-65.

—'The Meaning of Virgin', *NTS* 12 (1965–66), pp. 293-99.

—'The Rabbinic Background of St. Paul's Use of *hyperakmos* (1 Cor. vii.36)', *JJS* 17 (1965), pp. 89-91.

Forkman, G., *The Limits of the Religious Community: Expulsion from the Religious Com-munity within the Qumran Sect, within Rabbinic Judaism and within Primitive Chris-tianity* (trans. P. Sjölander; Lund: Gleerup, 1972).

Fox, R., *Kinship and Marriage: An Anthropological Perspective* (Harmondsworth: Penguin Books, 1967).

Frances, F.O., *Conflict at Colossae: A Problem in the Interpretation of Early Christianity Illustrated by Selected Modern Studies* (Missoula, MT: Scholars Press, rev. edn, 1975).

Frank, R.I., 'Augustus' Legislation on Marriage and Children', in R. Stroud and J. Palvel (eds.), *California Studies in Classical Antiquity* (8 vols.; Berkeley: University of Cali-fornia Press, 1976), VIII, pp. 41-52.

Friedl, E., 'The Position of Women: Appearance and Reality', *Anthropological Quarterly* 40 (1967), pp. 97-108.

Funk, R.W., 'The Watershed of the American Biblical Tradition: The Chicago School, First Phase, 1892–1920', *JBL* 95 (1976), pp. 4-22.

Furnish, V.P., *The Moral Teaching of Paul* (Nashville: Abingdon Press, 2nd edn, 1985).

Gage, J., *Matronalia: Essai sur les dévotions et les organisations cultuelles des femmes dans l'ancienne Rome* (Brussels: Latomus, 1963).

Gager, J.G. Jr, 'Body Symbols and Social Reality: Resurrection, Incarnation and Asceticism in Early Christianity', *Religion* 12 (1982), pp. 345-63.

—'Functional Diversity in Paul's Use of End-Time Language', *JBL* 89 (1970), pp. 325-37.

—*Kingdom and Community: The Social World of Early Christianity* (Englewood Cliffs, NJ: Prentice–Hall, 1975).

—'Shall We Marry Our Enemies? Sociology and the New Testament', *Int* 37 (1983), pp. 256-65.

—'Social Description and Sociological Explanation in the Study of Early Christianity: A Review Essay', in N. Gottwald (ed.), *The Bible and Liberation: Political and Social Hermeneutictics* (Maryknoll, NY: Orbis Books, 1983), pp. 428-40.

Gardner, J.F., *Women in Roman Law and Society* (Bloomington: Indiana University Press, 1986).

Garland, D.E., 'The Christian's Posture toward Marriage and Celibacy: 1 Corinthians 7', *RevExp* 80 (1983), pp. 351-62.

Garnsey, P., *Social Status and Legal Privilege in the Roman Empire* (Oxford: Clarendon Press, 1970).

Garnsey, P., and R. Saller, *The Roman Empire: Economy, Society and Culture* (Berkeley: University of California Press, 1987).

Geertz, C., ' "From a Native's Point of View": On the Nature of Anthropological Under-standing', in K. Basso and H. Selby (eds.), *Meaning in Anthropology* (Albuquerque: University of New Mexico Press, 1976), pp. 221-38.

—'Religion as a Cultural System', in M. Banton (ed.), *Anthropological Approaches to the Study of Culture* (London: Tavistock Publications, 1966), pp. 1-44.

—'Thick Description: Toward an Interpretive Theory of Culture', in *idem*, *The Interpretation of Culture* (New York: Basic Books, 1973).

Georgi, D., *The Opponents of Paul in Second Corinthians* (Philadelphia: Fortress Press, rev. edn., 1986).

Geytenbeek, A.C. van., *Musonius Rufus and Greek Diatribe* (trans. B.L. Hijmans, Jr; Assen: Van Gorcum, rev. edn, 1963).

Giblin, C.H., '1 Corinthians 7: A Negative Theology of Marriage and Celibacy', *TBT* 41 (1969), pp. 2839-55.

Gooch, P.E., 'Authority and Justification in Theological Ethics: A Study in 1 Corinthians 7', *JRE* 11 (1983), pp. 62-74.

—'Ethical Authorities: 1 Corinthians 7', in *idem*, *Partial Knowledge: Philosophical Studies in Paul* (Notre Dame: University of Notre Dame Press, 1987).

Goodspeed, E.J., *The Meaning of Ephesians* (Chicago: University of Chicago Press, 1933).

Goodwater, L., *Women in Antiquity: An Annotated Bibliography* (Metuchen, NJ: Scarecrow Press, 1975).

Goudge, H.L., *The First Epistle to the Corinthians* (Westminster Commentaries; London: Methuen, 3rd edn, 1911).

Grant, F., *The Economic Background of the Gospels* (London: Oxford University Press, 1926).

Gratwick, A.A., 'Free Or Not So Free? Wives and Daughters in the Late Roman Republic', in E.M. Craik (ed.), *Marriage and Property* (Aberdeen: Aberdeen University Press, 1984), pp. 30-53.

Grosheide, F.W., *Commentary on the First Epistle to the Corinthians* (NICNT; Grand Rapids, MI: Eerdmans, 1953).

Gross, J.L., and S. Rayner, *Measuring Culture: A Paradigm for the Analysis of Social Organization* (New York: Columbia University Press, 1985).

Grosvenor, M., *A Grammatical Analysis of the Greek New Testament* (Rome: Biblical Institute Press, 1981).

Gunther, J.J., *St. Paul's Opponents and their Background: A Study of Apocalyptic and Jewish Sectarian Teachings* (NovTSup, 35; Leiden: Brill, 1973).

Hadas, M., *Three Greek Romances* (Garden City, NY: Doubleday, 1953).

Hagg, T., *The Novel in Antiquity* (Berkeley: University of California Press, 1983).

Hallett, J.P., *Fathers and Daughters in Roman Society: Women and the Elite Family* (Princeton, NJ: Princeton University Press, 1984).

Hammond, M., *The City in the Ancient World* (Cambridge, MA: Harvard University Press, 1972).

Harrington, D.J., 'Second Testament Exegesis and the Social Sciences: A Bibliography', *BTB* 18 (1988), pp. 77-85.

—'Sociological Concepts and the Early Church: A Decade of Research', *TS* 41 (1980), pp. 181-90.

Harris, G., 'The Social World of Early Christianity', *Lexington Theological Quarterly* 19 (1984), pp. 102-14.

Hartman, L., 'Some Unorthodox Thoughts on the Household Code Form', in J. Neusner, P. Borgen, E. Frerichs, and R. Horsley (eds.), *The Social World of Formative Christianity and Judaism* (Philadelphia: Fortress Press, 1980), pp. 219-34.

Héring, J., *The First Epistle of Saint Paul to the Corinthians* (trans. A.W. Heathcote and P.J. Allcock; London: Epworth Press, 1962).

Herzog, W.R., 'Interpretation as Discovery and Creation: Sociological Dimensions of Biblical Hermeneutics', *American Baptist Quarterly* 2 (1983), pp. 105-18.

Heyob, S.K., *The Cult of Isis among Women in the Greco-Roman World* (Leiden: Brill, 1975).

Hill, M., 'Paul's Concept of Enkrateia', *RTR* 36 (1977), pp. 70-78.

Holmberg, B., *Paul and Power: The Structure of Authority in the Primitive Church as Reflected in the Pauline Epistles* (Philadelphia: Fortress Press, 1978).

Hoops, M.H., Review of Gerd Theissen, *Psychological Aspects of Pauline Theology*, *Int* 42 (1988), p. 318, 320.

Hopkins, K., 'The Age of Roman Girls at Marriage', *Population Studies* 19 (1965), pp. 309-27.

—'Contraception in the Roman Empire', *Comparative Studies in Society and History* 8 (1965), pp. 124-51.

—*Death and Renewal* (Cambridge: Cambridge University Press, 1983).

Horsley, R.A., 'Gnosis in Corinth: 1 Cor. 8.1-6', *NTS* 27 (1980), pp. 32-51.

—'How Can Some of you Say that there Is no Resurrection of the Dead? Spiritual Elitism in Corinth', *NovT* 20 (1978), pp. 203-31.

—'Pneumatikos vs Psychikos: Distinctions of Spiritual Status among the Corinthians', *HTR* 69 (1976), pp. 269-88.

—'Spiritual Marriage with Sophia', *VC* 33 (1979), pp. 30-54.

—'Wisdom of Word and Words of Wisdom in Corinth', *CBQ* 39 (1977), pp. 224-39.

Howe, M., 'Interpretations of Paul in the Acts of Paul and Thecla', in D.A. Hagner and M.J. Harris (eds.), *Pauline Studies* (Exeter: Paternoster Press, 1980), pp. 33-49.

Hurd, J.C., *The Origin of I Corinthians* (Macon, GA: Mercer University Press, 2nd edn, 1983).

Hynes, W.J., *Shirley Jackson Case and the Chicago School* (Chico, CA: Scholars Press, 1981).

Isenberg, S.R., 'Some Uses and Limitations of Social Scientific Methodology in the Study of Early Christianity', *SBLSP* (Chico, CA: Scholars Press, 1980), pp. 28-49.

Isenberg, S.R., and D.E. Owen, 'Bodies, Natural and Contrived: The Work of Mary Douglas', *RelSRev* 3 (1977), pp. 1-16.

Jeffers, J., 'The Influence of the Roman Family and Social Structure on Early Christianity in Rome', in D.J. Lull (ed.), *SBLSP* (Chico, CA: Scholars Press, 1988), pp. 370-84.

Jensen, J., 'Does Porneia Mean Fornication?', *NovT* 20 (1978), pp. 161-84.

Jeremias, J., 'Die missionarische Aufgabe in der Mischehe (1 Kor. 7,16)', in W. Eltester (ed.), *Neutestamentliche Studien für Rudolf Bultmann zu seinem 70 Geburtstag* (BZNW, 21; Berlin: Töpelmann, 2nd rev. edn, 1957), pp. 255-60.

Jeremias, Joachim, 'Nochmals: War Paulus Witwer ?', *ZNW* 28 (1929), pp. 321-23.

—'War Paulus Witwer?', *ZNW* 25 (1926), pp. 310-12.

Jewett, R., 'The Sexual Liberation of the Apostle Paul', *JAAR* 47 (1979), pp. 55-87.

Jolowicz, H., *Historical Introduction to the Study of Roman Law* (Cambridge: Cambridge University Press, 1967).

Jones, A.H.M., *The Cities of the Eastern Roman Provinces* (Oxford: Clarendon Press, 1937).

—*The Greek City from Alexander to Justinian* (repr.; Oxford: Clarendon Press, 1979 [1940]).

—*The Roman Economy* (Oxford: Basil Blackwell, 1974).

Judge, E.A., 'The Early Christians as a Scholastic Community, Part 1', *JRH* 1 (1960), pp. 4-15.

—'The Early Christians as a Scholastic Community, Part II', *JRH* 1 (1961), pp. 125-37.

—'St. Paul and Classical Society', *JAC* 15 (1972), pp. 19-36.

—'The Social Identity of the First Christians: A Question of Method in Religious History', *JRH* 11 (1980), pp. 201-17.

—*The Social Pattern of Christian Groups in the First Century* (London: Tyndale Press, 1960).

Kajanto, I., 'On Divorce among the Common People of Rome', *Revue des Etudes Latines* 47 (1970), pp. 99-113.

Kampen, N., *Image and Status: Representations of Roman Working Women at Ostia* (Berlin: Mann, 1981).

Karris, R.J., 'The Background and Significance of the Polemic of the Pastoral Epistles', *JBL* 92 (1973), pp. 549-64.

Käsemann, E., 'On Paul's Anthropology', in *Perspectives on Paul* (trans. M. Kohl; Philadelphia: Fortress Press, 1971), pp. 1-31.

Keck, L.E., 'Ethos and Ethics in the New Testament', in J. Gaffney (ed.), *Essays in Morality and Ethics* (New York: Paulist Press, 1980), pp. 29-49.

—'On the Ethos of Early Christians', *JAAR* 42 (1974), pp. 435-51.

Kee, H.C., *Christian Origins in Sociological Perspective: Methods and Resources* (Philadelphia: Westminster Press, 1980).

Keesing, R.M., *Kin Groups and Social Structure* (New York: Holt, Rinehart & Winston, 1975).

Keesing, R.M., and F.M. Keesing, *New Perspectives in Cultural Anthropology* (New York: Holt, Rinehart & Winston, 1971).

Kent, J.H., *Corinth viii/3: The Inscriptions 1926–1950* (Princeton: American School of Classical Studies at Athens, 1966).

Klassen, W., 'Musonius Rufus, Jesus and Paul: Three First Century Feminists', in P. Richardson and J.C. Hurd (eds.), *From Jesus to Paul: Studies in Honor of Frances Wright Beare* (Waterloo: Wilfred Laurier University Press, 1984), pp. 185-206.

Koester, H., 'Gnomai Diaphoroi: The Origin and Nature of Diversification in the History of Early Christianity', in J.M.K Robinson and H. Koester (eds.), *Trajectories through Early Christianity* (Philadelphia: Fortress Press, 1971), pp. 114-57.

—'New Testament Introduction: A Critique of a Discipline', in J. Neusner (ed.), *Christianity, Judaism and Other Greco-Roman Cults: Studies for Morton Smith at Sixty*. I. *The New Testament* (Leiden: Brill, 1975), pp. 1-20.

Kraemer, R., 'Ecstatics and Ascetics: Studies in the Function of Religious Activities for Women in the Greco-Roman World' (PhD dissertation, Princeton University, 1976).

Kraemer, R.S., 'Ecstasy and Possession: The Attraction of Women to the Cult of Dionysus', *HTR* 72 (1979), pp. 55-80.

—'Women in the Religions of the Greco-Roman World', *RelSRev* 9 (1983), pp. 127-39.

Kraft, R.A., 'Judaism on the World Scene', in S. Benko and J.J. O'Rourke (eds.), *The Catacombs and the Colosseum: The Roman Empire as the Setting of Primitive Christianity* (Valley Forge, PA: Judson Press, 1971), pp. 31-98.

Kubo, S., '1 Corinthians VII.16: Optimistic or Pessimistic?', *NTS* 24 (1978), pp. 539-44.

Kugelman, R., '1 Cor. 7.36-38', *CBQ* 19 (1948), pp. 63-71.

Kümmel, W.G., *Introduction to the New Testament* (trans. H.C. Kee; Nashville: Abingdon Press, 1975).

Kunkel, W., *An Introduction to Roman Legal and Constitutional History* (Oxford: Clarendon Press, 1966).

Lacey, W.K., *The Family in Classical Greece* (London: A. & C. Black, 1964).

Lake, K., *The Earlier Epistles of St Paul: Their Motive and Origin* (London: Rivingtons, 1914).

Lampe, G.W.H., 'Church Discipline and the Interpretation of the Epistles to the Corinthians', in W. Farmer, C.F.D. Moule and R.R. Niebuhr (eds.), *Christian History and*

Interpretation: Studies Presented to John Knox (Cambridge: Cambridge University Press, 1967), pp. 337-62.

Lamphere, L., 'Strategies, Cooperation and Conflict among Women in Domestic Groups', in M. Rosaldo and L. Lamphere (eds.), *Women, Culture and Society* (Stanford: Stanford University Press, 1974), pp. 97-112.

Laney, J.C., 'Paul and the Permanence of Marriage in 1 Corinthians 7', *JETS* 25 (1982), pp. 283-94.

Leach, E., 'Anthropological Approaches to the Study of the Bible during the Twentieth Century', in G.M. Tucher and D.A. Knight (eds.), *Humanizing America's Iconic Book* (Chico, CA: Scholars Press, 1982), pp. 73-94.

Leduc, C., 'Marrage in Ancient Greece', in G. Duby and M. Perrot (gen. eds.), *A History of Women in the West. I. From Ancient Goddesses to Christian Saints* (ed. P. Schmitt Pantel; trans. A. Goldhammer; Cambridge, MA: Harvard University Press, 1992), pp. 235-95.

Lefkowitz, M.R. and M.B. Fant, *Women's Life in Greece and Rome: A Source Book in Translation* (Baltimore: The Johns Hopkins University Press, 1982).

Lenski, G., 'Status Crystallization: A Non-Vertical Dimension of Social Status', *American Sociological Review* 19 (1954), pp. 405-13.

— *A Theory of Social Stratification* (New York: McGraw–Hill, 1966).

Levick, B.M., *Roman Colonies in Southern Asia Minor* (Oxford: Clarendon Press, 1967).

Levine, L.I., *Caesarea under Roman Rule* (Leiden: Brill, 1975).

Lewis, N., *Life in Egypt under Roman Rule* (Oxford: Clarendon Press, 1983).

Lightman, M., and W. Zeisel, 'Univira: An Example of Continuity and Change in Roman Society', *CH* 46 (1977), pp. 19-32.

Lohse, E., *Colossians and Philemon* (Philadelphia: Fortress Press, 1971).

Long, A.A., *Hellenistic Philosophy: Stoics, Epicureans, Sceptics* (New York: Charles Scribner's Sons, 1974).

Lund, N., *Chiasmus in the New Testament: A Study in Formgeschichte* (Chapel Hill: University of North Carolina Press, 1942).

Lutz, C.E., *Musonius Rufus* (New Haven: Yale University Press, 1947).

MacDonald, D.R., *The Legend and the Apostle: The Battle for Paul in Story and Canon* (Philadelphia: Westminster Press, 1983).

—*There Is No Male and Female: The Fate of a Dominical Saying in Paul and Gnosticism* (Philadelphia: Fortress Press, 1987).

—'Virgins, Widows and Paul in Second Century Asia Minor', in P.J. Achtemeier (ed.), *SBLSP* (Missoula, MT: Scholars Press, 1979), pp. 169-84.

MacDonald, M.Y., *The Pauline Churches: A Socio-Historical Study of Institutionalization in the Pauline and Deutero-Pauline Writings* (Cambridge: Cambridge University Press, 1988).

MacMullen, R., *Enemies of the Roman Order: Treason, Unrest and Alienation in the Empire* (Cambridge, MA: Harvard University Press, 1975).

— *Paganism in the Roman Empire* (New Haven: Yale University Press, 1981).

—*Roman Social Relations 50 BC to AD 284* (New Haven: Yale University Press, 1974).

—'Women in Public in the Roman Empire', *Historia* 29 (1981), pp. 208-18.

Magie, D., *Roman Rule in Asia Minor* (Princeton, NJ: Princeton University Press, 1950).

Malherbe, A., 'Antisthenes and Odysseus, and Paul at War', *HTR* 76 (1983) pp. 143-73.

—*The Cynic Epistles: A Study Edition* (trans. Abraham; Missoula, MT: Scholars Press, 1977).

—*Moral Exhortation: A Greco-Roman Sourcebook* (Philadelphia: Westminster Press, 1986).

—*Social Aspects of Early Christianity* (Philadelphia: Fortress Press, 2nd edn, 1983).

Malina, B., *Christian Origins and Cultural Anthropology: Practical Models for Biblical Interpretation* (Atlanta: John Knox, 1986).

—'Does Porneia Mean Fornication?', *NovT* 14 (1972), pp. 10-17.

—'Freedom: A Theological Inquiry into the Dimension of a Symbol', *BTB* 8 (1978), pp. 62-76.

—*The Gospel of John in Sociolinguistic Perspective* (Berkeley: Center for Hermeneutical Studies, 1984).

—'The Individual and the Community: Personality in the Social World of Early Christianity', *BTB* 9 (1979), pp. 126-38.

—'Interpreting the Bible with Anthropology: The Case of the Poor and the Rich', *Listening* 21 (1986), pp. 148-59.

—*The New Testament World: Insights from Cultural Anthropology* (Atlanta: John Knox, 1981).

—'Normative Dissonance and Christian Origins', *Semeia* 35 (1986), pp. 35-58.

—Review of G. Theissen, *Sociology of Early Palestinian Christianity*, *CBQ* 41 (1979), pp. 176-78.

—'The Social Sciences and Biblical Interpretation', in N.K. Gottwald (ed.), *The Bible and Liberation: Political and Social Hermeneutics* (Maryknoll, NY: Orbis Books, 1983), pp. 11-25.

—'Why Interpret the Bible with the Social Sciences?', *American Baptist Quarterly* 2, (1983), pp. 119-33.

Manson, T.W., 'The Corinthian Correspondence I', in *Studies in the Gospels and Epistles* (Manchester: Manchester University Press, 1962), pp. 190-209.

Marrou, H., *The History of Education in Antiquity* (trans. G. Lamb; New York: Sheed and Ward, 1956).

Marshall, A.J., 'Roman Women in the Provinces', *Ancient Society* 6 (1975), pp. 109-28.

Martin, R., *Colossians and Philemon* (London: Oliphants, 1974).

—*1 and 2 Corinthians, Galatians* (Grand Rapids: Eerdmans, 1968).

McCown, C.C., 'Shirley Jackson Case's Contribution to the Theory of Sociohistorical Interpretation', *JR* 29 (1949), pp. 15-29.

Meeks, W.A., and R.L. Wilken, *Jews and Christians in Antioch in the First Four Centuries of the Common Era* (Missoula, MT: Scholars Press, 1978).

Meeks, W., *The First Urban Christians: The Social World of the Apostle Paul* (New Haven: Yale University Press, 1983).

—'The Image of the Androgyne: Some Uses of a Symbol in Earliest Christianity', *HR* 13 (1974), pp. 165-208.

—'The Man from Heaven in Johannine Sectarianism', *JBL* 41 (1972), pp. 44-72.

— *The Moral World of the First Christians* (Philadelphia: Westminster Press, 1986).

—'Since Then you Would Need to Go out of the World: Group Boundaries in Pauline Christianity', in T. Ryan (ed.), *Critical History and Biblical Faith: New Testament Perspectives* (Villanova: Edward Brothers, 1979), pp. 4-29.

—'The Social Context of Pauline Theology', *Int* 37 (1983), pp. 266-77.

—'Social Functions of Apocalyptic Language in Pauline Christianity', in *Apocalypticism in the Mediterranean World and the Near East: Proceedings of the International Colloquium on Apocalypticism Uppsala, August 12–17, 1979*, (Tübingen: J.C.B. Mohr, 1982), pp. 687-706.

Metzger, B., *A Textual Commentary on the Greek New Testament: A Companion Volume to the United Bible Societies' Greek New Testament* (London: United Bible Societies, 3rd edn, 1971).

Meyer, R., *The Golden Age of Augustus* (Toronto: Samuel Stevens, 1978).

Mitchell, M., 'Response to O.L. Yarborough, "Elitist Sexual Ethics in Corinth"' (unpublished paper presented at SBL, Bible and Ethics Consultation, Boston, MA, 6 December 1987).

Mitton, C.L., *The Epistle to the Ephesians* (London: Marshall, Morgan & Scott, 1973).

Moffatt, J. *The First Epistle of Paul to the Corinthians* (London: Hodder & Stoughton, 2nd edn, 1959).

Moiser, J., 'Reassessment of Paul's View of Marriage with Reference to 1 Cor. 7', *JSNT* 18 (1983), pp. 103-22.

Momigliano, A., 'The Social Structure of the Ancient City', in S.C. Humphreys (ed.), *Anthropology and the Greeks* (London: Routledge & Kegan Paul, 1978), pp. 177-93.

Morris, L., *The First Epistle of Paul to the Corinthians: An Introduction and Commentary* (The Tyndale New Testament Commentaries; London: Tyndale Press, 1958).

Moulden, J.L., *The Pastoral Epistles: 1 and 2 Timothy, Titus* (Harmondsworth: Penguin Books, 1976).

Moule, C.F.D., *An Idiom Book of the New Testament Greek* (Cambridge: Cambridge University Press, 1960).

Munck, J., 'The Church without Factions: Studies in 1 Corinthians 1–4', in *Paul and the Salvation of Mankind* (London: SCM Press, 1959), ch. 5.

Murphy-O'Connor, J., 'The Divorced Woman in 1 Cor. 7.10-11', *JBL* 100 (1981), pp. 601-606.

—*1 Corinthians* (New Testament Message; Wilmington: Michael Glazier, 1979).

—*St. Paul's Corinth: Texts and Archaeology* (Good News Studies, 6; Wilmington, DE: Michael Glazier, 1983).

Needham, R., 'Remarks on the Analysis of Kinship and Marriage', in *Rethinking Kinship and Marriage* (London: Tavistock Publications, 1971).

Neyrey, J., 'Bewitched in Galatia: Paul and Cultural Anthropology', *CBQ* 50 (1988), pp. 72-100.

—'Body Language in 1 Corinthians: The Use of Anthropological Models for Understanding Paul and his Opponents', *Semeia* 35 (1986), pp. 129-70.

—'Witchcraft Accusations in 2 Cor. 10-13: Paul in Social Science Perspective', *Listening* 21 (1986), pp. 160-70.

Neyrey, J., and B. Malina, *Calling Jesus Names: The Social Value of Labels in Matthew* (Sonoma, CA: Polebridge Press, 1988).

Nock, A.D., 'Religious Developments from the Close of the Republic to the Death of Nero', in S.A. Cook, F.E. Adcock, M.P. Charlesworth (eds.), *The Cambridge Ancient History* V.X: *The Augustan Empire 44 B.C.–A.D. 70* (Cambridge: Cambridge University Press, 1934), pp. 465-511.

Omanson, R.L., 'Some Comments about Style and Meaning: I Corinthians 9.15 and 7.10', *BT* 34 (1983), pp. 135-39.

O'Rourke, J.J., 'A Note on an Exception: Mt. 5.32 and 1 Cor. 7.12 Compared', *HeyJ* 5 (1964), pp. 299-302.

—'Hypothesis regarding 1 Cor. 7.36-8', *CBQ* 20 (1958), pp. 292-98.

Orr, W., and J.A. Walther, *1 Corinthians: A New Translation* (AB; Garden City, NY: Doubleday, 1976).

Orr, W.F., 'Paul's Treatment of Marriage in 1 Corinthians 7', *Pittsburg Perspective* 8 (1967), pp. 5-22.

Osiek, C., Review of Norman R. Petersen, *Rediscovering Paul: Philemon and the Sociology of Paul's Narrative World*, *BTB* 17 (1978), p. 39.

—*What Are they Saying about the Social Setting of the New Testament?* (Ramsey, NJ: Paulist Press, 1984).

Ostrander, D., 'One-and-Two Dimensional Models of the Distribution of Beliefs', in M. Douglas (ed.), *Essays in the Sociology of Perception* (London: Routledge & Kegan Paul, 1982), pp. 1-29.

Owen, D.E, 'Spectral Evidence: The Witchcraft Cosmology of Salem Village in 1692', in M. Douglas (ed.), *Essays in the Sociology of Perception* (London: Routledge & Kegan Paul, 1982), pp. 265-301.

Pagels, E., 'Adam and Eve, Christ and the Church: A Survey of Second Century Controversies concerning Marriage', in A.J.M. Wedderburn and A.H.B. Logan (eds.), *The New Testament and Gnosis: Essays in Honor of Professor Robert McL. Wilson* (Edinburgh: T. & T. Clark, 1983), pp. 146-75.

—'Paul and Women: A Response to Recent Discussion', *JAAR* 42 (1974), pp. 538-49.

Pasternak, B., *Introduction to Kinship and Social Organization* (Englewood Cliffs, NJ: Prentice–Hall, 1976).

Pearson, B.A., *The Pneumatikos-Psychikos Terminology in 1 Corinthians: A Study in the Theology of the Corinthian Opponents of Paul and its Relation to Gnosticism* (SBLDS, 12; Missoula, MT: Society of Biblical Literature, 1973).

—'Hellenistic Jewish Wisdom Speculation and Paul', in R.L. Wilken (ed.), *Aspects of Wisdom in Judaism and Early Christianity* (Notre Dame: University of Notre Dame Press, 1975).

Pepper, S., *World Hypotheses: A Study in Evidence* (Berkeley: University of California Press, rev. edn 1972 [1942]).

Perkins, P., A Review of Bruce J. Malina's *New Testament World: Insights from Cultural Anthropology*, *CBQ* 45 (1983), pp. 498-99.

Perry, B.E., *The Ancient Romances: A Literary, Historical Account of their Origins* (Berkeley: University of California Press, 1967).

Petersen, N.R., *Rediscovering Paul: Philemon and the Sociology of Paul's Narrative World* (Philadelphia: Fortress Press, 1985).

Phillipson, M., 'Theory, Methodology and Conceptualization', in P. Filmer, M. Phillipson, D. Silverman and D. Walsh (eds.), *New Directions in Sociological Theory* (London: Macmillan, 1972).

Phipps, W.E., 'Is Paul's Attitude toward Sexual Relations Contained in 1 Cor. 7.1?', *NTS* 28 (1982), pp. 125-31.

Pomeroy, S., *Goddesses, Whores, Wives and Slaves: Women in Classical Antiquity* (New York: Schocken Books, 1975).

—'The Relationship of the Married Woman to her Blood Relatives in Rome', *Ancient Society* 7 (1976), pp. 215-27.

—'Selected Bibliography on Women in Antiquity', *Arethusa* 6 (1973), pp. 125-37.

Radcliffe-Brown, A.R., 'On Rules of Descent and Inter-Kin Behaviour', in N. Graburn (ed.), *Readings in Kinship and Social Structure* (New York: Harper & Row, 1971), pp. 87-94.

Radista L.F., 'Augustus' Legislation concerning Marriage, Procreation, Love Affairs and Adultery', *ANRW*, II, pp. 278-339.

Ramsay, W.M., 'Historical Commentary on the Epistles to the Corinthians', *The Expositor*, Series 6.1 (1900), pp. 19-31, 91-111, 203-17, 273-89, 380-87; 6.2 (1900), pp. 287-302, 368-81, 429-44; 6.3 (1901), pp. 93-110, 220-40, 343-60.

—'The Jews in Graeco-Asiatic Cities', *Expositor*, 6.5 (1902), pp. 19-33, 92-109.

Rawson, B., 'Roman Concubinage and Other De Facto Marriages', *Transactions and Proceedings of the American Philological Society* 104 (1974), pp. 279-305.

Rawson, B. (ed.), *The Family in Ancient Rome: New Perspectives* (Ithaca, NY: Cornell University Press, 1986).

—'Family Life among the Lower Classes at Rome in the First Two Centuries of the Empire', *Classical Philology* 61 (1966), pp. 71-83.

Reekmans, T., 'Juvenal's View on Social Classes', *Ancient Society* 2 (1971), pp. 117-61.

—'Usurpation of Status and Status Symbols in the Roman Empire', *Historia* 20 (1971), pp. 275-302.

Reid, S.B., 'Enoch: The Rising Elite of the Apocalyptic Movement', *SBLSP* (Missoula, MT: Scholars Press, 1983).

Remus, H., 'Sociology of Knowledge and the Study of Early Christianity', *SR* 11 (1982), pp. 45-56.

—Review Symposium: Wayne A. Meeks, *The First Urban Christians: The Social World of the Apostle Paul*, *Horizons* 10 (1983), pp. 352-65.

Rex, J., *Key Problems of Sociological Theory* (London: Routledge & Kegan Paul, 1961).

Richardson, C.C., 'An Early Christian Sermon: An Anonymous Sermon, Commonly Called Clement's Second Letter', in C.C. Richardson (ed.), *Early Christian Fathers I* (Philadelphia: Westminster Press, 1953), pp. 183-202 .

Richardson, C.C. (ed.), *Early Christian Fathers*, I (LCC; Philadelphia: Westminster Press, 1953).

Richardson, J. (ed.), *Models of Reality: Shaping Thought and Action* (Mt Airy, MD: Lomond Books, 1984).

Richardson, P., 'Judgement in Sexual Matters in 1 Corinthians 6.1-11', *NovT* 25 (1983), pp. 37-58.

—' "I Say, not the Lord": Personal Opinion, Apostolic Authority and the Development of Early Christian Halakah', *TynBul* 31 (1986), pp. 65-86.

—'Logia of Jesus in 1 Corinthians', in D. Wenham (ed.), *Gospel Perspectives: The Jesus Tradition outside the Gospels* (Sheffield: JSOT Press, 1985), V, pp. 39-62.

—'On the Absence of Anti-Judaism in 1 Corinthians', in P. Richardson with D. Granskou (eds.), *Anti-Judaism in Early Christianity*. I. *Paul and the Gospels* (Waterloo: Wilfred Laurier Press, 1986), pp. 59-74.

—'Pauline Inconsistency: 1 Corinthians 9.19-23 and Galatians 2.11-14', *NTS* 26 (1980), pp. 347-62.

—'St. Paul on the Strong and the Weak: A Study in the Resolution of Conflict', *Crux* 13 (1975–76), pp. 10-20.

—'The Thunderbolt in Q and the Wise Man in Corinth', in P. Richardson and J. Hurd (eds.), *From Jesus to Paul: Studies in Honor of F.W. Beare* (Waterloo: Wilfred Laurier Press, 1984), pp. 91-112.

Richardson, P., and P. Gooch, 'Accommodation Ethics', *TynBul* 29 (1978), pp. 89-142.

Richlin, A., 'Approaches to the Sources on Adultery at Rome', in H.P. Foley (ed.), *Reflections on Woman in Antiquity* (New York: Gordon and Breech Science Pub., 1981), pp. 379-404.

Richter, P.J., 'Recent Sociological Approaches to the Study of the New Testament', *Religion* 14 (1984), pp. 77-90.

Richter, D.C., 'Women in Classical Times', *Classical Journal* 67 (1971), pp. 1-8.

Ridderbos, H., *Paul, an Outline of his Theology* (Grand Rapids: Eerdmans, 1975).

Riley, M.W., *Sociological Research: A Case Approach* (New York: Harcourt, Brace & World, 1963).

Rivers, W.H.R., *Kinship and Social Organization* (London School of Economics Monographs on Social Anthropology, 34; London: Athlone Press, 1968).

Rivière, P.G., 'Marriage: A Reassessment', in R. Needham (ed.), *Rethinking Marriage and Kinship* (London: Tavistock Publications, 1971), ch. 3.

Roberts, A. and J. Donaldson (eds.), *The Anti-Nicene Fathers* (Grand Rapids, MI: Eerdmans, 1950).

Roberts, R.L. Jr, 'The Meaning of *Chorizo* and *Douloö* in 1 Corinthians 7.10-17', *ResQ* 8 (1965), pp. 179-84.

Robertson, A., and A. Plummer, *A Critical and Exegetical Commentary on the First Epistle of St. Paul to the Corinthians* (ICC; Edinburgh: T. & T. Clark, 2nd edn, 1914 [1911]).

Robertson, E.H., *Corinthians 1 and 2* (J.B. Phillips; New York: Macmillan, 1973).

Robinson, J., 'Introduction: The Dismantling and Reassembling of the Categories of New Testament Scholarship', in J.M. Robinson and H. Koester (eds.), *Trajectories through Early Christianity* (Philadelphia: Fortress Press, 1971), pp. 1-19.

Rodd, C.S., 'On Applying a Sociological Theory to Biblical Studies', *JSOT* 19 (1981), pp. 95-106.

Rogers, S.C., 'Women's Place: A Critical Review of Anthropological Theory', *Comparative Studies in Society and History* 20 (1978), pp. 145-47.

Rosaldo, M.Z., 'The Use and Abuse of Anthropology: Reflections on Feminism and Cross-Cultural Understanding', *Signs* 5 (1980), pp. 389-417.

Rosaldo, M.Z., and L. Lamphere (eds.), *Women, Culture and Society* (Stanford: Stanford University Press, 1976).

Ruef, J.S., *Paul's First Letter to Corinth* (Harmondsworth: Penguin Books, 1971).

Sacks, K., *Sisters and Wives: The Past and Future of Sexual Equality* (Chicago: University of Illinois Press, 1982).

Salmon, E.T., *Roman Colonization Under the Republic* (Ithaca, NY: Cornell University Press, 1970).

—*Wealthy Corinth: A History of the City to 338 BC* (Oxford: Clarendon Press, 1984).

Sampley, J.P., 'Paul, his Opponents in 2 Corinthians 10–13 and the Rhetorical Hand-books', in J. Neusner, P. Borgen, E.S. Frerichs and R. Horsley (eds.), *The Social World of Formative Christianity and Judaism: Essays in Tribute to Howard Clark Kee* (Philadelphia: Fortress Press, 1988), pp. 162-77.

Sanders, E.P., 'Literary Dependence in Colossians', *JBL* 85 (1966), pp. 25-45.

Schmithals, W., *Gnosticism in Corinth: An Investigation of the Letters to the Corinthians* (trans. J.E. Steely; Nashville: Abingdon Press, 1971).

Schrage, W., 'Die Stellung zur Welt bei Paulus, Epiktel und in der Apokalyptik: Ein Beitrag zu 1 Kor. 7.29-31', *ZTK* 61 (1964), pp. 125-54.

Schrenk, G., 'The Father Concept in Later Judaism', *TDNT*, V, pp. 974-75.

Schubert, P., 'Shirley Case Jackson, Historian of Early Christianity: An Appraisal', *JR* 29 (1949), pp. 30-47.

Schüssler Fiorenza, E., *In Memory of Her: A Feminist Theological Reconstruction of Christian Origins* (New York: Crossroads, 1983).

Schütz, J.H., 'Charisma and Social Reality in Primitive Christianity', *JR* 54 (1974), pp. 51-70.

—*Paul and the Anatomy of Apostolic Authority* (SNTSMS, 36; London: Cambridge University Press, 1975).

Schweitzer, E., *The Letter to the Colossians* (London: SPCK, 1982).

Scroggs, R., 'The Earliest Christian Communities as Sectarian Movements', in J. Neusner (ed.), *Christianity and Judaism and Other Greco-Roman Cults: Studies For Morton Smith at Sixty*. II. *Early Christianity* (Leiden: Brill, 1975), pp. 1- 23.

—*Paul for a New Day* (Philadelphia: Fortress Press, 1977).

—'The Sociological Interpretation of the New Testament: The Present State of Research', *NTS* 26 (1980), pp. 164-79.

—'Sociology and the New Testament', *Listening* 21 (1986), pp. 138-47.

—'Paul and The Eschatological Woman', *JAAR* 40 (1972), pp. 283-303.

—'Paul and the Eschatological Woman: Revisited', *JAAR* 42 (1974), pp. 532-37.

—'ΣΟΦΟΣ and ΠΝΕΥΜΑΤΙΚΟΣ', *NTS* 14 (1967–68), pp. 33-55.

Segal, R.A., 'The Application of Symbolic Anthropology to Religions of the Greco-Roman World', *RelSRev* 10 (1984), pp. 216-23.

Sevain, L, 'Paul on Celibacy', *Clergy Review* 51 (1966), pp. 785-91.

Shelton, J.-A., *As the Romans Did: A Sourcebook in Roman Social History* (New York: Oxford University Press, 1988).

Sherwin-White, A.N., *Roman Foreign Policy in the East 168 BC–AD 7* (Norman: University of Oklahoma Press, 1983).

Shore, M.G., *The Science of Social Redemption: McGill, the Chicago School and the Origins of Social Research in Canada* (Toronto: University of Toronto Press, 1987).

Simon, W.G.H., *The First Epistle to the Corinthians: Introduction and Commentary* (Torch Bible Commentaries; London: SCM Press, 1959).

Smallwood, M., *The Jews under Roman Rule: From Pompey to Diocletian* (Leiden: Brill, 1976).

Smith, D., *The Life and Letters of St Paul* (New York: Harper & Row, 1970).

Smith, D.E., 'The Egyptian Cults at Corinth', *HTR* 70 (1977), pp. 201-31.

Smith, J.Z., 'Birth Upside Down or Right Side Up?', *HR* 9 (1970), pp. 281-303.

—'The Social Description of Early Christianity', *RelSRev* 1 (1975), pp. 19-25.

—'Too Much Kingdom, Too Little Community', *Zygon* 13 (1978), pp. 123-30.

Smith, M., 'Pauline Worship as Seen by Pagans', *HTR* 73 (1980), pp. 241-50.

Spencer, A.B., *Paul's Literary Style: A Stylistic and Historical Comparison of II Corinthians 11.16–12.13, Romans 8.9-39 and Philippians 3.2–4.13* (Jackson: Evangelical Theological Society, 1984).

Spickard, J., 'Mary Douglas's Three Versions of Grid/Group Theory: A Tool for New Testament Scholarship' (unpublished paper presented at the Annual Meeting SBL, Boston, MA, 4–6 December 1987).

Stambaugh, J.E., and D.L. Balch, *The New Testament in its Social Environment* (Philadelphia: Westminster Press, 1986).

Stambaugh, J.E., 'Social Relations in the City of the Early Principate: State of Research', in P.J. Achtemeier (ed.), *SBLSP* (Missoula, MT: Scholars Press, 1980), pp. 75-90.

Stanley, D.M., ' "Become Imitators of Me": The Pauline Conception of Apostolic Tradition', *Bib* 40 (1959), pp. 859-77.

Stanley, J., 'The Sociology of Knowledge and New Testament Interpretation', in
    B. Hargrove (ed.), *Religion and the Sociology of Knowledge: Modernization and
    Pluralism in Christian Thought and Structure* (Lewiston, NY: Edwin Mellen Press,
    1984), pp. 123-52.
Stowers, S.K., 'Social Status, Public Speaking and Private Teaching: The Circumstances of
    Paul's Preaching Activity', *NovT* 26 (1984), pp. 59-82.
Talbert, C.H., *Reading Corinthians: A Literary and Theological Commentary on 1 and 2
    Corinthians* (New York: Crossroads, 1987).
Tannehill, R., 'Exploring Paul in New Ways: A Review', *Int* 44 (1987), pp. 76-78.
Theissen, G., *The First Followers of Jesus: A Sociological Analysis of Earliest Christianity*
    (trans. J. Bowden; London: SCM Press, 1978).
—*Psychological Aspects of Pauline Theology* (trans. J.P. Galvin; Philadelphia: Fortress
    Press, 1987).
—*The Social Setting of Pauline Christianity* (trans. and ed. J. Schütz; Philadelphia: Fortress
    Press, 1982).
—'The Sociological Interpretation of Religious Traditions: Its Methodological Problems as
    Exemplified in Early Christianity', in N.K Gottwald (ed.), *The Bible and Liberation:
    Political and Social Hermeneutics* (Maryknoll, NY: Orbis Books, 1983), pp. 38-58.
Thomas, G.S.R., Review of J.G. Gager, *Kingdom and Community: The Social World of
    Early Christianity*, *JRH* 10 (1978), pp. 95-96.
Thrall, M.E., *The First and Second Letters of Paul to the Corinthians* (Cambridge Bible
    Commentary; London: Cambridge University Press, 1965).
—*Greek Particles in the New Testament: Linguistic and Exegetical Studies* (Grand Rapids:
    Eerdmans, 1962).
Tracy, D., 'A Theological Response to "Kingdom and Community" ', *Zygon* 13 (1978), pp.
    131-35.
Treggiari, S., 'Consent to Roman Marriage: Some Aspects of Law and Reality', *Classical
    Views* 26 (1982), pp. 34-44.
—'Libertine Women', *Classical World* 64 (1971), pp. 196-98.
—'Roman Social History: Recent Interpretations', *Social History* 8 (1974–75), pp. 149-64.
Turner, J., *The Structure of Sociological Theory* (Homewood, IL: Dorsey Press, rev. edn,
    1978).
Turner, V., 'Betwixt and Between: The Liminal Period in *Rites de Passage*', in J. Helm
    (ed.), *Symposium on New Approaches to the Study of Religion* (Seattle: University of
    Washington Press, 1964), pp. 4-20.
—*Dramas, Fields and Metaphors: Symbolic Action in Human Society* (Ithaca, NY: Cornell
    University Press, 1974).
—'Forms of Symbolic Action', in R.F. Spencer (ed.), *Forms of Symbolic Action: Pro-
    ceedings of the 1969 Annual Spring Meeting of the American Ethnological Society*
    (Seattle: University of Washington Press, 1969), pp. 3-25.
—*On the Edge of the Bush: Anthropology as Experience* (Tucson: University of Arizona
    Press, 1985).
—*The Ritual Process: Structure and Anti-Structure* (Chicago: Aldine Publishing, 1969).
—*Schism and Continuity in an African Society: A Study of Ndembu Village Life* (Man-
    chester: Manchester University Press, 1964).
—'Social Dramas', *Critical Inquiry* 7 (1980), pp. 141-68.
Verner, D.C., *The Household of God: The Social World of the Pastoral Epistles* (Chico,
    CA: Scholars Press, 1983).

Veyne, P. (ed.), *From Pagan Rome to Byzantium*, I, in P. Aries and G. Duby (gen. eds.), *A History of Private Life* (trans. A. Goldhammer; Cambridge: The Belknap Press of Harvard University, 1987).

Von Dehsen, C.D., 'Sexual Relationships and the Church: An Exegetical Study of 1 Corinthians 5–7' (PhD dissertation, Union Theological Seminary, 1987).

Wallace-Hadrill, A., 'Family and Inheritance in the Augustan Marriage Laws', *Proceedings of the Cambridge Philosophical Society* 27 (1981), pp. 50-80.

Weiss, J., *Der erste Korintherbrief* (Meyer Commentaries; Göttingen: Vandenhoeck & Ruprecht, 1970 [1910]).

—*The History of Primitive Christianity* (trans. and ed. F. Grant, A.H. Forster, P.S. Kramer and S.E. Johnson; New York: Wilson Erickson, 1936).

Wellborn, L.T., 'On the Discord in Corinth: 1 Corinthians 1–4 and Ancient Politics', *JBL* 106 (1987), pp. 85-111.

White, L.J., 'Grid and Group in Matthew's Community: The Righteousness/Honor Code in the Sermon on the Mount', *Semeia* 35 (1986), pp. 61-90.

Wilckens, U., *Weisheit und Torheit: Eine exegetische religionsgeschichtliche Untersuchung zu 1 Kor. 1 und 2* (Tübingen: Mohr, 1959).

Wilken, R.L, 'Towards a Social Interpretation of Early Christian Apologetics', *CH* 39 (1970), pp. 1-22.

Wilken, R., 'Collegia, Philosophical Schools and Theology', in S. Benko and J.J. O'Rourke (eds.), *The Catacombs and the Coloseum: The Roman Empire as the Setting of Primitive Christianity* (Valley Forge, PA: Judson, 1971), pp. 268-91.

Williams, G., 'Some Aspects of Roman Marriage Ceremonies and Ideals', *JRS* 48 (1959), pp. 16-29.

Wilson, R.McL., 'How Gnostic Were the Corinthians?', *NTS* 27 (1981), pp. 593-604.

Wilson-Kastner, P., and R. Rader, *A Lost Tradition: Women Writers of the Early Church* (Washington: University Press of America, 1981).

Wimbush, V.L., *Paul, the Wordly Ascetic: Response to the World and Self-Understanding according to 1 Corinthians 7* (Macon, GA: Mercer University Press, 1987).

Wink, W., *The Bible in Human Transformation* (Philadelphia, Fortress Press, 1973).

Wire, A., Review of John H. Elliott, *Home for the Homeless: A Sociological Exegesis of 1 Peter, its Situation and Strategy*; D.L. Balch, *Let Wives Be Submissive: The Domestic Code in 1 Peter*, *RelSRev* 10 (1984), pp. 209-16.

Wiseman, J., 'Corinth and Rome 1: 228 BC–AD 267', in H. Temporini and W. Haase (eds.), *ANRW*, II, 7.1, pp. 438-548.

Witherington, B., 'Rite and Rights for Women: Galatians 3.28', *NTS* 27 (1981), pp. 593-604.

—*Women in the Earliest Churches* (Cambridge: Cambridge University Press, 1988).

Worgul, George, Jr, 'Anthropological Consciousness and Biblical Theology', *BTB* 9 (1974), pp. 3-12.

Wuellner, W., 'Greek Rhetoric and Pauline Argumentation', in W. Schoedel and R.L. Wilken (eds.), *Early Christian Literature and the Classical Intellectual Tradition: In Honorum Robert M. Grant* (Paris: Beauchesne, 1979), pp. 177-88.

Yarborough, L.O., 'Elitist Sexual Ethics in Corinth' (unpublished paper presented at the SBL, Bible and Ethics Consultation, Boston, MA, 6 December 1987).

—*Not Like the Gentiles: Marriage Rules in the Letters of Paul* (Atlanta: Scholars Press, 1985).

Young, F., and D.F. Ford, *Meaning and Truth in 2 Corinthians* (Grand Rapids: Eerdmans, 1987).

Zerwick, M., and M. Grosvenor, *A Grammatical Analysis of the Greek New Testament* (Rome: Biblical Institute Press, 1981).

INDEXES

INDEX OF REFERENCES

Sister or Wife?

OTHER ANCIENT REFERENCES

INDEX OF AUTHORS

JOURNAL FOR THE STUDY OF THE NEW TESTAMENT
SUPPLEMENT SERIES